Jeremiah 1–29

JOHN M. BRACKE

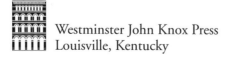
Westminster John Knox Press
Louisville, Kentucky

Scripture quotations, unless otherwise indicated, are from the New Revised Standard Version of the Bible, copyright © 1989 by the Division of Christian Education of the National Council of the Churches of Christ in the U.S.A., and are used by permission.

Book design by Publishers' WorkGroup
Cover design by Drew Stevens

First edition

Published by Westminster John Knox Press
Louisville, Kentucky

This book is printed on acid-free paper that meets the American National Standards Institute Z39.48 standard. ♾

PRINTED IN THE UNITED STATES OF AMERICA
00 01 02 03 04 05 06 07 08 09 — 10 9 8 7 6 5 4 3 2

Library of Congress Cataloging-in-Publication Data

Bracke, John M. (John Martin), 1947–
    Jeremiah 1–29 / John M. Bracke.
        p.   cm. — (Westminster Bible Companion)
    Includes bibliographical references.
    ISBN 0-664-25582-5 (pbk. : alk. paper)
    1. Bible. O.T. Jeremiah I–XXIX—Commentaries.   I. Title.
II. Series.
BS1525.3.B73   1999
224'.2207—dc21   99-43130

Jeremiah 1–29

Westminster Bible Companion

Series Editors

Patrick D. Miller
David L. Bartlett

Contents

Series Foreword

This series of study guides to the Bible is offered to the church and more specifically to the laity. In daily devotions, in church school classes, and in listening to the preached word, individual Christians turn to the Bible for a sustaining word, a challenging word, and a sense of direction. The word that scripture brings may be highly personal as one deals with the demands and surprises, the joys and sorrows, of daily life. It also may have broader dimensions as people wrestle with moral and theological issues that involve us all. In every congregation and denomination, controversies arise that send ministry and laity alike back to the Word of God to find direction for dealing with difficult matters that confront us.

A significant number of lay women and men in the church also find themselves called to the service of teaching. Most of the time they will be teaching the Bible. In many churches, the primary sustained attention to the Bible and the discovery of its riches for our lives have come from the ongoing teaching of the Bible by persons who have not engaged in formal theological education. They have been willing, and often eager, to study the Bible in order to help others drink from its living water.

This volume is part of a series of books, the Westminster Bible Companion, intended to help the laity of the church read the Bible more clearly and intelligently. Whether such reading is for personal direction or for the teaching of others, the reader cannot avoid the difficulties of trying to understand these words from long ago. The scriptures are clear and clearly available to everyone as they call us to faith in the God who is revealed in Jesus Christ and as they offer to every human being the word of salvation. No companion volumes are necessary in order to hear such words truly. Yet every reader of scripture who pauses to ponder and think further about any text has questions that are not immediately answerable simply by reading the text of scripture. Such questions may be about historical and geographical details or about words that are obscure or so loaded with meaning that one cannot tell at a glance what is at stake. They may be about the fundamental meaning of a passage or about what connection a particular text might have to our contemporary world. Or a teacher preparing for a church school class may simply want to know: What should I say about this biblical passage when I have to teach it next Sunday? It is our hope that these volumes, written by teachers and pastors with long experience studying and teaching the Bible in the church, will help members of the church who want and need to study the Bible with their questions.

The New Revised Standard Version of the Bible is the basis for the interpretive comments that each author provides. The NRSV text is presented at the beginning of the discussion so that the reader may have at hand in a single volume both the scripture passage and the exposition of its meaning. In some instances, where inclusion of the entire passage is not necessary for understanding either the text or the interpreter's discussion, the presentation of the NRSV text may be abbreviated. Usually, the whole of the biblical text is given.

We hope this series will serve the community of faith, opening the Word of God to all the people, so that they may be sustained and guided by it.

Introduction

The book of Jeremiah recounts the role of the prophet Jeremiah in the life of Judah in the years preceding and immediately following the fall of Jerusalem to Babylon in 587 B.C.

THE PROPHET JEREMIAH

Jeremiah was the "son of Hilkiah, of the priests who were in Anathoth in the land of Benjamin" (1:1). Though from a priestly family, Jeremiah was a prophet. The origins of Israelite prophecy are difficult to trace, and prophets were not unique to ancient Israel. For instance, in the ancient Near Eastern kingdom of Mari, persons functioned much like Israel's prophets several hundred years before the time of David and Solomon. In the Old Testament, prophets were most prominent during the centuries when kings ruled Israel and Judah (950–587 B.C.).

In our time, prophets are popularly thought of as (1) persons able to predict the future, (2) persons who are passionate advocates for justice issues, (3) persons who announce judgment and doom. In the Old Testament, prophets are messengers and spokespersons for God. Typically, prophetic speeches begin, "Thus says the Lord . . ." We will see often in the book of Jeremiah that Jeremiah is presented as one who announced the "word of the Lord." The primary concern of Israel's prophets was the relationship between God and God's people in a particular time and circumstance.

Certainly, Old Testament prophets spoke of future events. For instance, the prophet Jeremiah spoke repeatedly of the coming destruction of Jerusalem (1:14ff.; 4:5ff.; etc.). However, when Old Testament prophets like Jeremiah spoke of the future, they did so in two particular ways. First, prophets gave careful attention to the historical situation of their time.

Jeremiah was keenly aware of the rise of Babylon as a great power in the ancient Near Eastern world and of the threat Babylon was to Judah. Second, prophets understood that through the historical events of their day, God was at work. So, as God's spokesperson, Jeremiah announced that Babylon's invasion of Judah was God's doing. As Babylon attacked Jerusalem, Jeremiah, speaking for God, said, "I will bring them together into the center of this city" (21:4; compare Isa. 10:5–6 where Isaiah calls Assyria the "rod of my [God's] anger"). Thus, Old Testament prophets did not so much predict the future as they saw that God was at work in the unfolding events of their time.

Often, Old Testament prophets were outspoken advocates for justice for the poor and weaker members of society. Amos is the most notable example of such prophetic concern (for example, Amos 5:10–13), and there is prophetic concern for justice for the poor in the book of Jeremiah as well (for example, 8:10; 22:16–17). Yet, it will not do to define Old Testament prophets by a concern for justice. Even when prophets were explicitly concerned with justice for the poor, their social concern was rooted in God's own concern for the poor and oppressed, most evident in the deliverance of slaves from Egypt (Jer. 2:4–7; Amos. 2:9–10). To exploit or oppress the poor was to violate relationship with God. Prophetic social concern was rooted in theology, in an understanding of who God was and what God intended. Further, not all prophets had social justice as their primary concern. Hosea, for instance, had as a primary concern the relationship between God and God's people, which was explored through familial images (Hosea 2—husband and wife; Hosea 11—parent-child); in Hosea, the social consequences of Israel's broken relationship with God are not developed to nearly the extent as in Amos. The book of Jeremiah is more like Hosea than Amos.

Finally, prophets often spoke of God's judgment. That is certainly evident in the book of Jeremiah as the prophet announced the destruction of Judah and Jerusalem. Yet, because the primary concern of prophets was the relationship of God and God's people, the prophetic books of the Old Testament are not content to assert only judgment. They also imagine how, after God had called Israel to account through judgment, the relationship might continue (cf. Isaiah 40–55; Amos 9:11ff.). While there is an emphasis on judgment in the book of Jeremiah, the book is also concerned with the time after judgment, when God would "restore the fortunes" of God's people (30:3). In prophetic books, it is debatable if the concern for restoration after judgment reflects the interests of the actual prophets or the interests of those who later edited the prophets' speeches into books.

In either case, in reading the book of Jeremiah, we hear of both God's judgment and restoration, and the ways in which these are related.

In the book of Jeremiah, the prophet Jeremiah is portrayed as God's spokesperson who focused on the relationship between the people and God. The word of the Lord that Jeremiah spoke concerned the ways in which God was responding to Judah and the nations, for judgment and finally for restoration.

THE COMPOSITION AND TEXT
OF THE BOOK OF JEREMIAH

The final form of the book of Jeremiah is the result of a very complicated process that occurred over a long period of time. The book contains materials with different literary styles and different points of view about God, Israel, the exile, and the future of God's people. For instance, there are short, rhythmic poems, particularly in the first twenty-five chapters, that have frequently been attributed to the actual prophet Jeremiah. However, other poetry in the book is thought to be from later editors and not from Jeremiah himself, because it resembles material in Isaiah 40–55, which is widely assumed to have been written during the Babylonian exile and after Jeremiah's death. The prose in the book of Jeremiah also has different literary styles. Some material begins by noting the date and circumstance of an event involving Jeremiah (by reference to a year in the reign of a particular king) and concludes by reporting the response to the oracle Jeremiah delivered (for example, Jeremiah 26, 36). Many scholars have attributed this material to Jeremiah's scribe, Baruch. Other prose lacks the note of the date and circumstance of the event narrated, though in other ways, such as vocabulary and point of view, it resembles the prose described above (for example, Jeremiah 7). The similarities of the prose material in Jeremiah to the body of Old Testament literature called "Deuteronomistic," that is, the books of Deuteronomy, Joshua, Judges, Samuel, Kings, have long been observed. It is certain that Jeremiah himself did not write the entire book of Jeremiah as we now know it. Just as certainly, some of the material in the book is from the prophet, even if there is disagreement about precisely which sections of the book these may be.

It is not clear how the Book of Jeremiah, composed of poetry and prose of different kinds, came together. Within the book is an indication that even during the prophet's lifetime there was more than one collection of his words. Jeremiah 36 recounts an occasion when the prophet, banned from the Temple, sent Baruch, his scribe, to read a scroll. The scroll was seized, taken to Judah's King Jehoiakim, and read to him. As the scroll was read, its message so angered Jehoiakim that he cut it apart and threw it into a fire. When Jeremiah heard what had happened, he dictated another scroll to Baruch to which "many similar words were added" (36:32). If this account is reliable, it suggests that even while the prophet was living, his oracles were recorded and re-recorded, and that the second edition of the prophet's words included material not contained in the first edition.

There are other indications about the complex process by which the book of Jeremiah came to its final form. Some material seems to be gathered together in the book because of a common theme: Jeremiah 21:11–23:8 concerns the "house of David"; Jeremiah 23:9–40 concerns the prophets; Jeremiah 30–33 concerns the coming days when God would "restore the fortunes" of God's people; Jeremiah 45–51 consists of oracles against the nations. Some sections of the book seem to be organized by a catchword, a particular word repeated to hold several sections of the text together. (In Jeremiah 2–3, a Hebrew word meaning to walk, go, follow, or lead is such a catchword: v. 2, "you *followed* me"; v. 5, "*went far* from me"; v. 6, "*led* us"; etc.) Some passages are repeated in different sections of the book with some slight changes (for example, 23:5–6 and 33:14–16).

A further indication about the complex process of the book's formation is that there are two distinct versions of the book. In the Greek translation of the Old Testament (called the Septuagint), the book of Jeremiah is about one-eighth shorter than the standard Hebrew text of the Old Testament (called the Masoretic Text), on which the New Revised Standard Version translation is based. Further, the Greek and Hebrew texts differ regarding the placement of some material, most notably, the oracles against the nations (Jeremiah 45–51 in the NRSV). Portions of the book of Jeremiah found at Qumran among the Dead Sea Scrolls are more like the shorter, Greek text than the standard Hebrew text, suggesting that the shorter version may be older.

One of the most significant challenges in reading the book of Jeremiah is that the process by which the book was composed and reached its final form was very complicated and long. In the final form of the book, we are confronted with what will often seem a helter-skelter, patchwork quilt whose logic, sense, and coherence are not clear. So, it is not surprising that interpreters have gone about interpreting the book in different ways.

APPROACHES TO THE INTERPRETATION
OF THE BOOK OF JEREMIAH

There have been three primary approaches to the interpretation of the book of Jeremiah:

1. One approach has focused primarily on *the prophet Jeremiah*, the oracles he himself may have spoken, and how he may have addressed the particular historical situation in which he lived. This approach has dominated study of the book of Jeremiah for the last 150 years. That is, since the late nineteenth century, the attempt has been to determine as precisely as possible what the prophet Jeremiah said and how he addressed his situation in the late seventh and early sixth centuries B.C. This approach has assumed that the book of Jeremiah contains the original words of the historical prophet Jeremiah as well as material from later editors. The effort has been to recover the authentic words of the prophet Jeremiah that are somewhere embedded within the present book. Further, this approach has sought to relate, as far as is possible, the authentic words of the prophet to the specific historical setting in which the prophet spoke them. This approach has helped us better understand how Jeremiah may have related to his historical setting. However, it has not always taken seriously substantial portions of the book of Jeremiah that are not thought to be the authentic words of Jeremiah. Further, it has often been difficult to determine the exact historical situation addressed by those sections of the book deemed to be authentic.

2. The second approach has focused on *the work of the editors* of the book of Jeremiah, the theological traditions on which those who compiled the book drew, and how they shaped and reworked the traditions about the prophet Jeremiah to address the crisis of Judah's Babylonian exile. This approach assumes that within the book are the authentic words of the prophet as well as additions included by unknown persons. Most commonly, this approach has concluded that much in the book needs to be understood as the work of these later editors. These editors are understood to have been influenced by Deuteronomistic theology, such as is found in the book of Deuteronomy or as is evident in other books heavily edited by Deuteronomistic writers—Joshua, Judges, Samuel, Kings, or even parts of prophetic books such as Hosea and Amos. Often persons who take this approach draw a distinction between the theology of the historical Jeremiah and the theology of the editors of the book in the exile and see an unresolved tension between these perspectives in the book's final form.

3. The third approach focuses on *the book of Jeremiah as it is given us in its final form*, the ways in which the different kinds of material in the book

might cohere, and the theological sense of the book as a whole. This approach has two primary features:

a. The first feature is a concern for the coherence of the book. While recognizing that there are different kinds of literary materials in the book of Jeremiah, one asks if, in all its diversity and complexity, the book can be read as a whole. What evidence is there of literary coherence, so the book can be read as more than a loosely organized collection of divergent materials? Further, in what ways does the book of Jeremiah develop a cohesive theological perspective and hold together theological viewpoints that at first reading may seem to be in tension?

b. The second aspect of this approach is the recognition that the book is theological and functions in the church and synagogue to call forth faithful communities of God's people generation after generation. The first two approaches described above attempt to get behind the book to recover either the historical Jeremiah and his historical setting or the editors of the book and their historical setting in the exile. The concern for the historical circumstances behind the text has meant that the book of Jeremiah has often been read and studied as a historical record: as an account of what happened in Judah and to Jeremiah leading to the exile of 587 B.C., or as material that gives us insight into the nature of the community in exile and tries to make sense of the tragedy that befell them. The theological concern of the first two approaches is also historical. The concern is either for the theology of the historical Jeremiah or for the theology of the exilic editors of the book.

With the third approach, the focus shifts away from what the book meant in the context of the ancient world and asks how the book interprets the church and calls the church to faithfulness before God. The following comment by Walter Brueggemann reflects this way of reading the book of Jeremiah:

> The text does not require "interpretation or "application" so that it can be brought near our experience and circumstance. Rather, the text is so powerful and compelling, so passionate and uncompromising in its anguish and hope, that it requires we submit our experience to it and thereby reenter our experience on new terms, namely the terms of the text. (Brueggemann, *Jeremiah 1–25*, p. 17)

When the book of Jeremiah is approached as Christian scripture, the church is invited to stand open before it to hear its continuing witness to God's ways in the world and to heed its call to be a faithful community of God's people.

All three approaches to Jeremiah contribute to our understanding of it, and all will be evident in this commentary. The primary approach of this commentary is the third approach, an effort to understand the coherence of the final form of the book of Jeremiah. However, the insights gained from understanding the text as pointing to the historical Jeremiah or as reflecting the editors of the Jeremiah tradition in exile are used to enrich our understanding of the book. In what follows, the book is read like a story, the story of God working through Jeremiah to bring about the exile of Judah. As the story of the book unfolds, much of the material is read as if it were the speech of the prophet Jeremiah, even though it is likely that much material actually came from later editors.

THEOLOGICAL THEMES

The book of Jeremiah has as its central concern God: Who is God? What is the character of God? How does God relate to and act in the world? What does God purpose for the creation? Because theological concerns are so important to the book, I want to indicate what I consider the central theological concerns of Jeremiah. Three perspectives about God are particularly important:

1. In the book of Jeremiah, God is sovereign over creation, the nations, Israel, and the prophet Jeremiah. God spoke, and the course of history was changed. A central claim of the final form of the book is that God is watching over God's word to perform it (1:12). Most often in the book of Jeremiah, God watches over God's word "to pluck up and pull down, to destroy and to overthrow," but also "to build and to plant" (1:10; 18:7–8; 34:6; 31:28; 42:10; 45:4). God's word changes history both through judgment—plucking up and pulling down—and through restoration—building and planting. God is sovereign.

The book insists that God holds accountable the creation, the nations, Israel, and Jeremiah. In God's order stork, turtledove, swallow, and crane all have their "times," which they are to observe—and do!—in contrast to God's chosen people (8:7–8). Nations were summoned for God's purposes (4:13–18) but were also called to judgment for their pride (45:8 and various texts in Jeremiah 45–51). Israel was once saved by God from Pharaoh and given the promised land. However, they forgot God's goodness and rejected the Lord (Jeremiah 2), failed to heed God's instruction (translated by the NRSV as "law" in 8:8), broke covenant (Jeremiah 11), and so would be exiled. Jeremiah's complaints to God are met with a rebuke to "turn back

. . . utter what is precious, not what is worthless" (15:19). God called the world to account and in so doing was ready to pluck up and pull down.

Yet, the book of Jeremiah affirms that the God who has called to account is also gracious and merciful. God, who would make Judah and Jerusalem a desolation and ruin, in the coming days will restore the fortunes of the people, the land, and the city (30:3). The land will be restored, the Temple rebuilt, the broken covenant made new (Jeremiah 30–33). Other nations, too, called to account by God, will in time have their fortunes restored. God transforms the world through plucking up and pulling down, but then also through building and planting.

In the drama of the book of Jeremiah, the stress on God's sovereignty is affirmed against a theological alternative. This alternative is represented in the book by the prophets, priests, and royalty of the Jerusalem religious and political establishment. These held that God's people lived with divine guarantees of well-being (for instance, 6:14) and the security of divine presence forever ("the temple of the Lord," 7:4). These assurances blunted much seriousness about accountability before history's Sovereign.

2. In the book of Jeremiah, the Lord who holds peoples and nations accountable also experiences hurt and disappointment. So for instance, the Lord is portrayed as a husband who has been rejected by his beloved (2:29–32; cf. 2:2–3); or again, as a nurturing "Father" hurt because rebellious Judah and Israel refused to respond or follow (3:19–20). Anguished and pained by Israel's rejection, God must "pluck up and pull down." Yet the suffering of Israel and Judah in judgment, even if deserved, cause God further anguish. When Israel and Judah are punished, the Lord weeps over them (8:22ff.; 9:10, 17–18; 14:17) and remembers and is "deeply moved" for them (31:20).

In this connection, the laments of the prophet Jeremiah need to be mentioned (these are found in 11:18–20; 12:1–4; 15:15–18; 17:14–18; 20:7–18). The most obvious way to read these laments is to hear in them the anguish of the prophet himself, rejected and persecuted by his friends and neighbors. However, a closer reading suggests something more complex. In the book of Jeremiah, the prophet above all else speaks for the Lord. Jeremiah's words reveal God. Because in the book so much similarity exists between laments that are the direct speech of God and the laments spoken by the prophet, it seems likely that the laments of Jeremiah need to be heard as reflecting God's hurt and pain. As Terence Fretheim has argued:

> Given the fact that the laments of the prophet and God are so similar in their
> form and general orientation, in fact sometimes standing side-by-side, it is

difficult to avoid the conclusion that the prophet's laments are a mirror of the laments of God. In and through the lamenting of the prophet one can hear the anguish of God over what has happened in his relationship with his people. (Fretheim, *Suffering of God,* p. 158)

In the book of Jeremiah, the laments of the prophet Jeremiah mirror the anguish of God.

This concern with God's anguish does not allow us to read in the book a simple retribution theology: Do well and be blessed by God; disobey and be punished by God. To this retribution equation, the book of Jeremiah adds God's anguish. Because God both holds accountable and laments over Israel and Judah, the book understands there is no easy calculus about how the suffering, sovereign Lord will respond to the world. Thus, one of the challenges of studying the book of Jeremiah is to see how the Lord's judgment of and suffering over Israel and Judah are related.

3. Finally, the book of Jeremiah understands that God ultimately intends building and planting (1:10). While much of the book anticipates judgment, it also knows that the pained Sovereign who calls peoples and nations to account ultimately will work for a restored relationship with Israel and for the well-being of all peoples. God plucks up and pulls down but also builds and plants (1:10; 31:28), promising to restore the fortunes of Israel and the nations (29:14 and many texts in Jeremiah 30–33 regarding Israel; cf. 48:47; 49:6, 39 regarding the nations). This promised restoration is not accomplished by the conclusion of the book. However, there are indications that the book of Jeremiah believes God will watch over this word of promise, too, until building and planting are complete.

As this commentary seeks to understand the theological coherence of the book of Jeremiah, three theological tensions need to be held together:

1. There is a tension between the sovereign God who holds the world accountable, on the one hand, and the world of theological certainty and security represented by the Jerusalem political and religious establishment, on the other.
2. There is a tension between the Lord's judgment of Israel and Judah and God's anguish and suffering.
3. There is tension between God's word of plucking up and pulling down and the word of building and planting.

Amid these tensions we hear the book of Jeremiah as God's word to the church—the Word of the pained Sovereign of the creation, who directs the course of history through plucking up and tearing down and through building and planting.

AS WE BEGIN TO READ

As we begin to read and think about the book of Jeremiah, it is helpful to keep in mind several points that can be confusing:

1. Our intention is to understand the book of Jeremiah in its final form. So we read and discuss the book as the story of how and why God shaped the history of Judah toward exile in Babylon. We attempt to follow the plot of the story as it unfolds in the book. Mostly, the story is carried along by the speeches the prophet Jeremiah makes as God's spokesperson. The discussion refers to Jeremiah as the speaker wherever the book indicates that the prophet is to be understood as the speaker. Of course, the research done on the book of Jeremiah over the last century and a half (discussed above) suggests that the composition of the book was complicated, and not everything attributed to Jeremiah was actually said by him. While recognizing the conclusions of this research, in this discussion, where the book is read as a coherent story, there will not be great emphasis given to sorting out the authentic words of the prophet from material added by later editors.

2. It is confusing that the book speaks of both Israel and Judah. Jeremiah was a prophet in Judah almost one hundred years after the Northern Kingdom, Israel, had fallen to Assyria (see pp. 12–15). Nonetheless, the book sometimes records speeches of Jeremiah addressed to the Northern Kingdom. This may have happened for several reasons: (*a*) often in the Bible, even after Judah and Israel were two separate kingdoms, "Israel" was used to speak of the two kingdoms together; (*b*) Jeremiah seems sometimes to be remembering a time when Israel and Judah both still existed, or when there was only a single entity, "Israel"—when David and Solomon were kings or even before that, all the way back to the early settlement of the promised land; (*c*) during Jeremiah's time there was an effort to reestablish Israel—both Judah in the south, which continued to exist, and Israel in the north, which existed only as a vassal state of Assyria—as a united kingdom, as it was during the time of David and Solomon. Jeremiah may have at times had these efforts in mind.

Remember, Jeremiah was a prophet to Judah but did sometimes speak of "Israel."

3. The name for God in the Old Testament and in the book of Jeremiah can also be confusing. God (with a capital *G*, to distinguish the God

of Israel from the gods of the nations) was God's generic name, the simplest name for God. However, God also had what we might call a proper name or a particular name in the Old Testament and in the book of Jeremiah. This name was Yahweh, a name God revealed to Moses before the exodus (Exodus 3). However, the name Yahweh was considered so sacred, and still is by our Jewish brothers and sisters, that it was and is not spoken by them. Instead, when the name Yahweh appears in a text, they say "Adonai," which means "Lord." So, in the text of the NRSV, when "the Lord" is used, that is a translation of God's particular name, Yahweh. Sometimes in the discussion of the book herein the name Yahweh or the designation "the Lord" is used.

4. This discussion of the book of Jeremiah uses the NRSV of the Bible. However, in some places it is not possible to appreciate what is being said without referring to the Hebrew on which the English translation is based. It will be obvious when this is being done.

The Word of God
Jeremiah 1

Jeremiah 1 introduces us to the book of Jeremiah and announces its central theme: God is sovereign over the world. The prophet Jeremiah is introduced as God's spokesperson to whom "the word of the Lord came" (1:2) and whose "words" (1:1) are central to the book. The book develops as the "word of the Lord," spoken through the words of the prophet Jeremiah, is shown to direct the course of history.

Jeremiah 1:1–3

1:1 **The words of Jeremiah son of Hilkiah, of the priests who were in Anathoth in the land of Benjamin,** 2 **to whom the word of the LORD came in the days of King Josiah son of Amon of Judah, in the thirteenth year of his reign.** 3 **It came also in the days of King Jehoiakim son of Josiah of Judah, and until the end of the eleventh year of King Zedekiah son of Josiah of Judah, until the captivity of Jerusalem in the fifth month.**

These verses introduce the prophet Jeremiah and the historical setting for the book. They provide important clues about the concerns of the book of Jeremiah as a whole.

JEREMIAH'S ORIGINS AND HISTORICAL SETTING

The prophet Jeremiah was from a priestly family from Anathoth in the land of Benjamin. Jeremiah's family stood in the tradition of the priest Abiathar, exiled to Anathoth by King Solomon at the beginning of his reign. When David was king, there were two priests in Jerusalem. Abiathar was a priest connected with Israel's earlier tribal era. He represented a theological tradition rooted in the exodus that was concerned about oppression and injustice and that was suspicious of monarchy. The origins of Zadok,

David's other priest, are obscure. Zadok appears to have had connections with the political and religious establishment of Jerusalem at the time David captured the city from the Jebusites. Zadok strongly supported the monarchy. It is not surprising that Solomon chose Zadok as priest and banished Abiathar, since Abiathar had supported Adonijah, a rival of Solomon, to succeed David as king. This identification of Jeremiah with Abiathar, a priest at odds with the Davidic monarchy in Jerusalem, gives an early hint about what will be a major theme in the book of Jeremiah, the conflict between the prophet and the Davidic kings of Jerusalem.

Jeremiah was from Anathoth, a village that was located somewhat northeast of Jerusalem in the hill country of the tribe of Benjamin. After the empire of David and Solomon divided into the kingdoms of Israel (north) and Judah (south), Benjamin was politically part of Judah. By the time of Jeremiah, the territory of Benjamin and the town of Anathoth had become centers of opposition to the Jerusalem establishment, and in particular, to Judah's final king, Zedekiah.

The historical setting for the book is identified in verses 1–3 as the period from the thirteenth year of King Josiah (627 B.C.) until the Babylonian captivity of Jerusalem (587 B.C.). These were traumatic years in Judah's life. After nearly a century of Assyrian domination, the Assyrian Empire began to collapse. When, in 640 B.C., Josiah became king (2 Kings 22; he was a young boy, and his mother, Jedidah, likely functioned initially as his regent), a brief period followed for Judah to reassert her political independence. Under King Josiah there was a religious revival, whose most tangible expression was the restoration of the Jerusalem Temple. It is widely assumed that as part of this religious revival, the core of what is now the book of Deuteronomy was written. Politically, Josiah seems to have envisioned the reunification of the Southern Kingdom, Judah, with the Northern Kingdom, Israel (defeated in 722 B.C. by Assyria and an Assyrian province after that). The reign of Josiah began in the hope that Israel would be restored to the glory of the days of David and Solomon.

Tragically, Josiah was killed in a battle against Egypt in 609 B.C. (2 Kings 23:28–30). The years after Josiah's death were difficult. Pharaoh Neco of Egypt deposed Josiah's oldest son as his successor and installed another of Josiah's sons on the throne, Eliakim, to whom Neco gave the name Jehoiakim (the renaming was an act of sovereignty by the Egyptian pharaoh). Jehoiakim, who began his reign as a subject king of Egypt, soon had to contend with a new power in the ancient Near East: Babylon. Jehoiakim paid tribute to King Nebuchadnezzar of Babylon, but when Babylon was threatened by Egypt (about 601 B.C.), Jehoiakim rebelled

THE ERA OF THE PROPHET JEREMIAH

(640 TO 538 B.C.)

640   Josiah becomes king of Judah (his mother is initially his regent)
The Assyrian Empire begins to collapse

620   "Josiah's reform" underway in Judah, including remodeling of the Temple

609   Josiah killed in a battle with the Egyptian army
The oldest son, King Josiah, is king for three months
Egypt installs another of Josiah's sons as king: Jehoiakim
Judah is a vassal state of Egypt

The early speeches of Jeremiah are dated to these years

605   Judah becomes a vassal state of Babylon

598–97 King Jehoiakim dies and his successor is his son, Jehoiachin

597   In response to an earlier rebellion by Jehoiakim, Babylon sacks Jerusalem
Captives are taken to Babylon, including King Jehoiachin
Babylon installs a son of Josiah as king and gives him the name Zedekiah

Jeremiah is an active prophet and meets much resistance

587   Babylon destroys Jerusalem to punish a rebellion by Zedekiah
Jerusalem's wall is breached and the Temple burned
Zedekiah's sons are killed, and Zedekiah with many others are deported to Babylon
Gedaliah becomes "governor" of Judah

Jeremiah is taken against his will to Egypt by a group of Judaeans, where he likely dies

538   Persia overthrows Babylon, and Cyrus issues an edict allowing exiles to return to Judah; few do so

against Babylon (2 Kings 24:1–2). Babylon quickly dealt with the Egyptian threat and soon moved to punish those vassal states, including Judah, that had rebelled. As Babylon moved on Jerusalem, King Jehoiakim died.

Jehoiakim's son, Jehoiachin, succeeded his father and at once faced an attack on Jerusalem by Babylon. In 597 B.C., King Jehoiachin surrendered. The Babylonians looted the Temple and took leaders in Jerusalem, including King Jehoiachin, as captives to Babylon. Jehoiachin's uncle, Mattaniah (a son of Josiah), was installed by Babylon as king in Jerusalem and given the name Zedekiah by the Babylonians (2 Kings 24). Zedekiah struggled unsuccessfully to find a way through the continuing conflict between Babylon and Egypt that dominated ancient Near Eastern politics. He was himself indecisive and lacked the support of skilled advisers. He finally chose to rebel against Babylon, but the decision proved a disaster. In 587 B.C., Babylon again attacked Jerusalem. The city was sacked and burned, the Temple destroyed, and more captives were taken to Babylon. Zedekiah was made to witness the execution of his own sons, then was blinded and taken to Babylon (2 Kings 25:6–7; Jer. 39:4–8).

The career of the prophet Jeremiah corresponds to these events. It is not clear that Jeremiah had begun his prophetic activities during the reign of Josiah (the uncertainty concerns whether the reference to the "thirteenth year" of Josiah's reign (1:2) marks Jeremiah's birth or the beginning of his prophetic activity). However, Jeremiah certainly was active during the reigns of Jehoiakim, Jehoiachin, and Zedekiah and was a witness to the fall of Jerusalem. After the fall of Jerusalem, Jeremiah was forced to accompany a group of Judaeans seeking to escape Babylonian domination in Egypt (Jeremiah 43–44). His prophetic career and life apparently ended as an exile in Egypt.

As we read the book of Jeremiah, we are reminded frequently of the persons and events that led to the Babylonian capture of Jerusalem, and of the role of Jeremiah in these events. However, a word of caution is necessary as we think about the prophet Jeremiah as a historical figure. In the book of Jeremiah, much of the material has been shaped by persons living during or after the Babylonian exile who used the words and accounts of the prophet Jeremiah as a starting point for their own theological reflections about the exile and about the future of God's people. The history of the composition of the book is complicated (see Introduction). It is not possible to read a "history" or "biography" of Jeremiah from the book. As one scholar has said, what the book of Jeremiah presents is a "portrait" of the prophet Jeremiah that is neither slavishly bound to history nor cut loose from history, but that is instead a theological interpretation of the prophet (Brueggemann, "Book of Jeremiah," 131–32).

JEREMIAH'S WORDS AND THE WORD OF GOD

Certainly, the book of Jeremiah is interested in the historical characters and circumstances that led toward "the captivity of Jerusalem" (v. 3). Yet, in the first verses of the book, interest in Israel's history is set alongside the claim that Jerusalem's captivity had to do with "the words of Jeremiah . . . to whom the word of the Lord came" (v. 1). Verses 1–3 indicate that the book is not merely a historical report about how the exile occurred or an analysis of the international politics of the ancient Near Eastern world that led to the defeat of Judah by Babylon. Instead, the book of Jeremiah invites us to discern how "the captivity of Jerusalem," "the words of Jeremiah," and "the word of the Lord" are related.

From the outset, the book of Jeremiah is concerned with the sovereign word of God conveyed through words of Jeremiah that moved Judah's history toward the Babylonian exile. Yet the text is subtle. The first verses of the book are careful not to equate "the words of Jeremiah" with "the word of the Lord"; nor is the word of the Lord identified with the words of the book. Further, the text makes no effort to explain how the words of the prophet and the word of the Lord might have shaped history toward the captivity of Jerusalem. As readers, we are put on notice by verses 1–3 that the book we are reading concerns the words of the prophet Jeremiah, and that the words of Jeremiah are connected with the word of the Lord that moves history toward the captivity of Jerusalem. To discern how this may be so, we are invited to read further.

Jeremiah 1:4–10

1:4 **Now the word of the LORD came to me saying,**

5 **"Before I formed you in the womb I knew you,**
and before you were born I consecrated you;
I appointed you a prophet to the nations."

6 **Then I said, "Ah, Lord GOD! Truly I do not know how to speak,**
for I am only a boy."

7 **But the LORD said to me,**
"Do not say, 'I am only a boy';
for you shall go to all to whom I send you,
and you shall speak whatever I command you.

8 **Do not be afraid of them,**
for I am with you to deliver you,

says the LORD."

9 **Then the LORD put out his hand and touched my mouth; and the**
LORD said to me,

"Now I have put my words in your mouth.
10 See, today I appoint you over nations and over kingdoms,
to pluck up and to pull down,
to destroy and to overthrow,
to build and to plant."

Jeremiah is the spokesperson for God's word. These verses recount the call of Jeremiah to be God's prophet and how the word of the Lord came to Jeremiah (v. 4). In God's relationship with Jeremiah, the initiative is God's. Only once is it reported that Jeremiah himself speaks (v. 6). Jeremiah is God's person—formed, known, consecrated, and appointed for the particular task of being "a prophet to the nations" (v. 5). The appointment of Jeremiah as a prophet to the nations anticipates the broad vision of God's dominion claimed in the book. Not only Judah but the nations are subject to God's will and purposes, announced by Jeremiah. Throughout the book, but especially in Jeremiah 45–51, there are prophetic speeches concerning the nations. Twice more in Jeremiah 1, in verses 10 and 15, the claim is made that Jeremiah is a prophet to the nations. In the book of Jeremiah, nations and kingdoms are subject to God's sovereign purposes, which Jeremiah is to announce.

Jeremiah contests his readiness for the task to which God appoints him, a task Jeremiah immediately associates with speech: "Ah, Lord God! Truly I do not know how to speak, for I am only a boy" (v. 6). Jeremiah's objection is reminiscent of Moses, who, when sent by God to Pharaoh, claimed he was unfit because he was "slow of speech and slow of tongue" (Exod. 4:10). However, the Lord immediately counters Jeremiah's objection with a demand and a promise. The demand is that Jeremiah go and speak; the promise is an assurance of God's presence and deliverance. Much is expected of Jeremiah, but God's expectations are supported by an assurance of divine help. At the conclusion of Matthew's Gospel we find something similar. Jesus had great expectations, that his disciples go and make disciples of all nations. Jesus also promised his disciples his continuing presence with them, saying, "I am with you always" (Matt. 28:20). God expects much of those called to serve but also promises much.

In the first three verses of the book we are told that God's word spoken through the words of Jeremiah will lead Jerusalem toward captivity by Babylon. In verses 4–10 we see "the word of the Lord" also leads Jeremiah to God's service. God's admonition to Jeremiah not to be afraid, along with God's promise to deliver Jeremiah, anticipates another theme in the book. As God's spokesperson, Jeremiah meets resistance, rejection, and threats of death for announcing God's word of judgment. Of course, since Jeremiah is God's spokesperson, the resistance to and rejection of the prophet are resistance to and rejection of God. Judah's rejection of God and God's spokesperson Jeremiah are important reasons that the Lord directed history toward the captivity of Jerusalem.

These verses show concern with the prophet himself only secondarily. Their primary concern is with the power of God to direct the course of history. Thus, at the conclusion of these verses, the word of the Lord is placed in the prophet's mouth (v. 9), and Jeremiah becomes God's spokesperson. God's authorization of the prophet is reinforced in verse 10 with the announcement that Jeremiah is appointed a prophet over the nations. In the Old Testament, the word *appoint* is used to designate persons for positions of oversight. (For example, Joseph is appointed overseer in Gen. 39:4, and Levites are appointed to their office in Num. 1:50.) God's appointment of Jeremiah as prophet to the nations ties their future to their response to the word of the Lord that Jeremiah is to announce.

At the conclusion of verse 10, the word of the Lord that Jeremiah is to speak to the nations is made more specific. The intention of God that Jeremiah is to announce is both judgment and restoration for the nations. Plucking up and pulling down stand together with building and planting. The book of Jeremiah as a whole helps us understand how these contrasting intentions of God are related. The explicit terms from Jeremiah 1:10 (in some variation) occur five more times in the book: 18:7–10; 24:6; 31:27–28; 42:10; 45:4. However, God's activity to judge and restore—to pluck up and pull down, to build and plant—is pervasive in the book, and we need to examine the interplay of these divine acts much more extensively than their explicit expression in the phrases from Jeremiah 1:10.

Jeremiah 1:1–10 expresses a central theme of the book, that God is sovereign over the nations and directs history. This claim may well conflict with how we have come to view history. In his book *Foolishness to Greeks: The Gospel and Western Culture*, Lesslie Newbigin reflects on the typical view of history in our modern world:

It is possible, and in our culture normal, to exclude the name of God altogether from our account of public affairs, and to construe history as a continuum of cause and effect, an arena where "historical forces" are at work and events take place in accordance with regularities that can be scientifically established, or at least an arena in which the only purposes at work are those of individual human beings. (P. 51)

In the church today, we are inclined to analyze closely historical causes and effects: the impact of congressional actions in creating a more just society, the consequences of a president's economic or foreign policy on developing third-world countries, the ways in which a zoning board decision will impact on our congregation and its neighborhood. We need to be concerned about such matters even as the book of Jeremiah is concerned with the policies of and policy makers in Jerusalem.

Yet in the book of Jeremiah history is not seen as a continuum of cause and effect whose outcome is determined solely by the interplay of historical forces. Rather, the world is seen to be governed and directed by God in ways that Jeremiah is to announce. There is awareness in the book of developments in international politics, such as the emergence of Babylon as a world power and the decision of the leaders of Judah in Jerusalem to resist Babylon. Yet the book spends little time attempting to analyze the interplay of these political activities. The claim of the book is that God is sovereign over history and will judge the nations, including Judah—pluck up and pull down. Then, God will restore them—build and plant.

This view of history found in the book of Jeremiah is the dominant view of history in the Bible. For instance, the book of Acts also knows that history is not to be understood as a continuum of cause and effect but as God's acts to direct history's course. In Acts, even Jesus' rejection and crucifixion are interpreted to reveal God's purposeful leading of the world and God's triumph over human efforts to subvert God's purposes:

> This man, handed over to you according to the definite plan and foreknowledge of God, you crucified and killed by the hands of those outside the law. But God raised him up, having freed him from death, because it was impossible for him to be held in its power. (Acts 2:23–24)

According to our modern worldview, "events take place in accordance with regularities that can be scientifically established" (Newbigin, *Foolishness to Greeks*, p. 51). In the books of Jeremiah and Acts, God directs history. Hence, the church affirms, "But God raised him up, having freed him from death, because it was impossible for him to be held in its power" (Acts 2:24).

The initial verses of the book of Jeremiah call us in the church to rethink how it is we understand history. Newbigin summarizes this matter:

> The question is whether the faith that finds its focus in Jesus is the faith with which we seek to understand the whole of history, or whether we limit this

faith to a private world of religion and hand over the public history of the world to other principles of explanation. (*Foolishness to Greeks*, p. 61)

The book of Jeremiah understands that God is sovereign over the world and directs history.

Jeremiah 1:11–16

1:11 **The word of the LORD came to me, saying, "Jeremiah, what do you see?" And I said, "I see a branch of an almond tree."** [12] **Then the LORD said to me, "You have seen well, for I am watching over my word to perform it."** [13] **The word of the LORD came to me a second time, saying, "What do you see?" And I said, "I see a boiling pot, tilted away from the north."**

[14] **Then the LORD said to me: Out of the north disaster shall break out on all the inhabitants of the land.** [15] **For now I am calling all the tribes of the kingdoms of the north, says the LORD; and they shall come and all of them shall set their thrones at the entrance of the gates of Jerusalem, against all its surrounding walls and against all the cities of Judah.** [16] **And I will utter my judgments against them, for all their wickedness in forsaking me; they have made offerings to other gods, and worshiped the works of their own hands.**

The call of Jeremiah is continued in the two visions reported in verses 11–16. Each vision is identified as the coming of "the word of the Lord" to Jeremiah. The vision of the almond tree in verses 11–12 utilizes a Hebrew wordplay. Jeremiah reports that he sees an "almond tree" (*shāqēd* in Hebrew), and God interprets, "You have seen well, for I am watching [*shōqēd* in Hebrew] over my word to perform it." The vision of the almond tree with its wordplay leads to the declaration that what the Lord intends will be accomplished: "I am watching over my word to perform it." In the first vision, the intention of "my word" is not made specific and could as easily refer to plucking up and pulling down as to building and planting (1:10).

However, in the vision reported in verses 13–16, the word of the Lord is clearly about God's judgment. Jeremiah sees a "boiling pot, tilted away from the north" (v. 13). This vision of a boiling pot points to a threat to Judah coming from the north. We are reminded that the book of Jeremiah concerns "the word of the Lord" leading to "the captivity of Jerusalem" (1:2–3). The advance of an unnamed enemy from the north against Jerusalem is the work of the Lord, and the defeat of Judah and Jerusalem is God's intention. In this second vision, the stress is clearly on plucking up and pulling down. The judgment threatened in verse 15, that enemies will set up their thrones in the gates of Jerusalem, closely parallels Jeremiah 39:3 (at the beginning of a narrative about the fall of Jerusalem): "When Jerusalem was taken, all the officials of the king of Babylon came and sat in the middle gate." The vision of the boiling pot in Jeremiah 1:13–16 foreshadows the direction of the book toward the captivity of Jerusalem (v. 3).

The vision of the pot concludes with a statement indicating the reason for God's judgment of Jerusalem: "I will utter my judgments against them, for all their wickedness in forsaking me; they have made offerings to other gods, and worshiped the works of their own hands" (v. 16) God threatens disaster (v. 14) because Judah committed wickedness (in v. 16; the NRSV translates as "wickedness" the Hebrew word that in v. 14 is translated "disaster"). In other words, Israel's wickedness of forsaking God will result in judgment, the "disaster" (the same Hebrew word as for wickedness) of an enemy advance to destroy Jerusalem.

"Forsaking" God is a theme developed extensively in the book of Jeremiah (2:13, 17, 19; 5:7, 19; 9:13; 16:11; 17:13; 19:4; 22:9). This concern is closely related to the understanding of forsaking God in the book of Deuteronomy, where it is connected with covenant curses (Deut. 28:20; 29:25; and 31:16). The book of Deuteronomy understands that God delivered Israel from slavery in Egypt and gave the people the promised land. God's deliverance was the basis for a "covenant," a formal relationship between God and Israel that indicated how Israel was to respond to God's deliverance and the gift of the land. A summary of the covenantal obligations or stipulations is found in the Ten Commandments (Deuteronomy 5; cf. Exodus 20), and a more specific indication of covenant expectations follows in Deuteronomy 12–26 (cf. Exodus 21–23). Deuteronomy understands that when Israel obeys, God will continue to bless the people so they may long remain in the land (see Deut. 5:33; 6:18). However, if Israel disobeys God and breaks covenant, for instance, by violating the First Commandment and forsaking God, then Deuteronomy understands that Israel risks God's judgment and covenant curse, particularly the loss of the land (Deut. 28:21, 64). Like the book of Deuteronomy, the book of Jeremiah claims that the consequences of forsaking God will be judgment and, specifically, captivity.

Some caution is needed at this point so we do not hear that we must somehow earn our status with God, a demand for "works righteousness." Both Deuteronomy and Jeremiah assume that the Lord has been gracious to Israel in many ways. God took the initiative in establishing a relationship with Israel, particularly in delivering them from Egypt and giving them the promised land (see Deuteronomy 1–11; Jer. 2:5–7). Because God has taken a gracious initiative to establish a relationship with God's people, the books of Deuteronomy and Jeremiah understand that Israel needs to respond to God:

You shall love the LORD your God with all your heart, and with all your soul, and with all your might. (Deut. 6:5, and pervasively in the first eleven chapters of Deuteronomy)

> I thought
>> how I would set you among my children,
> and give you a pleasant land,
>> the most beautiful heritage of all the nations.
> And I thought you would call me, My Father,
>> and would not turn from following me.
>
> (Jer. 3:19)

These books never imagine that people can "earn" God's favor. They do understand that if persons seriously "counted their blessings" from God, it would lead to trust in and obedience of God. However, the book of Jeremiah makes the accusation that Judah and Israel have forsaken the Lord.

Jeremiah 1:17–19

1:17 But you, gird up your loins; stand up and tell them everything that I command you. Do not break down before them, or I will break you before them. ¹⁸ And I for my part have made you today a fortified city, an iron pillar, and a bronze wall, against the whole land—against the kings of Judah, its princes, its priests, and the people of the land. ¹⁹ They will fight against you; but they shall not prevail against you, for I am with you, says the LORD, to deliver you.

Jeremiah 1 concludes with assurances and encouragement to the prophet. However, as in verses 4–10, these verses are primarily not about the prophet but about God. The fortified walls of Jerusalem and the cities of Judah (1:15) will fall because Judah has forsaken God. By contrast, Jeremiah will be made by God "a fortified city" able to stand against the whole land (v. 18), and God's intentions will prevail despite the resistance to God by prophets, priests, kings, and people of the land.

Jeremiah 1 begins with an affirmation that the word of the Lord will bring about the captivity of Jerusalem. Jeremiah 1 concludes with a warning that the word of the Lord, spoken by God's messenger, Jeremiah, will be resisted by the Jerusalem religious and political establishment, who have forsaken God (1:16). Thus, Jeremiah 1 sets in motion the central dynamics of the book as a whole: the sovereignty of God over history, a charge to Jeremiah to be the spokesperson for the word of the Lord, the claim that Judah has forsaken God, and the warning that the Jerusalem leaders will resist God's word and the prophet who announces it. It is through the development of these themes that the book of Jeremiah unfolds.

"They Have Forsaken Me"
(Jeremiah 2–3)

Jeremiah 2–3 elaborates on the accusation from Jeremiah 1:16 that Judah and Jerusalem have forsaken God. Jeremiah 2:1–3 describes God's initial relationship with Israel. The remainder of Jeremiah 2 indicates the ways in which the people have distorted their relationship with the Lord and in so doing forfeited the life and blessings God intended for them. Jeremiah 3 concerns God's response to being forsaken. The chapter expresses God's pained disappointment and suggests the lengths to which the Lord is willing to go to restore relationship with God's people.

There are only some general historical references in Jeremiah 2–3 (2:10, 16–18, 36, 3:6–11), and they are not specific enough to help in identifying the historical situation Jeremiah may have addressed through these speeches. Again, these chapters of the book of Jeremiah move us toward a theological understanding of "the captivity of Jerusalem" (1:3).

Jeremiah 2:1–3

> 2:1 **The word of the LORD came to me, saying:** [2] **Go and proclaim in the hearing of Jerusalem, Thus says the LORD:**
> > **I remember the devotion of your youth,**
> > **your love as a bride,**
> > **how you followed me in the wilderness,**
> > **in a land not sown.**
> > [3] **Israel was holy to the LORD,**
> > **the first fruits of his harvest.**
> > **All who ate of it were held guilty;**
> > **disaster came upon them,**
>
> > > **says the LORD.**

Verses 2–3 use two images to characterize the initial relationship between God and Israel. First, God remembers "the devotion" of the people's youth and Israel's "love as a bride" when they followed after God in the wilderness. This image reflects an ancient Near Eastern marriage ceremony in which a bride followed her husband from her abode to his and points to Israel's original faithfulness or loyalty to God. The use of the Hebrew word translated in the NRSV as "devotion" to describe the relationship of Israel and the Lord is particularly striking. In the vast majority of Old Testament uses of this word, it is God's faithfulness, in contrast to Israel's, that is stressed. Here, Israel's faithfulness or devotion to God is affirmed. By comparing Israel's wilderness relationship with the Lord to that of a bride who follows after her husband, a positive view of Israel's initial relationship with God is presented. (In these verses and throughout the early chapters of the book, remember that "Israel" is used to speak of the united kingdoms of Israel and Judah, the whole people of God. Israel divides into two kingdoms after King Solomon—Judah [south] and Israel [north]. As we read further, the focus is increasingly on Judah.)

The second way in which God's initial relationship with Israel is characterized is through the image of "first fruits." For Israel, the first fruits of the harvest belonged to God and were to be presented as an offering (see Deut. 26:1–15). God identifies Israel with the first fruits of the harvest and so calls Israel "holy." The word *holy* indicates a relationship between God and Israel in which Israel is set apart for or devoted exclusively to God. The assertion that God's people are "holy to the Lord" and "the first fruits of his harvest" leads to an assurance of God's protection. Those who "ate"—the Hebrew verb can mean either "eat" or, in a military sense, "devour"—the first fruits belonging to God will be held guilty, and "disaster" will come on them (cf. 1:14, 16). God pledges protection against any nation that might attempt to harm Israel.

The two ways in which God remembers the initial relationship with Israel at the beginning of Jeremiah 2 complement each other. The bridal imagery stresses Israel's loyalty to God, while the first-fruits imagery stresses God's loyalty to Israel. Yet this very positive view of the original relationship between God and Israel serves as a foil for what follows. The remainder of Jeremiah 2–3 concerns the ways in which God is forsaken by Israel. As we read Jeremiah 2–3, we are challenged to reflect on God's loyalty to the church and the ways in which we in the church may forsake the Lord.

Jeremiah 2:4–13

2:4 **Hear the word of the LORD, O house of Jacob, and all the families of the house of Israel.** 5 **Thus says the LORD:**
What wrong did your ancestors find in me

that they went far from me,
and went after worthless things,
and became worthless themselves?
6 They did not say, "Where is the LORD
who brought us up from the land of Egypt,
who led us in the wilderness,
in a land of deserts and pits,
in a land of drought and deep darkness,
in a land that no one passes through,
where no one lives?"
7 I brought you into a plentiful land
to eat its fruits and its good things.
But when you entered you defiled my land,
and made my heritage an abomination.
8 The priests did not say, "Where is the LORD?"
Those who handle the law did not know me;
the rulers transgressed against me;
the prophets prophesied by Baal,
and went after things that do not profit.

9 Therefore once more I accuse you,
                                        says the LORD,
and I accuse your children's children.

10 Cross to the coasts of Cyprus and look,
send to Kedar and examine with care;
see if there has ever been such a thing.
11 Has a nation changed its gods,
even though they are no gods?
But my people have changed their glory
for something that does not profit.
12 Be appalled, O heavens, at this,
be shocked, be utterly desolate,
                                        says the LORD,

13 for my people have committed two evils:
they have forsaken me,
the fountain of living water,
and dug out cisterns for themselves,
cracked cisterns
that can hold no water.

In Jeremiah 2:4–13, Jeremiah announces a lawsuit brought by God against Israel. In this lawsuit, God is the prosecutor and, finally, the judge;

God's people are the accused. God brings charges against the people (vv. 4–9), conducts an interrogation (vv. 10–11), appeals to witnesses (v. 12), and finally renders a verdict (v. 13). These verses develop from Jeremiah 2:2–3 by the repetition of a key- or catchword. In Jeremiah 2:2, God remembers that initially Israel "followed me" in the wilderness. The same Hebrew verb translated as "followed" in Jeremiah 2:2 occurs three times in verses 4–8 (and in 2:14–25 three additional times). By looking at the three uses of this catchword, we can follow the argument of these verses.

1. The Hebrew verb translated in verse 2 as "followed" is translated in verse 5 as "went after" and is used by God to accuse Israel of idolatry: "they . . . went after worthless things." "Worthless things" is widely recognized as a euphemism for the fertility gods. These gods, such as Baal and his consort Asherah, were understood in the world of the ancient Near East to be responsible for the fertility of crops and herds. Fertility cults included ritual prostitution to remind or even coerce the gods into sexual activity, which was understood as necessary for the earth's fertility. Israel had long rejected the fertility cults and their deities and insisted that the Lord alone was the source of life. At the core of God's accusation against Israel is that they had violated the First Commandment, "You shall have no other gods before me" (Exod. 20:3; Deut. 5:7; but also see 1 Kings 18). God asserts that the once-devoted bride has turned to others, and the consequence of Israel's reliance on the fertility deities will be that the once-holy people will become "worthless" like the fertility gods to whom they have become devoted (vv. 4–5).

2. The Hebrew verb from verse 2 occurs again in verse 6 in the phrase "who led us in the wilderness." God led Israel from places of death, Egypt and the wilderness, and brought Israel to a place of life and blessing, "into a plentiful land to eat its fruits and its good things" (v.7). However, God brings the charge that the people no longer asked, "Where is the Lord who brought us up from the land of Egypt?" (v. 6). God's saving deeds on behalf of Israel—exodus deliverance, wilderness guidance, the gift of land—are no longer remembered, and the Lord is no longer understood as the source of Israel's well-being. Israel not only turned to the fertility gods but also turned away from the Lord. They forgot that it was the Lord who had led them from death to life.

God's accusations against Israel are intensified with the charge that they have "defiled" the land entrusted to them and made it "an abomination." In Leviticus 18, defilement and abomination are linked with improper sexual activity, with the consequence being exile: "the land vomited out its inhabitants" (18:25). The charge in Jeremiah 2 that Israel "defiled my land,

and made my heritage an abomination" is linked to ritual prostitution at the cults of the fertility gods. The accusation that the people who were a devoted bride have forsaken the Lord and made the land an abomination builds a ʻcase for the loss of the land and the captivity of Jerusalem.

3. God's indictment is concluded in verse 8 with the third occurrence of the verb from verse 2, here translated again as "went after." Again, the charge is that Israel has forsaken the Lord for the fertility deities; they "went after worthless things." The leadership of Judah is particularly held accountable. Priests, rulers (shepherds), and prophets are accused of not saying, "Where is the Lord?" It is no wonder that Israel does not remember God's saving deeds when the community leaders, those responsible for teaching, worship, and the public order, have forgotten God. The accusation that the community leaders "went after things that do not profit" parallels the accusation of verse 5 that Israel "went after worthless things, and became worthless themselves," that is, they turned from the Lord who had saved them to the fertility deities, who can do nothing.

God's accusation is that Israel violated the First Commandment; the people turned from the Lord and went after other gods. Once Israel followed God in the wilderness and was holy to God. However, Israel chose to follow worthlessness and became worthless. Once, the Lord led Israel through the wilderness to the land where God offered life and blessings. However, Israel went after the fertility deities, and by so doing, defiled God's land and made God's heritage an abomination.

The lawsuit of God that Jeremiah announces is concluded with a three-part summation of the case against Israel (vv. 11–13). First, God compares Israel negatively to the nations who, though their gods cannot compare to the Lord, nonetheless do not change their gods (vv. 10–12). Israel has been fickle like no other people in relationship to their God. Second, God calls on the heavens, urging that they "be appalled" at the charges God has brought (v. 12). Again, this text assumes a courtroom drama of cosmic proportions. As the concluding argument develops, God appeals to the heavens to act as witnesses to the case being presented, to be "shocked" at the behavior of the accused. Finally, God concludes the prosecution argument with the charge that the people have committed two "evils" (v. 13; the word for evil in this verse is the same Hebrew word translated as "disaster" and "wickedness" in 1:14, 16). The first evil is that "they have forsaken me, the fountain of living water." Israel once followed God in the wilderness, once was led by the Lord "up from the land of Egypt . . . [through] the land of drought and deep darkness . . . into a plentiful land to eat its fruits and its good things" (vv. 6–7). The Lord has been "the fountain of living water" to Israel, a source of life that the people have inexplicably forsaken. The second evil is that they turned to other gods, who are likened to "cracked cisterns." In an arid land, springs are far preferable to cisterns. Israel has not only forsaken "the fountain of living water" but has chosen "cracked cisterns that can hold no water," the fertility deities who are incapable of sustaining Israel's well-being in the land. In the exchange of the Lord for the fertility gods, Israel acted in a way that would lead to death, to "the captivity of Jerusalem" (1:3).

The oracles that follow in Jeremiah 2 reinforce and intensify God's accusations made in verses 4–13. However, before reading further, we need to reflect on how these verses, so important to the book of Jeremiah, might address the church. In addressing the church at Corinth about food offered to idols, Paul wrote:

> Indeed, even though there may be so-called gods in heaven and on earth— as in fact there are many gods and many lords—yet for us there is one God, the Father, for whom are all things and for whom we exist, and one Lord, Jesus Christ, through whom are all things and through whom we exist. (1 Cor. 8:5–6)

The problem of many gods and many lords is precisely the problem addressed in Jeremiah 2:4–13, and throughout much of the book of Jeremiah. Will Israel "follow after" the God who saved them from slavery in Egypt and gave them the land of milk and honey, or will the people forsake God for the Baals? Will Israel's devotion be to God or to worthless fertility gods? Martin Luther reflected about the problem of God and the gods like this:

> When do men have other gods?
> 　Men have other gods—
> 　. . . . .
> 　c. When they fear, love, or trust in any person or thing as they should fear, love and trust in God alone.
> 　　　　　　　　　　　　　(Luther, *Small Catechism*, pp. 50–51)

Jeremiah 2:4–13 makes us ask, What do we fear, love, and trust? To whom or what do we look for saving power and security, for meaning and authority?

In the book *Following Christ in a Consumer Society*, John Kavanaugh has written of the idolatrous temptations with which Christians must contend in the affluence of the Western world. Noting how Christianity is often co-opted to legitimate the interests of particular cultures and their institutions, Kavanaugh observes of the American life:

> Achievement and wealth become endowed with redemptive, even salvific, power. Poverty and marginality, which should serve as signals of grace, are inevitably interpreted as the just deserts of "those lazy people who cannot take care of themselves." Thus the substantive teachings of Christ concerning justice, compassion, and generosity lose their clarity and power in a web of slickly spiritualized, but still racist and class-oriented, market myth. (p. 105)

Jesus called his disciples to follow after him. Kavanaugh's observation about the idolatrous claims of economic achievement and success in our society echoes the concern of Jeremiah 2:4–13 and confronts us with the troubling possibility that we who are part of a consumer culture, instead of following Jesus, may go after that which is worthless and does not profit.

Jeremiah 2:14–19

2:14 Is Israel a slave? Is he a homeborn servant?
    Why then has he become plunder?
15 The lions have roared against him,
    they have roared loudly.
    They have made his land a waste;
    his cities are in ruins, without inhabitant.
16 Moreover, the people of Memphis and Tahpanhes
    have broken the crown of your head.
17 Have you not brought this upon yourself
    by forsaking the LORD your God,
    while he led you in the way?
18 What then do you gain by going to Egypt,
    to drink the waters of the Nile?
    Or what do you gain by going to Assyria,
    to drink the waters of the Euphrates?
19 Your wickedness will punish you,
    and your apostasies will convict you.
    Know and see that it is evil and bitter
    for you to forsake the LORD your God;
    the fear of me is not in you,
               says the Lord GOD of hosts.

The prophet identifies a further distortion in the relationship between God and Israel. Somehow Israel has become a slave and an object of plunder (vv. 14–15). God did not intend for Israel to be a slave! We have already

been reminded that it was God who delivered Israel from slavery in Egypt
(2:6). So the question is posed: If Israel was not a slave, how have they
become one?

This tragedy is explained by the prophet through a twice-stated accusation (vv. 17, 19) that Israel has forsaken God (cf. 2:6). This accusation
surrounds two additional questions posed in verse 18 that make more specific the charge against Israel:

> Why are you on the way to Egypt,
> to drink the waters of the Nile?
> Why are you on the way to Assyria,
> to drink the waters of the Euphrates?
> (author's translation)

The prophet charges that Israel has forsaken the Lord and sought security
in political alliances. Once the Lord was the "fountain of living water" to
Israel (2:13). Jeremiah accuses Israel of seeking water for themselves—life
and security in political alliances with Egypt and Assyria. Again, once it
was the Lord led Israel "in the way" (v. 17), but Jeremiah accuses Israel of
choosing its own way. Ironically, it is a way to Egypt and Assyria, nations
by whom Israel and Judah had been subjugated over many decades. By
seeking security in alliances with Egypt and Assyria, Israel has chosen to
become a "slave" (v. 14), and the promised land, once a land of plenty (v.
7), has become "ruins" and a "waste" like the wilderness land of drought,
"without inhabitant" (v. 15; cf. 2:6).

As the prophet's speech is concluded, he describes God with a Hebrew
word that is translated in the NRSV as "Lord" in the sense of a slave's master. (Note that "Lord" here is not a translation of Yahweh, God's proper
name.) Israel is a slave after all, but Israel's "master" (Lord) is the God of
the exodus, and not Egypt or Assyria. With Master Yahweh, "the fountain
of living water," there is life and blessing for Israel in the land. Drinking
the waters of Egypt and Assyria has brought only death, and the land has
become a "waste" and "ruins." Israel, set free by the Lord, has chosen to
become a slave once more through political alliances with Egypt and
Assyria. God intends Israel to be free, but they have chosen a path that will
lead to captivity, first to Egypt and Assyria but finally to Babylon.

These verses express a paradox that runs deep in the Christian tradition.
God's freedom—from the oppression of slavery in Egypt, from the power
of sin and death—is freedom to be in relationship with and commit one's
life to the Lord, who is the source of life and blessing. There is always the
danger, as this text from Jeremiah suggests, that God's people will use the

freedom the Lord has given for self-serving ends. So, Paul said to the church at Galatia,

> you were called to freedom, brothers and sisters; only do not use your freedom as an opportunity for self-indulgence, but through love become slaves to one another. For the whole law is summed up in a single commandment, "You shall love your neighbor as yourself." (Gal. 5:13–14)

God offers freedom, the life-giving freedom to live in relationship with the Lord. In the freedom God has given, Israel chooses to enter enslaving alliances with Egypt and Assyria. Paul warns us in the church of the danger of using our freedom in the gospel of Jesus Christ for "self-indulgence."

The familiar hymn "Make me a captive, Lord" expresses well for the church the paradox about freedom and submission to God:

> Make me a captive, Lord,
> And then I shall be free;
> Force me to render up my sword,
> And I shall conqueror be.
>
> I sink in life's alarms
> When by myself I stand;
> Imprison me within Thine arms,
> And strong shall be my hand.

Jeremiah 2:20–25

2:20 **For long ago you broke your yoke**
      and burst your bonds,
      and you said, "I will not serve!"
  On every high hill
      and under every green tree
      you sprawled and played the whore.
21 **Yet I planted you as a choice vine,**
      from the purest stock.
  How then did you turn degenerate
      and become a wild vine?
22 **Though you wash yourself with lye**
      and use much soap,
  the stain of your guilt is still before me,
                says the Lord GOD.
23 **How can you say, "I am not defiled,**
      I have not gone after the Baals"?

> Look at your way in the valley;
> know what you have done—
> a restive young camel interlacing her tracks,
> ²⁴ a wild ass at home in the wilderness,
> in her heat sniffing the wind!
> Who can restrain her lust?
> None who seek her need weary themselves;
> in her month they will find her.
> ²⁵ Keep your feet from going unshod
> and your throat from thirst.
> But you said, "It is hopeless,
> for I have loved strangers,
> and after them I will go."

Jeremiah's perception of the distorted relationship between God and Israel is further developed through a series of harsh and even offensive images that express the extreme perversion in Israel's life. Although God can remember when Israel was a devoted youth and loving bride, in these verses Israel is compared to a whore, a wild vine, a restive young camel, a wild ass in heat. With great sarcasm these verses characterize the distortion of Israel's relationship with God, and in turn, the distortion of Israel's identity.

The distortion of Israel's relationship with God portrayed from the beginning of Jeremiah 2 is emphasized by the repetition of the Hebrew verb from verse 2 whose basic meaning is to walk, go, or follow:

2:2   as a bride, Israel *followed* the Lord in the wilderness
2:6   Israel *went after* worthlessness
2:6   They did not say, "Where is the Lord, who *led* us in the wilderness . . ."
2:8   prophets *went after* things that do not profit
2:17   Israel forsook the Lord who *led* them in the wilderness
2:23   God's people have *gone after* Baals
2:25   Israel says, "I have loved strangers and after them I will *go*."

Once, Israel was devoted to the Lord and in the wilderness followed as a loving bride; the Lord led Israel from Egypt, through the wilderness, and to the land. God saved Israel from death for life. However, Israel forsook the Lord and went after the fertility deities, who were incapable of sustaining Israel, who were "worthless" and did "not profit." In a reference to the prostitution associated with the fertility cults, Jeremiah charges that Israel has become a harlot who follows strangers, the fertility gods, whom she loves. The final three sections of Jeremiah 2—verses 26–28, 29–32, and 33–37—present additional ways that Israel has distorted relationship with God.

Jeremiah 2:26–28

The central accusation of Jeremiah 2 is that Israel has forsaken the Lord and sought well-being through the fertility gods and in political alliances. In these verses, the prophets, rulers, and priests who no longer ask, "Where is the Lord?" (2:8) are quoted as they address their new gods, saying "to a tree, 'You are my Father,' and to a stone, 'You gave me birth' " (v. 27). On the one hand, Israel has forsaken the Lord for the fertility gods that are worthless and cannot save them. On the other hand, those who have forsaken the Lord and turned to other gods for their well-being are not consistent, and in their time of trouble they turn to the Lord and plead, "Come and save us!" Like many people, Judah was not serious about their relationship with the Lord until there was a crisis. In times of trouble, their devotion to God was ardent. No wonder God was moving history toward the captivity of Jerusalem, when Israel would finally be caught and shamed for how they related to the Lord.

Jeremiah 2:29–32

2:29 **Why do you complain against me?**
        You have all rebelled against me,

                                                says the LORD.

30 **In vain I have struck down your children;**
      they accepted no correction.
      Your own sword devoured your prophets
      like a ravening lion.
31 **And you, O generation, behold the word of the LORD!**
      Have I been a wilderness to Israel,
      or a land of thick darkness?
      Why then do my people say, "We are free,
      we will come to you no more"?
32 **Can a girl forget her ornaments,**
      or a bride her attire?
      Yet my people have forgotten me,
      days without number.

There is a close connection between these verses and Jeremiah 2:1–13. While in Jeremiah 2:9, God declares against Israel, "I accuse you," in these verses God refutes a "complaint" (v. 29, the same Hebrew word translated "accuse" in 2:9) brought by God's people. Israel has charged God with desertion, with being "a wilderness to Israel, or a land of thick darkness" (v. 31). Because Israel thought that God had become a source of death and chaos, they felt justified to declare, "We are free, we will come to you no more" (cf. 2:14, 20). This exchange reflects the profound distortion in Israel's relationship with the Lord. God, who led Israel through the wilderness, "a land of . . . deep darkness" (2:6), is accused by Israel of being a "wilderness" and a "land of thick darkness." God's people have turned their relationship with the Lord upside down and backward. They have forsaken God but accuse God of forsaking them.

The prophet concludes this oracle by returning to the bridal imagery from Jeremiah 2:2. God remembers Israel as a loving bride (2:2), and brides do not forget they are brides, that is, they do not forget their ornaments and attire. The Lord remembers Israel, but they have forgotten God.

Jeremiah 2:33–37

2:33 **How well you direct your course**
　　　　　to seek lovers!
　　　　So that even to wicked women
　　　　you have taught your ways.
　34 **Also on your skirts is found**
　　　　the lifeblood of the innocent poor,
　　　　though you did not catch them breaking in.
　　　　Yet in spite of all these things
　35 **you say, "I am innocent;**
　　　　surely his anger has turned from me."
　　　　Now I am bringing you to judgment
　　　　for saying, "I have not sinned."
　36 **How lightly you gad about,**
　　　　changing your ways!
　　　　You shall be put to shame by Egypt
　　　　as you were put to shame by Assyria.
　37 **From there also you will come away**
　　　　with your hands on your head;
　　　　for the LORD has rejected those in whom you trust,
　　　　and you will not prosper through them.

These concluding verses of Jeremiah 2 draw together themes and images from throughout the chapter. In verse 33 the prophet charges that Israel has directed their "course to seek lovers." The phrase suggests that the people have turned both to fertility gods and to political alliances for security. Israel's political and religious promiscuity has become so notorious that even "wicked women" (remember the whore image of v. 20) learn from Israel. Israel, which should have modeled for the nations a way of relating to God, has become the worst kind of example (cf. v. 11).

In addition to charges of religious and political promiscuity, the prophet accuses Israel of exploiting the innocent poor, who are charged with theft even though they have not been caught breaking in (v. 34; cf. 2:26, "As a thief . . . "). God's judgment will occur because Israel declares, "I am innocent," as the accused poor actually are, and "I have not sinned," when Israel has sinned blatantly by forsaking the Lord (that is, they gadded about changing their "ways," v. 36; cf. 2:18).

Finally, the prophet announces that by God's judgment Israel will be put to "shame" (v. 36; cf. 2:26) by Egypt and Assyria, allies trusted by Israel (cf. 2:18, 33). The book of Jeremiah repeatedly affirms that God is sovereign over the nations. At least for a time, Assyria and Egypt serve God's purpose of judgment against Judah and Israel. From Egypt and Assyria, Israel will come away with "her hands on her head" (v. 37). There may be a parallel to the story of Tamar and Amnon in 2 Samuel 13:

> After Tamar is violated, Amnon hates her; she is "sent away" (v 16 there), the door is bolted against her, she "goes off" . . . with her hands on her head (v 19 there). The "hands on your head" in the present passage is then an expression of humiliation and despair; does [Jeremiah] imply that Egypt will rape Israel as Amnon took advantage of Tamar? (Holladay, *Jeremiah 1*, pp. 111–12)

The "lovers" to whom Israel has turned for help and security will be instead a source of abuse and harm.

Jeremiah 2 concerns the ways in which the people have distorted their relationship with God by forsaking God and seeking their well-being with the fertility deities and in political alliances. The chapter is bold, harsh, and, at the end, brutal in portraying the distorted relationship between God and Israel. The people have turned from the God of the exodus and sought their well-being and security in the fertility deities and in political alliances.

The trap into which Israel fell is also a threat to the church today. The church can easily forget its identity, distort its relationship with God, and seek well-being and security in ways that are popular in our culture. James Wallis has written of the church:

> Our churches are now, in most every instance, bearing the marks of a paralyzing conformity to the world that has crippled our life and our witness. We

have adopted the structure and values of the large corporation in our organizational patterns. Having become like other institutions and bureaucracies, we employ the same techniques and methods. The ordinary social values are reproduced rather than reversed in the churches, and we have substituted a captive civil religion for the clear proclamation of the Word of God. . . . Basic and primary to the task of Christians today is to recover the biblical vision of the church as the people of God—a new social reality in the midst of the life of the world. The biblical metaphors for the people of God—aliens, exile, pilgrims, sojourners, strangers, salt, light—must be revived and made real again in our everyday experience. If that salt loses its savor, if the light is swallowed up in darkness, they no longer fulfill their intended purpose and are good for nothing. The church's service and mission in the world is absolutely dependent on its being different from the world, being in the world but not of the world. (*Agenda for Biblical People*, pp. 100–101)

The prophet Jeremiah made the accusation that Israel had conformed to the world of the ancient Near East and so had become salt that had lost its savor. Jeremiah still speaks to us in the church, urging that we remember whose we are and who we are.

Jeremiah 3:1–10

3:1 **If a man divorces his wife**
     and she goes from him
     and becomes another man's wife,
     will he return to her?
     Would not such a land be greatly polluted?
     You have played the whore with many lovers;
     and would you return to me?
                              says the LORD.
  2 **Look up to the bare heights, and see!**
     Where have you not been lain with?
     By the waysides you have sat waiting for lovers,
     like a nomad in the wilderness.
     You have polluted the land
     with your whoring and wickedness.
  3 **Therefore the showers have been withheld,**
     and the spring rain has not come;
     yet you have the forehead of a whore,
     you refuse to be ashamed.
  4 **Have you not just now called to me,**
     "My Father, you are the friend of my youth—
  5 **will he be angry forever,**

will he be indignant to the end?"
This is how you have spoken,
but you have done all the evil that you could.
⁶ The LORD said to me in the days of King Josiah: Have you seen what she did, that faithless one, Israel, how she went up on every high hill and under every green tree, and played the whore there? ⁷And I thought, "After she has done all this she will return to me"; but she did not return, and her false sister Judah saw it. ⁸ She saw that for all the adulteries of that faithless one, Israel, I had sent her away with a decree of divorce; yet her false sister Judah did not fear, but she too went and played the whore. ⁹ Because she took her whoredom so lightly, she polluted the land, committing adultery with stone and tree. ¹⁰ Yet for all this her false sister Judah did not return to me with her whole heart, but only in pretense, says the LORD.

Jeremiah 3 develops particularly from the claim of Jeremiah 2:2 that Israel is the Lord's bride. The background of Jeremiah 3:1–10 is the divorce law of Deuteronomy 24:1–4. Deuteronomy 24 stipulates that should a man divorce his wife and she subsequently marry and divorce a second man, the first husband may not take her back. Such a woman is considered "defiled" (the same word that occurs in Jeremiah 2:7 regarding the land), and to take her back would be "abhorrent" to the Lord and bring "guilt" on the land. It is difficult to know why Israel may have thought of remarriage in this negative manner, but this law does underlie Jeremiah 3.

Jeremiah 3:1–2 applies this law from Deuteronomy 24 to Israel. In fact, Israel's situation is much worse than the case imagined in Deuteronomy 24. The Lord has not sent Israel away, but instead, as we know from Jeremiah 2, Israel has forsaken God. The once-faithful bride has "played the whore with many lovers" (cf. 2:20, 25, 33), "polluted the land with . . . whoring and wickedness" (v. 2), and instead of following the Lord in the wilderness (2:2), "sat waiting for lovers . . . in the wilderness" (v. 2; cf. 2:6, 24, 31). It is not God who has abandoned Israel, but Israel that has forsaken the Lord. Given Israel's behavior, the stipulation from Deuteronomy rules out any chance that God's once-devoted bride can return, that God's relationship with Israel can be restored.

In fact, these verses indicate that the behavior of Israel results in covenant curse: "Therefore the showers have been withheld, and the spring rain has not come" (v. 3). In Deuteronomy 28, one consequence of forsaking God (28:20) is drought:

The sky over your head shall be bronze, and the earth under you iron. The LORD will change the rain of our land into powder, and only dust shall come down upon you from the sky until you are destroyed. (Deut. 28:23–24)

The irony is that the fertility gods to which Israel turned were intended to ensure there would be rain. The Lord offered Israel life and blessing, but they chose death and curse. Further, the people are portrayed in these verses as intransigent. Israel continues to play the whore and refuses to be "ashamed" (Jer. 3:3; cf. 2:26, 36); and again, Israel calls to God, "My father . . . ," yet continues to do "all the evil that you could" (vv. 4–5). In calling Yahweh "My Father," Israel verbally affirms a proper relationship with God. However, in seeking security through the fertility deities and political alliances, the people's actions belied their words. The relationship between God and the people was hopelessly broken, and a restoration of the relationship was prohibited by stipulations God had established (Deuteronomy 24).

The prophet's portrayal of the relationship between God and Israel as a broken marriage is reinforced and deepened in verses 6–10. In contrast to the image of Israel as the devoted youth (2:3), Israel and Judah are called "faithless." The mention of King Josiah (v. 6) suggests that Judah's "return" in these verses referred to Josiah's reform, intended to reunify Judah and Israel. Judah saw how God had sent Israel away "with a decree of divorce" (v. 8), a reference to the destruction of Israel by Assyria in 722 B.C. Yet Judah would not return and is twice characterized by Jeremiah as "false," an accusation whose meaning is made specific in verse 10: "false . . . Judah did not return to me with her whole heart, but only in pretense, says the Lord" (cf. vv. 4–5). Judah played at their relationship with God; it was pretend, not sincere and deep. Jeremiah presents the relationship between God and Judah as hopelessly and irreparably broken. The restoration of the relationship is beyond what God's stipulations allow (vv. 1–5) but also beyond Israel's will or ability.

Yet there is one clue in these verses that the Lord still hopes for a restored relationship. Despite all evidence, God reflects (v. 7): "And I thought, 'After she has done all this, she will return to me.' " Like a jilted lover, God hopes Judah might yet return. However, quickly God must admit that "she did not return." God's hope that Judah might repent is disappointed.

Jeremiah 3:11–14

3:11 **Then the LORD said to me: Faithless Israel has shown herself less guilty than false Judah.** [12] **Go, and proclaim these words toward the north, and say:**
> **Return, faithless Israel,**
>
> > **says the LORD.**
>
> **I will not look on you in anger,**
> **for I am merciful,**
>
> > **says the LORD;**

I will not be angry forever.
13 Only acknowledge your guilt,
that you have rebelled against the LORD your God,
and scattered your favors among strangers under every green tree,
and have not obeyed my voice,

                                                  says the LORD.
14 Return, O faithless children,

                                                  says the LORD,

for I am your master;
I will take you, one from a city and two from a family,
and I will bring you to Zion.

What was only hinted in Jeremiah 3:7 comes to full expression in verses 11–14. The Lord, who had been forsaken by "faithless Israel," nonetheless makes a startling and undeserved offer: "Return, faithless Israel. . . . Return, O faithless children. . . . " (vv. 12, 14). The Lord reinforces this unexpected invitation for faithless Israel to return, even in violation of covenant stipulations, through three statements: (1) "I will not look on you in anger," (2) "for I am merciful," (3) "I will not be angry forever" (v. 12). A restoration of relationship is possible because the Lord's anger is tempered by "mercy"—the same Hebrew word translated as "devotion" in reference to God's people in Jeremiah 2:2. Israel was once devoted to God but is so no longer. Now, it is only God's mercy (perhaps better translated "devotion" to match 2:2) that makes a restored relationship possible. Israel's devotion to God waned, but the Lord's devotion to Israel is steadfast. Though it is against stipulations established by the Lord, God nonetheless makes a startling offer to Israel: "Return." The Lord so wants a relationship with Israel that God is willing to violate God's own law.

While God offers to allow Israel to return (vv. 12, 14), the offer does carry conditions (v. 13). Guilt and covenant disobedience need to be acknowledged, and Israel's return needs to be with "her whole heart" (see v. 10). The Lord will risk violation of covenant stipulations to restore relationship with the people. Still, the "faithless one" needs to "return" to the Lord. In verse 14, God declares: "I am your master." The Hebrew word here can be translated as either "master" or "husband," and in the context of Jeremiah 2–3, both are appropriate. Israel has a husband/master, but it is God, not the fertility deities or Judah's foreign allies. God's people are already in a committed relationship with the Lord, their master or husband, and it is to this relationship that they are called to return.

Jeremiah 3:15–18

Having opened the possibility for a restored relationship, the Lord indicates what might occur should Israel repent or "return." In place of the rulers (shepherds) who have forgotten God's saving deeds and Israel's dependence on God (2:8, 26) the Lord will provide rulers devoted to God (3:15). In the once-plentiful land (2:7) where showers have been withheld (3:3), there will again be increase (3:16). In judgment, enemies will set their thrones in Jerusalem's gates (1:15); when God restores Israel, Jerusalem will be known as the "throne of the Lord," where the nations will gather (3:17). God's "heritage," the land, made abominable by Israel, will be restored (v. 18; cf. 2:7). Thus, in the future and after the captivity of Jerusalem (1:3)—"at that time" and "in those days"—God intends a restored relationship, life and blessing for God's people, building and planting (1:10). This text likely reflects an expression of hope that arose among those who edited the book of Jeremiah after the time of the prophet and during the period of Babylonian captivity.

Jeremiah 3:19–20

God intended to restore Israel and hoped that they would repent. However, in these verses God's thoughts shift from imagining what might have been to a pained reflection on the current state of the relationship. There is a contrast between the Lord's intention for relationship (v. 19) and Israel's response to God (v. 20). The Lord's intention for Israel is expressed by a double use of "I thought . . . " (v. 19): that when Israel was given the land (heritage), they would call God "Father" and follow after God. The Lord is a generous parent who most of all desires relationship with these children (cf. Hos. 11:1–11).

Yet, from Jeremiah 2–3 we know about these children. So we are not surprised to learn that God's offer of a restored relationship is shunned. God recognizes that instead of calling the Lord "Father," Israel has been "faithless." The double expression of God's intention (v. 19, "I thought . . . I thought . . . ") is matched by a double use of "faithless" to describe Israel (v. 20). Thus, God suffers the rebuke of unresponsive children and is seen through this text as a pained and disappointed parent.

The depth of God's willingness to restore relationship with Israel dominates Jeremiah 3. God is willing to take the people back even when doing so violates God's own covenant stipulations. God's desire for relationship, evident in these verses, anticipates the gospel we know in Jesus Christ. Paul expresses this good news in this way:

But now, apart from the law, the righteousness of God has been disclosed, and is attested by the law and the prophets, the righteousness of God through faith in Jesus Christ for all who believe. For there is no distinction, since all have sinned and fall short of the glory of God; they are now justified by his grace as a gift. (Rom. 3:21–24)

It is "apart from the law" and "by his grace as a gift" that we hear God's offer for Israel to return in Jeremiah 3. The book of Jeremiah knows us well. The devotion of God's people is always fickle. What is certain is God's devotion, which seeks us out and invites us back into relationship. Then, God waits to see if we who are "justified by [God's] grace as a gift" will accept this gracious offer.

Jeremiah 3:21–24

3:21 **A voice on the bare heights is heard,**
the plaintive weeping of Israel's children,
because they have perverted their way,
they have forgotten the LORD their God:
²² **Return, O faithless children,**
I will heal your faithlessness.

"Here we come to you;
for you are the LORD our God.
²³ **Truly the hills are a delusion,**
the orgies on the mountains.
Truly in the LORD our God
is the salvation of Israel.
²⁴ **"But from our youth the shameful thing has devoured all for which**
our ancestors had labored, their flocks and their herds, their sons and
their daughters. ²⁵ **Let us lie down in our shame, and let our dishonor**
cover us; for we have sinned against the LORD our God, we and our
ancestors, from our youth even to this day; and we have not obeyed the
voice of the LORD our God."

The final verses of Jeremiah 3 report a confession of sin by Israel and another call from the Lord for Israel and Judah to return. What is difficult about these verses is how to understand the confession that the people voice.

In verse 21, we are told that Israel is weeping because they recognize they have perverted their way (see 2:17, 23, 33, 36; 3:2) and forgotten the Lord their God (cf. 2:2, 13, 32). God calls again for these faithless children to return, and Israel responds (3:22–25) by acknowledging that "the hills are a delusion," that the fertility gods are worthless. It is, God's people affirm, the Lord who is "the salvation of Israel." This response is a confession of sin and recognition of covenant violation. Jeremiah 2 begins with God remembering of Israel "the devotion of your youth." Jeremiah 3 ends with Israel remembering the distortion of their relationship with God "from our youth." At the beginning of Jeremiah 2, God promises to hold guilty all "who ate" Israel, the first fruits of God's harvest (2:3). At the end of Jeremiah 3, Israel recognizes they have been "devoured" (the same Hebrew verb as "ate" in 2:3) as a consequence of their idolatry. This confession suggests that some within Judah were linking a military defeat with forsaking God. However, it is not possible to discern from this text just what events in Judah's history may have led to this kind of confession.

If this was a sincere confession, it was a proper response to God's call to "return to me" (3:10). Yet we have also seen in Jeremiah 3 the portrayal of God's people who returned, "but only in pretense" (3:10), who called God "My Father" but then continued to do evil (3:5). Little in Jeremiah 2–3 suggests these verses should be read as a sincere confession. The Lord offered Israel a chance to "return," and despite this confession, little indicates that God's offer was accepted.

These last verses of Jeremiah 3 remind us that sincere repentance, leaving one's old ways and turning to Christ, is never easy. When Jesus challenged the rich young ruler to repent by surrendering his great riches and to follow Jesus, the ruler went away sorrowful (Luke 18:18–25). Repentance and submission to God's rule demanded too much. Yet as Jeremiah knew, life before God demands radical repentance.

Jeremiah called Israel to leave behind their fertility cults and foreign alliances as sources of security and well-being and to return to God. The Lord watched to see how they would respond. Jeremiah still calls us to leave behind violence and power, race and sex, wealth and class as sources of our security and to return to God. The Lord waits to see how we disciples will heed our Lord's call to us to "repent, for the kingdom of heaven has come near" (Matt. 3:2).

"My Wrath Will Go Forth like Fire"
(Jeremiah 4–6)

God's call for Israel to "return," sounded at the end of Jeremiah 3, is heard again as Jeremiah 4 begins. Several themes run through Jeremiah 4–6: Israel is called to return to God and warned that if they do not, they will face God's fierce anger, which will burn like fire. God's judgment is portrayed as the invasion of an enemy from the north, plundering the land and attacking its cities. God's sovereign governance of the world is affirmed while the people are presented as senseless and foolish, blind to their guilt and misled by their leaders in Jerusalem to think that all is well.

Jeremiah 4:1–4

4:1 **If you return, O Israel,**

says the LORD,

> **if you return to me,**
> **if you remove your abominations from my presence,**
> **and do not waver,**
> 2 **and if you swear, "As the LORD lives!"**
> **in truth, in justice, and in uprightness,**
> **then nations shall be blessed by him,**
> **and by him they shall boast.**
> 3 **For thus says the LORD to the people of Judah and to the inhabitants of Jerusalem:**
> **Break up your fallow ground,**
> **and do not sow among thorns.**
> 4 **Circumcise yourselves to the LORD,**
> **remove the foreskin of your hearts,**
> **O people of Judah and inhabitants of Jerusalem,**
> **or else my wrath will go forth like fire,**
> **and burn with no one to quench it,**
> **because of the evil of your doings.**

In Jeremiah 4:1–4, God again calls for Israel to return. These verses hold out two options for Israel: one positive, should they return, and one negative, should they refuse.

1. Should Israel return to God (vv. 1–2), they are offered the possibility of fulfilling the purpose for which God had called their ancestor Abraham: "nations shall be blessed by him, and by him they shall boast" (v. 2; cf. Gen. 12:1–3 and esp. Gen. 22:18; 26:4). However, God offers this possibility only conditionally (Jer. 4:2): "if you return . . . then nations shall be blessed." God's people need to submit to God if, through them, the nations are to be blessed as God intends.

2. Should God's people refuse to return (vv. 3–4), they are confronted with the prospect of God's judgment. Verse 3 alludes to a text from Hosea to indicate what Israel must do to avoid God's judgment:

> Sow for yourselves righteousness;
>   reap steadfast love;
>   break up your fallow ground;
> for it is time to seek the LORD
>   that he may come and rain righteousness upon you.
>   (Hos. 10:12)

The call in Hosea for Israel to "seek the Lord" complements the call to return in Jeremiah 4:1. God's demand that the people "circumcise yourselves to the Lord" is a call for total submission to God. In the Old Testament, the heart is not, as we often think in our culture, the seat of emotions. Rather, the heart is the center of will or volition (so Ps. 51:10, "Create in me a clean heart, O God"). Circumcision is a ritual by which persons are committed or dedicated to God (see Gen. 17:9–14). So, to circumcise one's heart is to commit one's will to God. In Jeremiah 4:3–4, as in 4:1–2, God calls Israel to submit to God. However, verses 3–4 conclude with not a promise but a warning. Israel is called to submit to the Lord or else to face God's judgment, described as "wrath [which] will go forth like fire, and burn with no one to quench it."

In these verses, Israel is called to embrace the vocation to which God called Abram and Sarai, to be agents of God's blessing in the world (Gen. 12:1–4). Hans Walter Wolff has argued that it was during the time of David and Solomon that Israel began to understand that they were blessed by God and commanded by God to be a blessing to the nations. This sense of mission was expressed by a person or persons in ancient Israel that Wolff identified as the "Yahwist," responsible for an early edition of the first four books of the Old Testament. Toward the conclusion of his article, Wolff notes the use of the blessing theme in Jeremiah 4:1–4 and comments:

> Jeremiah says here that Israel can fulfill her redemptive assignment . . . in the world—her task ever since Genesis 12:3b—only when she herself confesses God with undivided loyalty and uprightness of life. (Wolff, *Kerygma of the Yahwist*," p. 64)

As this section of the book unfolds, the issues of the "loyalty and uprightness" of Israel's life will be central concerns.

Jeremiah 4:5–8

4:5 **Declare in Judah, and proclaim in Jerusalem, and say:**
Blow the trumpet through the land;
shout aloud and say,
"Gather together, and let us go
into the fortified cities!"
6 **Raise a standard toward Zion,**
flee for safety, do not delay,
for I am bringing evil from the north,
and a great destruction.
7 **A lion has gone up from its thicket,**
a destroyer of nations has set out;
he has gone out from his place
to make your land a waste;
your cities will be ruins
without inhabitant.
8 **Because of this put on sackcloth,**
lament and wail:
"The fierce anger of the LORD
has not turned away from us."

The prophet offers a word picture of God's fierce anger (v. 8; also see 4:4) that Judah will face if they fail to repent. Jeremiah imagines that God's anger will be expressed through military threat. An army is imagined invading Judah, an alarm is sounded ("Blow the trumpet through the land"), and a call goes out: "Gather together, and let us go into the fortified cities . . . flee for safety, do not delay" (vv. 5–6). Those who lived in outlying areas need to seek protection in the walled cities. The agent of God's anger will be an enemy from the north that will attack Judah (v. 6; compare 1:13). The invader is described (4:7) with language similar to that in Jeremiah 2:15, as "a lion" who goes up from its "thicket" to make the land a "waste" and its cities "ruins without inhabitant."

By linking God's anger with the invasion of an enemy from the north, these verses make clear that Judah's destruction is not to be understood as simply some historical accident. Rather, God is directing the course of Judah's history so that "the evil of your doings" (4:5) will result in "evil from the north" (4:6; cf. 1:14 and 16). The invasion is also related to Israel's failure to repent or return to the Lord (v. 8). Because Judah will not "return" to the Lord, God's fierce anger will not "turn away" (the same Hebrew word translated as "return") from Israel, and the land will be destroyed.

Jeremiah 4:9–10

4:9 **On that day, says the LORD, courage shall fail the king and the officials; the priests shall be appalled and the prophets astounded.** [10] **Then I said, "Ah, Lord GOD, how utterly you have deceived this people and Jerusalem, saying, 'It shall be well with you,' even while the sword is at the throat!"**

Verses 9–10 are linked to the description of Judah's invasion (vv. 5–8) by the words "on that day." Thus, these verses are to be read as presenting the aftermath of the invasion of Judah described in the preceding verses. The leaders of Judah (prophets, priests, kings; cf. 2:8, 26) are portrayed as "appalled" and "astonished" at the invasion. They had thought that all was well but had no sense of their accountability before God.

Jeremiah complains that God has deceived Judah (4:10). In Jeremiah's perception, God should not have allowed Judah's leaders, perhaps those who claimed to be prophets especially, to continue to assert that all is well. The leaders in Jerusalem claimed to represent God and speak for God. Thus, Jeremiah's logic is that God also is responsible for the tragedy that is about to befall Judah, by allowing these leaders to deceive the people into thinking all is well. Jeremiah as a prophet spoke the word of the Lord to Israel. However, Jeremiah did not hesitate to speak to the Lord on behalf of Israel when the situation demanded. Surely, Judah deserved judgment, but Jeremiah believed that in allowing the Jerusalem leaders to claim that all was well, God had been deceptive.

Jeremiah was God's spokesperson, but he also spoke honestly with the Lord to voice his objection about God's way with Judah. Jeremiah's forthrightness is a model of prayer that engages in honest conversation, in the confidence that God can deal with our disappointment and anger as well as praise.

Jeremiah 4:11–18

Verses 11–12, introduced by the phrase "at that time," also refer back to verses 5–8 and the invasion of the land. However, the meteorological image of these verses—"hot wind"—points ahead and also links verses 11–12 to verses 13–18. God will send a "hot wind" toward the people. This image, consistent with that in 4:4 of God's wrath that burns like fire, leads to the announcement that God will come toward Judah in judgment.

Using meteorological images, the prophet portrays the advance of an enemy as like "clouds" and a "whirlwind," an irresistible, uncontrollable, destructive force. As this enemy advances, Israel will be reduced to lamentation: "woe to us, for we are ruined" (v. 13). The prophet presses deeper his description of an invader (vv. 15–16). An alarm will be sounded from the north, whence "besiegers" approach. This description of an enemy is another occasion for Jeremiah to call on Judah to repent (v. 14). As in God's call to repentance in Jeremiah 4:4, Jeremiah is concerned with Judah's "heart." The prophet announces that the heart of God's people—their will or volition—needs to be washed of its "wickedness." The problem with Judah is that they do not will to be responsive to God's goodness toward them, do not intend covenantal obedience. In fact, Jeremiah sees that their heart is so wicked that only by a change in heart can God's people "be saved" (v. 14; see also 2:27–28; 3:23). Judah's heart condition is critical, if not fatal; they need a transplant, a new heart or will. But that is for later (see 31:31–34). Still, God offers the option of repentance, the possibility that the people might yet "remove the foreskin of [their] hearts" (4:4), that is, submit to God and avoid God's wrath.

Jeremiah raises the question about the heart of God's people, if they are willing to submit to God. These words of Jeremiah remind us that through Jesus Christ, God has made us a people of circumcised hearts, even though we do not always live as if that is who we are. So, as we gather to worship, we sing prayerfully that God will restore us as a people whose hearts are drawn to God:

> Blessed Jesus, at Your word
> We are gathered all to hear You;
> Let our hearts and souls be stirred
> Now to seek and love and fear You;
> By your teachings true and holy,
> Drawn from earth to love You solely.

Week by week, worship is the invitation to be the people God intends us to be, people who have surrendered ourselves to God.

Jeremiah 4:19–22

4:19 My anguish, my anguish! I writhe in pain!
Oh, the walls of my heart!
My heart is beating wildly;
I cannot keep silent;
for I hear the sound of the trumpet,
the alarm of war.
20 Disaster overtakes disaster,
the whole land is laid waste.
Suddenly my tents are destroyed,
my curtains in a moment.
21 How long must I see the standard,
and hear the sound of the trumpet?
22 "For my people are foolish,
they do not know me;
they are stupid children,
they have no understanding.
They are skilled in doing evil,
but do not know how to do good."

In these verses we hear for the first time the anguish of the prophet Jeremiah at the "disaster" (v. 20) he must announce and witness, the invasion of Judah. The invasion is signaled by a trumpet blast (v. 19). The prophet imagines that Judah will be totally destroyed. The reference to tents and curtains probably refers to the Jerusalem Temple, destroyed by Babylon in the invasion of Judah in 587 B.C. The theme of Judah's destruction by an invading army is familiar to us now.

What is interesting in these verses is Jeremiah's reaction to Judah's destruction. Prior verses have been concerned with Israel's wicked heart (4:14, 18) as the cause of God's judgment. Now it is the "heart" of the prophet that is stricken as he anticipates the coming judgment and so cries out in anguish (v. 19). How is this anguished cry of Jeremiah to be understood in the context of Jeremiah 4? Three levels of understanding are possible.

First, these verses can be understood to portray Jeremiah's own anguish. We see the prophet nearly overwhelmed by the task to which God has appointed him. The word of the Lord that Jeremiah must speak impacts on him personally. Jeremiah was a citizen of Judah; he knew Jerusalem and had worshiped in the Temple. Announcing the destruction of Judah and Jerusalem was not something that Jeremiah enjoyed having to do. We can hear in these verses the personal anguish of the prophet in announcing judgment on people and places dear to him.

At the second level, we can hear Jeremiah's anguish giving voice to the anguish that the people should feel. The prophet's response is appropriate to the severe crisis that Judah faces. However, the people of Judah have been deceived by the Jerusalem leaders to think that all is well (4:10), and so they are calm. All of Judah should be experiencing Jeremiah's anguish but is not. Often, prophets are those persons who express what should be felt by everyone in a community but is not. In our situation, for instance, all Christians should be deeply offended by the enduring racism of society and the abuse of the environment. Prophets are those among us who give expression to the anguish we all should feel. At this level, the pained heart of the prophet expresses the horror that the people should feel at the approaching disaster but do not.

At the third level, through the anguish of the prophet we witness God's own anguish. We are accustomed to hearing through Jeremiah, God's spokesperson, the thought, will, and intention of the Lord. Jeremiah is not his own person, and his words are more than his own expression. Jeremiah is the spokesperson for God. So, as we hear Jeremiah's anguished speech, we also hear the pathos of God. God needs to speak judgment against Israel (4:12), but to speak such judgment troubles God deeply.

Through the speech of Jeremiah we hear the prophet's anguish, the anguish that should have been felt by all in Judah, and God's own pain at Judah's judgment. Yet, the speech of these verses concludes on a different note. The anguish of God and Jeremiah does not blunt their harsh analysis of Judah. Regrettably, disaster will befall Judah because God's people have been foolish and done evil; most significant, they have forsaken the Lord and turned to the idols, so judgment is inescapable.

Jeremiah 4:23–28

4:23 I looked on the earth, and lo, it was waste and void;
    and to the heavens, and they had no light.
24 I looked on the mountains, and lo, they were quaking,
    and all the hills moved to and fro.
25 I looked, and lo, there was no one at all,
    and all the birds of the air had fled.
26 I looked, and lo, the fruitful land was a desert,
    and all its cities were laid in ruins
    before the LORD, before his fierce anger.
27 For thus says the LORD: The whole land shall be a desolation; yet I
    will not make a full end.
28 Because of this the earth shall mourn,
    and the heavens above grow black;

> **for I have spoken, I have purposed;**
> **I have not relented nor will I turn back.**

In verses 23–25 (each verse begins, "I looked . . . "), Jeremiah imagines the collapse of creation into chaos ("waste and void" and "no light" in v. 23 reflect Genesis 1). Through cosmic imagery the prophet attempts to make vivid the consequences of Israel's disobedience and failure to repent. The Lord's intention for creation (vv. 23–25), for the nations (4:2), and for God's people (v. 26) is portrayed at the point of collapse. Verse 26, the fourth and final time in these verses that the prophet declares, "I looked . . . ," summarizes the message. The "fruitful land" will become a desert and the cities will be in ruins (cf. 2:15; 4:7) before God's "fierce anger" (4:4, 8). The world of life and blessing that God intended will collapse into chaos. This collapse of creation and dissolution of history is not merely the result of natural processes. Israel will not "return," so God will not "turn back" the judgment of Judah (v. 28; the same Hebrew word is used for both "return" and "turn back"). The whole creation, the course of history, and the destiny of Israel are directed by God.

While the imagery of these verses may seem strange and exaggerated to us, we know the reality of which they speak. Human rebellion against God causes chaos. The failure to be caring of persons brings conflict and chaos to families and communities. Failure to care for the world God has entrusted to us, by pollution of the land, sea, and air, brings "the silent spring," as Rachel Carson phrased it. The failure to resolve international conflicts because of national pride or long-standing enmities can quickly result in horribly destructive wars and even bring the world to the brink of nuclear annihilation. We know well that to break relationship with God can threaten chaos and death on a massive scale.

Yet, amid these declarations of God's judgment and visions of the creation's collapse, one muted, alternative note is sounded: "yet I will not make a full end" (v. 27). There can be no mistaking the severity of God's judgment announced in these verses, God's seriousness about plucking up and pulling down (1:10). Still, the promise "yet I will not make a full end" keeps alive the possibility that what God purposes will not be complete in judgment alone for Judah.

Jeremiah 4:29–31

> 4:29 **At the noise of horseman and archer**
> **every town takes to flight;**
> **they enter thickets; they climb among rocks;**
> **all the towns are forsaken,**

and no one lives in them.

30 And you, O desolate one,
what do you mean that you dress in crimson,
that you deck yourself with ornaments of gold,
that you enlarge your eyes with paint?
In vain you beautify yourself.
Your lovers despise you;
they seek your life.

31 For I heard a cry as of a woman in labor,
anguish as of one bringing forth her first child,
the cry of daughter Zion gasping for breath,
stretching out her hands,
"Woe is me! I am fainting before killers!"

For the third time, Jeremiah imagines a battle scene. An army with horsemen and archers is portrayed attacking Judah's cities, so that Judah is left "desolate" (v. 30). It is surprising, then, that when desolate Judah is next presented in this scene, it is as a prostitute dressed in red clothes, bedecked in jewels, face heavy with makeup (v. 30; cf. 2:20, 33). What are we to make of this image?

Through this imagery, Jeremiah again comments upon the efforts of Judah to find security through political alliances (see 2:14–19 above). During the time of Jeremiah, Judah attempted to find protection by making pacts or entering into leagues with neighboring states. From this text, it is not possible to identify which incident Jeremiah may have had in mind. The book of Jeremiah later suggests an effort by Judah to seek help from Egypt as Babylon threatened (37:6–10) and to enter into an agreement with several neighboring states to resist Babylon (Jeremiah 27). These political and military allies that Judah seeks out are called "lovers" by Jeremiah (4:30). Obviously, in portraying Judah as a prostitute, Jeremiah is being quite derogatory. He may be suggesting that to be an attractive partner to Judah's neighbors, the nation sought to "beautify" itself, perhaps pretending to be a more attractive political and military ally than it was. Such efforts would have undoubtedly meant compromise in Judah's commitment to God. It was not unusual in the ancient Near East for treaties with foreign nations to require some acknowledgment of the new allies' gods, which would have compounded Israel's participation with the fertility cults. Thus, to enter political and military alliances in an effort to be secure, Judah may well have had to forsake the Lord for other gods. However, the Lord was Judah's rightful "husband" (see 2:2), so the prostitute image fits the situation well.

Tragically, prostitution is often dangerous and violent, and Jeremiah warns Judah that its "lovers," the allies it has attracted by whatever means, are likely to turn on Judah and become enemies (see 2:36). Perhaps the invasion described in 4:29 is not by Babylon but by one of Judah's supposed "lovers," an ally that turned against Judah.

With a shift of metaphor, the prophet concludes by presenting the daughter of Zion crying out like a woman in labor: "Woe is me! I am fainting before killers!" (4:31; cf. 4:8, 13). The fierce anger of the Lord will bring God's people to the point of death, yet in the background of this image of Judah as a woman in labor, a hint of birth and new life linger. God will pluck up and break down as Judah's history moves toward exile (1:3). Yet, God has given Jeremiah another word to speak in time, "build and plant." That other word can be heard faintly in these verses, behind the dominant theme of God's judgment.

Jeremiah 5:1–9

5:1 **Run to and fro through the streets of Jerusalem,**
     look around and take note!
     Search its squares and see
     if you can find one person
     who acts justly
     and seeks truth—
     so that I may pardon Jerusalem.
2   **Although they say, "As the LORD lives,"**
     yet they swear falsely.
3   **O LORD, do your eyes not look for truth?**
     You have struck them,
     but they felt no anguish;
     you have consumed them,
     but they refused to take correction.
     They have made their faces harder than rock;
     they have refused to turn back.

4   **Then I said, "These are only the poor,**
     they have no sense;
     for they do not know the way of the LORD,
     the law of their God.
5   **Let me go to the rich**
     and speak to them;
     surely they know the way of the LORD,
     the law of their God."
     But they all alike had broken the yoke,

they had burst the bonds.

6 Therefore a lion from the forest shall kill them,
a wolf from the desert shall destroy them.
A leopard is watching against their cities;
everyone who goes out of them shall be torn in pieces—
because their transgressions are many,
their apostasies are great.

7 How can I pardon you?
Your children have forsaken me,
and have sworn by those who are no gods.
When I fed them to the full,
they committed adultery
and trooped to the houses of prostitutes.
8 They were well-fed lusty stallions,
each neighing for his neighbor's wife.
9 Shall I not punish them for these things?

says the LORD;

and shall I not bring retribution
on a nation such as this?

Jeremiah 5 continues to develop God's call to repentance from Jeremiah 4:1–4. With the hope of being able to pardon Judah, God instructs Jeremiah to search Jerusalem for a person "who acts justly and seeks truth" (v. 1).

God's command that Jeremiah search Jerusalem reflects the story of Sodom and Gomorrah (Genesis 18–19). In the Genesis story, God announces to Abraham that the cities are to be destroyed because of their wickedness. However, Abraham inquires of God how many righteous persons he needs to find in order for the cities to be spared. Finally, Abraham is able to agree with God that if even ten righteous persons can be found, Sodom and Gomorrah will be saved. Of course, the ten could not be found, and Sodom and Gomorrah stand to this day as symbols of sin and evil. In the text before us, God is willing to pardon Jerusalem if Jeremiah can find even one person who acts justly and seeks truth. Some have suggested God's leniency in being satisfied with just one person is a comment on how evil Jerusalem had become.

Acting justly and seeking truth were core values in ancient Israel, ways of being and relating that were deemed fundamental marks of relationship with God. (Note that a similar expression is found in Micah 6:8: "do justice, and . . . love kindness, and . . . walk humbly with your God.") A Christian equivalent would be to love God and love neighbor, without which it is difficult to claim one is a disciple. In looking for a person in Jerusalem who acts justly and seeks truth, God is not expecting any extraordinary qualities but that which is to be expected of anyone in Israel, anyone part of the covenant community. One such person will do!

In ancient Israel, to act justly meant that one exhibited concern for the poor and disadvantaged, to see that they had an opportunity to share in the blessings and benefits of the creation and promised land. Concern for acting justly was rooted in the primary way that Israel knew the Lord, through the exodus deliverance of slaves from Egypt. This Old Testament notion of justice is different from our common idea of justice, which we portray through a blindfolded person holding balanced scales. Our idea of justice is that all in society are treated alike. The Old Testament idea of justice is that those at a disadvantage are to be given special consideration. This is perhaps like parents who, when one of their children has a special need, commit a disproportionate amount of time and family resources to respond. Such unequal concern for the poor and disadvantaged, like God's concern for the Hebrew slaves in Egypt, is what it means in the Old Testament to act justly.

Jeremiah was also to look for a person who "seeks truth." The Hebrew word translated in the NRSV as "truth" in verse 1 is, in other versions of the Bible, often translated as "integrity," or as one commentator has remarked, "the trait that enables one to keep one's word, to be counted on" (Holladay, *Jeremiah 1*, p. 176). Seeking the truth (or we might say, seeking to live with integrity) should probably be understood as more demanding than doing justice or as the basis from which one acts justly. Beyond doing justice, seeking the truth suggests a way of being, something at the core of one's life. In ancient Israel, seeking truth would have meant that one sought to live as a person who was totally committed to God, whose life embodied the Shema: "The Lord is our God, the Lord alone. You shall love the Lord your God with all your heart, and with all your soul, and with all your might" (Duet. 6:4), which today still has a central place in Jewish worship as an expression of what it means to live in covenant with God).

Regrettably, Jeremiah's initial search proves futile, particularly regarding the quality of seeking truth or integrity. Jeremiah reports to God that while many in Jerusalem invoke the Lord's name (5:2, "they say, 'As the Lord lives' "), "they swear falsely." Of course, we hear in this that the Third Commandment was being violated: "You shall not make wrongful use of the name of the Lord your God" (Exod 20:7; Deut. 5:11). The accusation may have both narrow and broad implications. More narrowly, in ancient Israel one swore an oath or pledge by invoking the Lord's name, likely suggesting God's judgment if one failed to keep the oath. Jeremiah's report may indicate that the residents of Jerusalem constantly were making oaths and invoking the Lord's name but then not keeping these oaths. This would have been a misuse of the Lord's name, and certainly a violation of integrity. More broadly, Jeremiah's accusation may suggest that in Jerusalem everyone claimed to be faithful to the Lord, but there was no evidence of faithfulness beyond the constant use of the Lord's name. No one, for example, acted justly. In a similar vein, Jesus said, "Not everyone who says to me, 'Lord, Lord,' will enter the kingdom of heaven, but only the one who does the will of my Father in heaven" (Matt. 7:21). Jeremiah's search for a person "who acts justly and seeks truth" is futile. There is no evidence that anyone in Jerusalem has returned to the Lord (5:3), and so there is no opportunity for God to pardon.

However, God is not ready to give up. Having failed to find any indication of repentance among the poor, God orders that the search next concentrate on the more well-to-do. In Jerusalem, the seat of government and the Temple, are the king and his advisers as well as the priests, those who have had much opportunity to study and know God's ways and God's law (vv. 4–5). The idea of the law may give us a wrong idea about the religion of ancient Israel. While there were certainly laws and stipulations that everyone was to keep, to know "way of the Lord, the law of God" (vv. 4–5) was to do more than obey some rules and regulations. Instead, it was to participate in God's purposes for the creation and all people. When Israel and Judah thought about God's ways, for instance, the story of the exodus was a primary model. God's ways included the end of oppression and suffering for those who mattered little to persons with power and position. Laws existed in ancient Israel, but they gave expression to God's ways of justice for the oppressed and downtrodden. The responsibility of the "rich" (v. 5) like the king and his advisers and the Temple priests was to guide God's people in the ways of the Lord (see Ps. 72:1–4, 12–14; cf. Jer 2:8). They should have known how to act justly and seek truth. However, the outcome of Jeremiah's search among the rich is futile. There is no evidence of repentance, and not a single person is found who can make possible the Lord's pardon.

The consequence of Israel's failure to return to God is imagined as death and destruction, now by three beasts, instead of a lion alone (v. 6; cf. 2:15; 4:7). There will be no escape. Two words are used to summarize God's accusations: *transgressions* and *apostasies.* The Hebrew word for "apostasies" has the same Hebrew root as the word for "return," used to call for repentance in Jeremiah 3 and in 4:1–4. God's people had not only "refused to turn back" (5:3) but committed apostasies; that is, they had turned from God (see 4:8).

Verses 7–8 specify these apostasies by linking together the charges that Israel has forsaken God and that they have committed adultery. While the combination of religious and sexual misconduct may surprise us, it well describes the situation encountered by Jeremiah, at two levels. On one level, forsaking God through the worship of the fertility deities involves cult prostitution (v. 7), though it has been suggested that cult prositution led to widespread practice of adultery that undermined Judah's social order (see Thompson, *Book of Jeremiah*, p. 180). Another scholar suggests bluntly that "their Baal worship results in nothing but a vast whorehouse" (Holladay, *Jeremiah I*, p. 180). Jeremiah has already charged that Judah violated the Third Commandment (v. 2), and here he points to a violation of the Seventh Commandment, against adultery. On a second level, Israel's participation in the fertility cults is adultery in the sense that it violates relationship with the Lord. That is, Israel has forsaken God for Baal (a violation of the First Commandment), but from the perspective that Israel is the bride of the Lord (2:2), forsaking God also constitutes adultery.

Nowhere in Jeremiah 5:1–8 is there evidence that Judah has repented. Nowhere is there evidence of persons who act justly and seek truth. To the contrary, there are charges that Israel has violated three of the Ten Commandments. So, when God finally poses the question "Shall I not punish them for these things?" (v. 9), the answer is clear. God cannot pardon (v. 7), and punishment is inevitable.

Jeremiah 5:10–19

5:10 **Go up through her vine-rows and destroy,**
       but do not make a full end;
       strip away her branches,
       for they are not the LORD's.
   11 **For the house of Israel and the house of Judah**
       have been utterly faithless to me,
                                    says the LORD.
   12 **They have spoken falsely of the LORD,**
       and have said, "He will do nothing.
       No evil will come upon us,
       and we shall not see sword or famine."
   13 **The prophets are nothing but wind,**
       for the word is not in them.

Thus shall it be done to them!

14 Therefore thus says the LORD, the God of hosts:
Because they have spoken this word,
I am now making my words in your mouth a fire,
and this people wood, and the fire shall devour them.

15 I am going to bring upon you
a nation from far away, O house of Israel,

> says the LORD.

It is an enduring nation,
it is an ancient nation,
a nation whose language you do not know,
nor can you understand what they say.

16 Their quiver is like an open tomb;
all of them are mighty warriors.

17 They shall eat up your harvest and your food;
they shall eat up your sons and your daughters;
they shall eat up your flocks and your herds;
they shall eat up your vines and your fig trees;
they shall destroy with the sword
your fortified cities in which you trust.

18 But even in those days, says the LORD, I will not make a full end of you.

19 And when your people say, "Why has the LORD our God done all these things to us?" you shall say to them, "As you have forsaken me and served foreign gods in your land, so you shall serve strangers in a land that is not yours."

Quickly, God orders punishment. The destruction of Judah is described using images of uprooting a vineyard. Earlier in the book, Israel is described as the first fruits of God's harvest. However, the prophet already has charged that Judah, "choice vine from the purest stock," has turned "degenerate and become a wild vine" (2:21; compare Isaiah 5). In these verses, God orders that the vine be cut down. We are reminded of Jesus saying in the Gospel of John, "I am the true vine, and my Father is the vinegrower. He removes every branch in me that bears no fruit" (John 15:1–2; but look at this passage as part of John 15:1–17). In addition to the use of the "first fruits" image, there seem to be other references to Jeremiah 2:1–3 in these verses. The people once "holy to the Lord" (2:3), that is, set apart by God, are now judged "not the Lord's" (5:10). The people once devoted to God (2:2) are now described as having been "utterly faithless" (5:11).

God's announcement of judgment at this point in the story does not come as a surprise, though once more God qualifies the judgment: "destroy, but do not make a full end" (v. 10). God is justified in pulling down and plucking up Judah as a degenerate vine. However, the qualification "but do not make a full end" is unexpected. Though accountability and judgment are clearly the dominant themes of these early chapters of the book, God's order not to make a full end indicates that God's purpose for Israel will not be completed by plucking up and tearing down.

Still, announcement of God's judgment dominates as the prophet accuses the people of false speech (vv. 12–13). This accusation needs to be heard in relation to God's search of Jerusalem for someone who seeks truth (v. 1). Instead of the integrity of total commitment to the Lord, Judah is confident that God "will do nothing," and that "no evil" will come on those who violate God's commandments or break covenant. In Judah there is a sense that obedience is not necessary because there will be no accountability; so there is no seriousness about relationship with the Lord, a disregard for God's covenant, and no integrity (truth) in the life of the community.

The falseness of prophetic speech is noted specifically (v. 13). False speech by prophets who are supposed to speak for God is a challenge to God's sovereignty. Such "false" prophets speak a word that God has not authorized. This false prophecy is met by a new word from God through the prophet Jeremiah (vv. 14–17). God's word is to be enacted in the processes and concreteness of history. The destroying fire of God will be "a nation from far away" (v. 15), and through them God's people will be devoured. Once it was those who ate the first fruits of God's harvest on whom God would send "disaster" (2:3). Now it is announced that God's "wrath . . . like fire" (see 4:4, 8) will "devour" (the same Hebrew word as "ate" in 2:3) Israel.

This text, so focused on God's destruction of Judah, concludes as it began. God declares once more, "But even in those days I will not make a full end" (5:18). God intends to "devour" Israel. Still, God purposes something more, "not a full end," though what this may suggest is not developed here.

For most Christians, these chapters of the book of Jeremiah with their considerable concern for God's judgment and wrath are very difficult. We, after all, imagine that our God is a God of love and not wrath. Often this contrast between God's love and wrath is used to distinguish in a too simple way the character of God in the Old Testament—a God of wrath—from the God of the New Testament revealed in Jesus—a God of love. Yet, if we imagine only a God whose love never calls the world to account, we risk engaging in the misunderstanding of the Jerusalem leadership, described in the book of Jeremiah as persons who imagine, "He will do nothing. No evil will come upon us" (5:12). Though it is difficult, this section of the book of Jeremiah challenges us to face the righteous judgment and the wrath of God.

The apostle Paul, who held steadfastly to the claim that God acted to save the world in Jesus Christ, nonetheless did not hesitate to speak of God's wrath:

> For the wrath of God is revealed from heaven against all ungodliness and wickedness of those who by their wickedness suppress the truth. For what can be known about God is plain to them, because God has shown it to them. Ever since the creation of the world his eternal power and divine nature, invisible through they are, have been understood and seen through the things he has made. So they [Gentiles] are without excuse; for though they knew God, they did not honor him as God or give thanks to him, but they became futile in their thinking, and their senseless minds were darkened. (Rom. 1:18–21)

For Paul, God is sovereign and holds all humanity accountable. All who are ungodly and wicked, who worship and serve "the creature rather than the Creator" (Rom. 1:25), risk God's wrath, God's righteous judgment. Much like the book of Jeremiah, Paul understood that humanity stands accountable before God, even as God reaches out to humanity in love that saves.

The noted African American theologian James Cone addresses the tension between God's righteous judgment and God's love in this way:

> Black theology then, asks not whether love is an essential element of the Christian interpretation of God, but whether the love of God itself can be properly understood without focusing equally on the biblical view of God's righteousness. Is it possible to understand what God's love means for the oppressed without making wrath an essential ingredient of that love? What could love possibly mean in a racist society except the righteous condemnation of everything racist? Most theological treatments of God's love fail to place the proper emphasis on God's wrath, suggesting that love is completely self-giving without any demand for obedience. Bonhoeffer called this "cheap grace." (James Cone, *A Black Theology of Liberation*, p. 69)

God's wrath is the essential complement to God's love for the oppressed—for those, in Cone's example, who suffer in a racist society. God's wrath also expresses God's redeeming love. Of course, many of us in American churches are part of the dominant white culture. We live in a position most like the Jerusalem leadership described in the book of Jeremiah, eager to hear "It shall be well with you!" (4:10; cf. 6:14–15) and "No evil will come upon us" (5:12). This section of the book of Jeremiah addresses our leanings toward "cheap grace" with the stern call to repent or return to God and with clear and vivid pictures of "the fierce anger of the Lord."

Yet there is the hint in this material as well that God's wrath contributes to a larger purpose of God. God orders, "Destroy, . . . but do not make a full end" (5:10; cf. Rom. 5:6–11, where Paul continues his discussion of God's wrath). Despite the clarity of the book of Jeremiah about God's wrath, the drama of God's way with people who will not return remains open: "but do not make a full end." How might God proceed?

Jeremiah 5:20–31

5:20 Declare this in the house of Jacob,
    proclaim it in Judah:
21 Hear this, O foolish and senseless people,
    who have eyes, but do not see,
    who have ears, but do not hear.
22 Do you not fear me? says the LORD;
    Do you not tremble before me?
    I placed the sand as a boundary for the sea,
    a perpetual barrier that it cannot pass;
    though the waves toss, they cannot prevail,
    though they roar, they cannot pass over it.
23 But this people has a stubborn and rebellious heart;
    they have turned aside and gone away.
24 They do not say in their hearts,
    "Let us fear the LORD our God,
    who gives the rain in its season,
    the autumn rain and the spring rain,
    and keeps for us
    the weeks appointed for the harvest."
25 Your iniquities have turned these away,
    and your sins have deprived you of good.
26 For scoundrels are found among my people;
    they take over the goods of others.
    Like fowlers they set a trap;
    they catch human beings.
27 Like a cage full of birds,
    their houses are full of treachery;
    therefore they have become great and rich,
28 they have grown fat and sleek.
    They know no limits in deeds of wickedness;
    they do not judge with justice

the cause of the orphan, to make it prosper,
and they do not defend the rights of the needy.
²⁹ Shall I not punish them for these things?
                                    says the LORD,
and shall I not bring retribution
on a nation such as this?
³⁰ An appalling and horrible thing
has happened in the land:
³¹ the prophets prophesy falsely,
and the priests rule as the prophets direct;
my people love to have it so,
but what will you do when the end comes?

At the beginning of this lengthy speech, God addresses Judah as a "fool-ish and senseless people" (v. 21), an address that echoes ideas already pres-ent in Jeremiah 4–5. The "foolish" people echoes Jeremiah 4:22, where God had characterized Israel as "stupid," the same Hebrew word as "fool-ish" in 5:21. By calling Judah "senseless," God charges that Judah has not been thinking clearly or thinking at all. A senseless people, in Hebrew, is literally a people with "no heart." This echoes God's demands of Judah "remove the foreskin of your hearts" and "wash your heart clean of wicked-ness" (4:4, 14) and suggests that Judah does not have the will to live in covenant with God. The implications of Judah being foolish and senseless are developed in subsequent verses.

Verses 22–25 describe God's sovereign ordering of the world for "good" and the creation's respect for the bounds God established. The sea and waves respect the boundary of the sand they "cannot pass over"; God gave the rains their season and appointed weeks for the harvest (v. 24). The creation knows what it means to "fear" and "tremble before" God (v. 22) and honors God's sovereignty. Yet Israel, God concludes, "has a stubborn and rebellious heart; they have turned aside and gone away" (v. 23) and do not fear God (vv. 22, 24). The creation honors God's sovereignty, but Judah does not.

The "sin" and "iniquity" of Judah, that is, the specific ways in which they fail to fear God, are described as the exploitation of persons (vv. 26–28). Some have become "great and rich" by exploiting the weakest per-sons in society. Such exploitation is hardly evidence of persons acting justly (v. 1) and suggests that Judah has overstepped the bounds of covenant rela-tionship with God. Such violation of covenant will result in the loss of the "good" God intended, God's blessings of the autumn and spring rains and the harvest (v. 24; cf. 3:3). So, God concludes that while the sea observes the boundary God has set, Judah knows "no limits in deeds of wickedness" (v. 28).

As Jeremiah 5 concludes, God asks hearers to draw their own conclusions about what must happen: "Shall I not punish them for these things? says the Lord" (v. 29). Only one conclusion can be drawn.

Jeremiah 6:1–8

6:1 **Flee for safety, O children of Benjamin,**
         from the midst of Jerusalem!
         Blow the trumpet in Tekoa,
         and raise a signal on Beth-haccherem;
         for evil looms out of the north,
         and great destruction.
   2 **I have likened daughter Zion**
         to the loveliest pasture.
   3 **Shepherds with their flocks shall come against her.**
         They shall pitch their tents around her;
         they shall pasture, all in their places.
   4 **"Prepare war against her;**
         up, and let us attack at noon!"
         "Woe to us, for the day declines,
         the shadows of evening lengthen!"
   5 **"Up, and let us attack by night,**
         and destroy her palaces!"
   6 **For thus says the LORD of hosts:**
         Cut down her trees;
         cast up a siege ramp against Jerusalem.
         This is the city that must be punished;
         there is nothing but oppression within her.
   7 **As a well keeps its water fresh,**
         so she keeps fresh her wickedness;
         violence and destruction are heard within her;
         sickness and wounds are ever before me.
   8 **Take warning, O Jerusalem,**
         or I shall turn from you in disgust,
         and make you a desolation,
         an uninhabited land.

Again, Jeremiah speaks of the impending invasion of an enemy. The enemy is imagined approaching Judah: "evil looms out of the north, and great destruction" (6:1; cf. 1:13–15; 4:6). Jeremiah uses the image of a shepherd to depict the occupation of an enemy king (6:3). "Shepherd" was a common designation for a king in the world of Jeremiah. The prophet imagines the enemy developing plans for a relentless attack, day and night (vv. 4a, 5). Once more, the cry "woe" will be heard from Judah (4:8, 13, 31).

Verses 6–8 intertwine further warnings of destruction with more accusations against Judah. God orders a siege of Jerusalem (6:6; cf. 1:15; 4:16) and gives as the rationale "there is nothing but oppression within her." Social injustice and exploitation (cf. 2:34; 5:26–28) are again identified as a problem; no one is acting justly. This speech concludes with the warning that God will abandon Judah and leave the land "a desolation, an uninhabited land" (6:8; see also 2:15; 4:7). In 6:8, the NRSV translates the Hebrew "take warning." A better translation would be "take correction." Twice, in Jeremiah 2:30 and 5:3, the Hebrew word translated in 6:8 as "take warning" has been used to indicate Israel's failure to accept correction. Given this refusal and the ample evidence of Judah's abiding "wickedness," God's continuing hope that they may yet take correction and repent is astonishing.

It is easy, given all the criticism of Judah in these early chapters, to overlook the book of Jeremiah's deep interest in God. The questions "Who is God?" and "What is God like?" are central concerns of the book. An obvious answer to the question "Who is God?" is that God is the righteous judge who holds accountable Judah and Israel, the nations, and indeed the whole creation. Yet there is another side of God's character that this section of the book wants us to see. God has every reason to despair that the people will ever repent, yet God still invites them to "take warning." Deep in the biblical understanding of God, and deep in the book of Jeremiah, is a recognition that God is more than a righteous judge who exacts judgment:

> The LORD, the LORD,
> a God merciful and gracious,
> slow to anger,
> and abounding in steadfast love and faithfulness,
> keeping steadfast love for the thousandth generation,
> forgiving iniquity and transgression and sin,
> yet by no means clearing the guilty,
> but visiting the iniquity of the parents
> upon the children
> and the children's children,
> to the third and fourth generation.
>
> (Exod 34:6–7)

The God of Jeremiah is "a God merciful and gracious" who keeps hoping humanity will "take warning." We in the church affirm that we know the God who is gracious through Jesus Christ, and by God's grace alone are we saved:

> For by grace you have been saved through faith, and this is not your own doing; it is the gift of God—not the result of works, so that no one may boast. (Eph. 2:8–9)

Jeremiah 6:9–15

6:9 Thus says the LORD of hosts:
   Glean thoroughly as a vine
   the remnant of Israel;
   like a grape-gatherer, pass your hand again
   over its branches.

10 To whom shall I speak and give warning,
   that they may hear?
   See, their ears are closed,
   they cannot listen.
   The word of the LORD is to them an object of scorn;
   they take no pleasure in it.
11 But I am full of the wrath of the LORD;
   I am weary of holding it in.

   Pour it out on the children in the street,
   and on the gatherings of young men as well;
   both husband and wife shall be taken,
   the old folk and the very aged.
12 Their houses shall be turned over to others,
   their fields and wives together;
   for I will stretch out my hand
   against the inhabitants of the land,
                              says the LORD.

13 For from the least to the greatest of them,
   everyone is greedy for unjust gain;
   and from prophet to priest,
   everyone deals falsely.
14 They have treated the wound of my people carelessly,
   saying, "Peace, peace,"
   when there is no peace.
15 They acted shamefully, they committed abomination;

yet they were not ashamed,
they did not know how to blush.
Therefore they shall fall among those who fall;
at the time that I punish them, they shall be overthrown,
                                          says the LORD.

Though hope has been held out that Israel might yet "take warning" (6:8), these verses despair of that possibility. Jeremiah announces God's judgment using the imagery of gleaning a vine (v. 9; see 5:10). The language suggests a thorough and severe judgment. Yet verse 10, a reflection by the prophet Jeremiah, indicates little response by God's people to this threat. No one has listened, and the ears of God's people, like their hearts, remained "uncircumcised" (cf. 4:4, 5:21). The NRSV translation "ears are closed" captures the sense of the text but misses the direct connection to Jeremiah 4:4 captured by a more literal translation of the Hebrew, "ears are uncircumcised." That is, though they hear the word of the Lord through Jeremiah, they are unwilling to submit to God and repent. So, the conclusion is drawn that God's word is "an object of scorn" to Judah in which "they take no pleasure" (v. 10). The people have rejected God's sovereign word, so the prophet has to speak another word, a word of God's "wrath" (vv. 11–12). God's outstretched hand (v. 12) that had once brought Israel from Egypt through the desert and to the land (Deut. 26:6–9; compare Jer. 2:6–7) will now be turned against them.

Verses 13–15 make specific the ways in which God's word has been rejected by Judah. The Jerusalem leadership (prophets and priests are specifically identified) are deeply involved in social injustice through acquiring "unjust gain" (v. 13; see, too, 2:8; 4:9; 5:31). While false dealings most evidently refer to unsavory economic practices (cf 2:34–35, 5:27–28), the prophetic and priestly falseness indicated in verse 14 suggests another dimension of this problem. Not only have there been false dealings socially and economically, but there is also falsehood in the subsequent response of the Jerusalem leadership to the seriousness of such dishonest economic practices, a cover-up if you will. The duty of the prophets and priests is to call Judah to be faithful to their covenant with God, who freed Israel from slavery in Egypt. Instead, this text suggests that the Jerusalem leadership have either ignored the situation or, worse, found a way to justify unscrupulous economic practices in the name of God, who had deep concern for the poor and disadvantaged. So, Jeremiah charges that the "wound" of God's people (6:14; cf. 6:7) is being treated "carelessly" by announcing " 'Peace, peace,' when there is no peace" (v. 14;

see 4:10). The exploitative economic schemes being practiced in Judah are a festering wound that threatens Judah's life, that will lead to defeat and exile. We know that to ignore the symptoms of illness and pretend we are well can seriously imperil our health and even lead to death. Jeremiah accuses Judah's prophets and priests of ignoring the social symptoms of a disease, a broken relationship with God, that threatens Judah's existence.

This warning about pronouncing a too-easy peace reminds us today that repentance is a demanding practice. It is not enough to feel sorry about our sin or to participate in a liturgy in which we confess our sin and share Christ's peace. Finally, repentance requires a change in heart and a change in how we relate to others in our social and economic dealings. Yet, demanding as repentance is, we know that the One to whom we confess invites us to return and does not intend to make a full end: "For I have no pleasure in the death of anyone, says the Lord God. Turn, then, and live" (Ezek. 18:32).

Jeremiah 6:16–21

16 Thus says the LORD:
Stand at the crossroads, and look,
and ask for the ancient paths,
where the good way lies; and walk in it,
and find rest for your souls.
But they said, "We will not walk in it."
17 Also I raised up sentinels for you:
"Give heed to the sound of the trumpet!"
But they said, "We will not give heed."
18 Therefore hear, O nations,
and know, O congregation, what will happen to them.
19 Hear, O earth; I am going to bring disaster on this people,
the fruit of their schemes,
because they have not given heed to my words;
and as for my teaching, they have rejected it.
20 Of what use to me is frankincense that comes from Sheba,
or sweet cane from a distant land?
Your burnt offerings are not acceptable,
nor are your sacrifices pleasing to me.
21 Therefore thus says the LORD:
See, I am laying before this people
stumbling blocks against which they shall stumble;
parents and children together,
neighbor and friend shall perish.

These verses need to be understood in relation to the material in verses 13–15, charging that Judah's leaders have ignored life-threatening social injustices that will lead to the nation's destruction. God commands Judah to "stand at the crossroads, . . . and ask . . . where the good way lies; and walk in it, and find rest for your souls" (v. 16). The "crossroads" and "ancient paths" refer to the ways of Moses, to the stipulations of the covenant that God had given at Sinai to guide Israel's life. Central to these stipulations are commands dealing with economic justice. For example, the Tenth Commandment, concerned with coveting (Exod. 20:17; Deut. 5:21) has to do not just with envy of neighbors' possessions but with legal maneuvering to secure a neighbor's property. King Ahab, with the help of his queen, Jezebel, violated the Tenth Commandment in the underhanded manner in which they seized Naboth's vineyard (1 Kings 21). Jeremiah repeatedly charges that Judah has strayed from the ways of Moses, "the ancient paths." For example, in verses 6:13–14, Jeremiah accuses Judah of economic injustice. Judah refuses to walk in the way of the Lord, who had delivered slaves from oppression, and instead has become a nation of oppressors themselves.

God's call to Judah to walk in the ancient paths is connected with the promise that they will "find rest." In the book of Deuteronomy, an obedient response to God's gracious deliverance of Israel from slavery means blessing and long life in the land of promise (Deut. 6:1–3; see Deut. 4:10; 5:29; 6:13; 10:12). William Holladay has suggested that the Hebrew word for rest used in verse 16 implies something like "national security" and relief from external, international threats (also see Isa. 28:12; Holladay, *Jeremiah I*, p. 221). Thus, God calls Judah to return to covenant obedience and promises that if they do so, the threats they face from Babylon will cease and they will have "rest," long life, and blessing in the land. Judah's prophets and priests offer a phoney cure to the nation's ills by pretending nothing is wrong. God's call through Jeremiah for Judah to return to covenant obedience is demanding but promises real healing and rest from the Babylonian destruction that threatens Judah's life.

Regretfully, God concludes that Judah refuses covenant obedience even when warned by "sentinels" (v. 17). It is, of course, God's spokesperson Jeremiah who has been warning Judah of their impending destruction as an enemy advances from the north and the trumpets sound in alarm (v. 17; but remember 4:5 and 6:1). Jeremiah is God's sentinel, but Judah refuses to heed his call. Jeremiah signals the lethal danger Judah faces as a result of their covenant disobedience, but other prophets speak an easier word that assures God's people all is well (v. 14; the conflict between Jeremiah and other prophets is picked up in Jeremiah 23 and 27–29). Judah faces a lethal danger but refuses to listen to the warnings of God's sentinel, Jeremiah, that an enemy is coming to destroy them.

The conclusion that Judah will neither walk in the ways of covenant obedience nor heed the warning of God's prophet prepares for the speech of judgment that is introduced by "Therefore" at 6:18. Verses 18–21 again unfold like a courtroom drama (see 2:1–13). While verse 19 is mostly a restatement of charges already presented in verses 16–17, verses 20–21 further develop God's case against Judah. Though God's people refuse covenant obedience and engage in economic exploitation (6:14), they nonetheless continue to offer sacrifices to God in their worship (v. 20). God declares that these sacrifices are not "pleasing."

In ancient Israel, sacrifices were understood to be a means by which God might be approached. Through sacrifices, God provided a way by which the people might express their thanksgiving to God or, in other cases, seek God's forgiveness and reconciliation. (Much of Leviticus 1–6 describes various kinds of offerings and sacrifices common in ancient Israel). However, there was never an assumption that sacrifices were in any way magical or that God could be manipulated by them. Rather, having made sacrifice as provided for by God, the people thought they would live as those who had been forgiven. For the people of Judah to have made sacrifices to God and yet continue to engage in economic exploitation of others was for them to live as if they had made no sacrifices. In the New Testament we find the same logic, for instance, in 1 John, where the writer argues, "Whoever says, 'I am in the light,' while hating a brother or sister, is still in the darkness" (1 John 2:9; cf. Matt. 5:23–35). With Judah's refusal to embrace covenantal obedience (Jer. 6:16–17), it is not at all surprising that God does not find the sacrifices pleasing. Perhaps sacrifices were among the ways in which the Jerusalem priests had been treating the wound of Judah carelessly (v. 14); the sacrifices were understood to be, by themselves, assurances that all was well, rather than prods leading to the reform of unjust economic practices.

We should not take God's rejection of Judah's sacrifices as a blanket condemnation of sacrifices. What makes the sacrifices not pleasing is the absence of a match between the sacrificial rituals, which express a renewed relationship with God, and Judah's social practice, which evidences blatant disregard for God. Other Old Testament prophets express a similar criticism of Israel's sacrifices, and in every case the criticism concerns the failure of God's people to live through their social dealings the relationship with God that they claim by offering sacrifices. So, for instance, Isaiah announces God's condemnation of Israel's worship and rejection of their sacrifices because they have failed to care for the socially disadvantaged, the widows and orphans (Isa. 1:10–17). Similarly, Micah announces that the primary covenantal obligations required by God are justice, kindness, and humble obedience, apart from which sacrifices are not pleasing to God (Micah 6:6–8; cf. Hos. 6:6).

We should not take from these condemnations of sacrifice that worship and ritual acts are not important to God. Worship and its rituals provide an opportunity to act out and model our relationship with God. We gather around the communion table to see acted out the drama of God's salvation through Jesus' life and death and resurrection; we experience how we are fed and nourished by God; we are invited to communion with our brothers and sisters; and we pledge that as God has served us at the table, we will leave worship renewed to serve God and neighbors in the world. However, the ritual of the sacrament is hollow if we come to the Lord's Table expecting nothing to change and leave with no intention of leading new lives as faithful disciples in the world. The sacrament will not nourish us if we come to the Lord's Table unwilling to see and hear of God's self-giving ways and leave unmoved to give ourselves for God and neighbor.

In Jeremiah 6:21, God, acting as the judge in this courtroom drama, pronounces sentence on Judah. The image of God placing stumbling blocks in the way of the people is shocking. We imagine God seeking the well-being of all people. There seems to be a clear connection between the beginning of this section, where God calls Judah to walk in "the ancient paths" (v. 16), that is, in the way of Moses and covenantal obedience, and the end of the section, where God threatens "stumbling blocks." Still, verse 21 does not make clear what the stumbling blocks or obstacles are that God will place before Judah. Some have suggested that the stumbling blocks are Judah's own apostasies, so that God will let the people trip themselves up and bring them to ruin by failing to rescue them from their own blunders, such as their foolish political alliances. Others have suggested more involvement by God and understand the stumbling block to be Babylon, which will cause Judah to perish. In any case, God has offered Judah life in covenantal obedience, but Judah has willfully chosen to reject God's offer. Thus, God will see to it that Judah perishes as they have chosen.

Jeremiah 6:22–26

6:22 Thus says the LORD:
See, a people is coming from the land of the north,
a great nation is stirring from the farthest parts of the earth.
23 They grasp the bow and the javelin,
they are cruel and have no mercy,
their sound is like the roaring sea;
they ride on horses,
equipped like a warrior for battle,
against you, O daughter Zion!

24 "We have heard news of them,
our hands fall helpless;
anguish has taken hold of us,
pain as of a woman in labor.
25 Do not go out into the field,
or walk on the road;
for the enemy has a sword,
terror is on every side."

26 O my poor people, put on sackcloth,
and roll in ashes;
make mourning as for an only child,
most bitter lamentation:
for suddenly the destroyer
will come upon us.

The punishment of God threatened in general terms in 6:9–15 and 16–21 is here made more specific. The enemy "from the land of the north" (v. 22; cf. 1:12; 4:6; 5:15; 6:1), "cruel" and with "no mercy," is imagined approaching Judah. Jeremiah warns that those who refuse to walk in the "good way" (6:16) should not dare "walk on the road" or go into a field, for the enemy will lurk there (v. 25). Before God's hand, stretched out in judgment (6:12), daughter Zion's hands "fall helpless" in the anguish and pain of a woman-in labor (v. 24; see 4:31). Those who assumed "we shall not see sword or famine" (5:12) will confront an enemy who "has a sword" that brings "terror . . . on every side" (6:25).

Through Jeremiah, God has done everything possible to warn Judah of their impending destruction by Babylon. Jeremiah called out on God's behalf, urging that Judah repent and return to covenantal obedience. However, Judah has not responded. In such a situation, our reaction may well be "I told you so." It is difficult to work up much sympathy when a misfortune befalls someone who has been repeatedly warned of danger but refuses to take heed. Yet, Jeremiah's reaction on hearing the news of an enemy advance on Judah is one of dismay. He cries out to God in profound grief ("mourning as for an only child," v. 26) that a "destroyer" approaches Judah. As we find Jeremiah grieving rather than gloating, we are made aware of the heavy responsibilities of his prophetic task. He yearns for the well-being of Judah and does not delight in pronouncing judgment even when judgment is well deserved.

However, the grief expressed in verse 26 may be heard in at least two other ways. Jeremiah expresses deep grief at the prospect of Judah's destruction, but from all indications, Judah is oblivious to the danger it faces. (See v. 14, for instance, where the prophets and priests insist that there is peace.) Given the circumstances, Jeremiah's grief is appropriate, and in a sense Jeremiah gives expression to the grief that Judah should feel, were they to face their situation honestly. Or, to say this somewhat differently, Jeremiah's grief anticipates that of Judah when Babylon finally will destroy them. We also need to remember that in hearing the grief of the prophet, we are hearing the grief of God. The loss caused by "the destroyer" will also be to God like the loss of an only child. In Jeremiah 3 we hear the Lord's expectation that Judah will call "Father" and remain loyal (3:19). Such a relationship does not develop, and the Lord faces the prospect that Judah, this beloved child, will perish.

Judah has chosen death but does not grieve. Instead, Jeremiah grieves, and his grief anticipates the grief that Judah will surely experience when destroyed by Babylon. Further, Jeremiah's grief gives us a glimpse into God's own pathos as the beloved child Judah is about to perish.

Jeremiah 6:27–30

6:27 **I have made you a tester and a refiner among my people**
so that you may know and test their ways.
28 **They are all stubbornly rebellious,**
going about with slanders;
they are bronze and iron,
all of them act corruptly.
29 **The bellows blow fiercely,**
the lead is consumed by the fire;
in vain the refining goes on,
for the wicked are not removed.
30 **They are called "rejected silver,"**
for the LORD has rejected them.

God appoints Jeremiah as "a tester and a refiner" (v. 27). The imagery is widely thought to come from the process by which silver is extracted from lead where it is present in minute amounts. The ore is heated, and when high enough temperatures are achieved, the lead is dissolved and the silver is separated out. God calls Jeremiah to refine Judah to "test their ways" (v. 27; cf. 6:16). The prophet is to help God discern if anything precious is left in Judah, some portion worth saving. Since the percentage of silver in lead is quite small (often 1 percent or less), the image of refining silver suggests a negative judgment about God's people; that is, the image suggests that God does not expect much (cf. 5:1–5 and the search for one righteous person). Of course, this is hardly surprising, given the indictments and charges brought against Judah in these early chapters of the book.

One is tempted to speculate about how Jeremiah was to undertake the task of refining and testing. Perhaps the refining was to take place through the prophet's announcement of the word of the Lord that brought Babylon down on Judah. The text, however, after defining the prophet's role as a refiner, provides no detail about the refining process but instead moves directly to Jeremiah's report about the outcome (vv. 28–30). Regrettably, despite a rigorous refining process, Jeremiah can find nothing of value among God's people, only rebellion, slanders, and corruption (v. 28). Judah, Jeremiah reports, is "rejected silver"—only wicked, with nothing of value left. The image of Jeremiah as a refiner and his conclusion that the refining has been "in vain" suggest Judah will be totally destroyed, and there is not even a small remnant worth saving.

In the preceding verses, we heard Jeremiah grieve Judah's destruction by an enemy and saw the pain of the prophet in having to announce the Lord's judgment. Further, in Jeremiah's grief we also glimpsed God's pathos. In verses 27–30, with their image of Jeremiah as tester and refiner, we see another side of the prophetic task. Judah's situation is analyzed and a hard judgment is rendered. Judah is all lead and no silver: unmitigated rebellion, slander, corruption, and wickedness. The judgment "rejected silver" is added to the growing list of images used to describe Judah's condition in the book of Jeremiah: an unfaithful bride, a choice vine turned degenerate, a child who has turned away from a parent, a holy people who commit abomination.

The image of refining God's people occurs in several places in the Old Testament. For instance, in Isaiah 48, God's refining of Israel in "adversity" seems to yield no more of value than in our text, though the Lord chooses to save Israel "for my own sake" (48:9–11). In Zechariah, the refining is successful, so that after God's judgment at least a remnant will be restored to relationship with God (Zech. 13:7–9). Similarly, in Malachi, in a text known through Handel's use of it in the *Messiah*, the Lord's coming is imagined as a rigorous refining, so that even the Levitical priests will be purified. However, the end of the process is imagined as renewal of God's people, who bring offerings pleasing to the Lord (Mal. 3:1–4). At least several uses of the image of refining in the Old Testament have a somewhat hopeful perspective. That is not the case with our text.

At the beginning of this section of the book, in Jeremiah 4, God's call for Israel and Judah to return held out two possibilities: (1) by returning, they might fulfill God's intention in calling Abram and Sarai; (2) should they fail to return, God's wrath will go forth like fire (4:1–4). Jeremiah 4–6 dares to imagine that God still hopes Judah and Israel will return, and that hope permeates these chapters. Yet at the end, these chapters recognize that the people have not returned to God, and there is nothing of value left in Judah. They are rejected by God and will have to face God's wrath. We are led another step in understanding "the captivity of Jerusalem" (1:3).

"Here You Are, Trusting Deceptive Words"
(Jeremiah 7–10)

Jeremiah 7–10 continues to develop accusations against God's people. In Jeremiah 2–3, the primary accusation is that the people have forsaken God; in Jeremiah 4–6 they are accused of failing to repent, of not heeding God's call to "return." In Jeremiah 7–10, accusations against Judah are developed by contrasting the people's self-perceptions and expectations with God's assessment of them. Various contrasts are developed in these chapters. For instance, the people imagine, "We are safe" (7:10; also see 8:20), while God announces, "Do not trust in deceptive words" (7:4, 8). Judah envisions that God will be with them ("Is the Lord not in Zion?" 8:19; cf. 7:4), but God declares, "If you truly amend your ways and your doings, . . . then I will dwell with you in this place" (7:5). The people think, "We are wise" (8:8), but God observes that "they have rejected the word of the Lord" and so asks, "What wisdom is in them?" (8:9). Judah expects "peace" (8:15; cf. 8:11), yet God sees that they have "sinned" and, rather than "healing," threatens "terror instead" (8:15). The people expect that God will pour wrath on the nations who "devoured Jacob" and made the land a waste (10:25), yet God judges that Judah has "not obeyed my voice" (9:13) and threatens to scatter them among the nations until they are consumed (9:16).

The primary concern of Jeremiah 7–10 is established in Jeremiah 7, where the prophet accuses Judah of trusting deceptive words by failing to hear (which also means, obey) God's word. This section of the book concludes in Jeremiah 10 with a lament by Judah. Jeremiah 10, which uses part of the communal lament for Jerusalem from Psalm 79, functions to underscore the way in which God's people trust in deceptive words.

Jeremiah 7:1–15

7:1 **The word that came to Jeremiah from the LORD:** 2 **Stand in the gate of the LORD's house, and proclaim there this word, and say, Hear the word of the LORD, all you people of Judah, you that enter these gates to worship the**

LORD. ³ Thus says the LORD of hosts, the God of Israel: Amend your ways and your doings, and let me dwell with you in this place. ⁴ Do not trust in these deceptive words: "This is the temple of the LORD, the temple of the LORD, the temple of the LORD."

⁵ For if you truly amend your ways and your doings, if you truly act justly one with another, ⁶ if you do not oppress the alien, the orphan, and the widow, or shed innocent blood in this place, and if you do not go after other gods to your own hurt, ⁷ then I will dwell with you in this place, in the land that I gave of old to your ancestors forever and ever.

⁸ Here you are, trusting in deceptive words to no avail. ⁹ Will you steal, murder, commit adultery, swear falsely, make offerings to Baal, and go after other gods that you have not known, ¹⁰ and then come and stand before me in this house, which is called by my name, and say, "We are safe!"—only to go on doing all these abominations? ¹¹ Has this house, which is called by my name, become a den of robbers in your sight? You know, I too am watching, says the LORD. ¹² Go now to my place that was in Shiloh, where I made my name dwell at first, and see what I did to it for the wickedness of my people Israel. ¹³ And now, because you have done all these things, says the LORD, and when I spoke to you persistently, you did not listen, and when I called you, you did not answer, ¹⁴ therefore I will do to the house that is called by my name, in which you trust, and to the place that I gave to you and to your ancestors, just what I did to Shiloh. ¹⁵ And I will cast you out of my sight, just as I cast out all your kinsfolk, all the off-spring of Ephraim.

The prophet Jeremiah is told by God to proclaim the word of the Lord at the gate of the Jerusalem Temple as Judah gathers for worship. The word that Jeremiah is to speak includes a double warning. First, Judah is called to "amend your ways and your doings." God's continued presence with Judah will require repentance. Thus, despite the conclusion of Jeremiah 6 that "the Lord has rejected them," God again holds out the possibility that Judah might yet repent.

Second, Jeremiah quotes words from the Temple liturgy, "This is the temple of the Lord" (7:4), to warn worshipers that they are not to assume that because the divine dwelling place has been in Jerusalem, God will always be present to protect Judah and Jerusalem. The deception of the words "this is the temple of the Lord" is evident when they are placed alongside God's warning "Amend your ways and your doings, and let me dwell with you" (7:3). God's continuing presence with and protection of Judah demand their repentance and obedience. God holds out no unconditional guarantees of security or protection. The options—either to amend their ways and their doings or to trust in deceptive words—are presented by Jeremiah as contrasting ways in which Judah might relate to God. Of course, it is clear which choice Jeremiah favors.

Verses 1–5, in addition to presenting Judah with two options, also contrast "deceptive words" and "the word of the Lord." The triple reference to the word of the Lord in verses 1–2 is matched by a triple repetition of the false words from the Temple worship quoted in verse 4: "the temple of the Lord." Judah faces the choice to "hear the word of the Lord" (v. 2) or to trust deceptive words (v. 4). In Jeremiah 7, the accusation against Judah is that they trust deceptive words (v. 8) but do not listen to (that is, obey) God's word (vv. 13, 23, 24, 26, 28; cf. 6:10, 19).

Jeremiah develops his first admonition by suggesting to Judah what amending their ways and doings entails (vv. 5–7). The prophet links the need to care for those who are the weakest in society with the demand for exclusive devotion to God. At one level, Judah needs to be concerned for relationships with the alien, widow, and orphan. These persons, the weakest in society and those most easily exploited or ignored, are not to be oppressed (vv. 5–6). The alien, widow, and orphan are often referred to in the Old Testament as examples of persons of particular concern to the God of Israel (see Exod. 22:22; Ps. 68:5; Isa. 1:17, 23; Jer. 22:3; Ezek. 22:7; Zech. 7:10).

Jeremiah links concern for the poor and weak with devotion to God alone, that is, to obedience of the First Commandment (v. 7:6–7). The Lord God of Israel was known as "the God who brought us out of Egypt" (Exod. 16:32; 18:1; Deut. 4:20; 6:23; 26:8, Josh. 24:5), who delivered slaves from oppression. Judah's foundational experience of God in the exodus showed that the Lord God of Israel was particularly concerned for persons who were exploited and oppressed. Judah, the heirs of those whom God saved from Pharaoh's exploitation, cannot exploit the weakest persons in their society and claim a relationship with the God of the exodus; or, to state the matter positively, for Judah to obey the First Commandment and be devoted to God alone (Exod. 20:3) means that they need to share God's concern for the weak and those most easily exploited, that is, the alien, widow, and orphan. There is a clear parallel to Jesus' summary of the greatest commandments, which also links love of God with love of neighbors: "The first is . . . 'you shall love the Lord your God with all your heart. . . .' The second is this, 'You shall love your neighbor as yourself'" (Mark 12:29–31).

Obedience to the First Commandment, to worship God alone, and concern for those most easily exploited in society are joined in the thinking of Jeremiah and are laid out as the necessary conditions if God is to continue to be present with Judah in the promised land (7:7). God's intent in giving the land was security "forever and ever" for Israel, former slaves who had been oppressed in Egypt. However, God's demands announced by Jeremiah (vv. 5–7) suggest that the realization of God's intent is dependent on Judah's repentance, so that they devote themselves to God alone and, in turn, cease to oppress the alien, widow, and orphan.

While verses 5–7 suggest change and repentance are still options for Judah, the introductory phrase of verse 8, "Here you are," indicates that in Jeremiah's judgment, Judah continues to ignore God's call to repent (vv. 3–4) and chooses instead to trust "deceptive words to no avail." The Hebrew word here translated "no avail" occurs in Jeremiah 2:8 and 11, where it is translated as "not profit." The use of this phrase suggests that Judah has turned from God, "the fountain of living water," to the fertility deities in whom there is "no profit." The accusation of idolatry, which is implicit in verse 7:8, is made explicit in 7:9 as Jeremiah charges that God's people make offerings to Baal and go after other gods.

As we have seen in verses 5–7, Jeremiah connects the worship of other gods with social practices that do not reflect the Lord's concern for those exploited and oppressed. Thus, we are not surprised to find that Jeremiah illustrates the accusation that Judah has trusted deceptive words by charging that Judah is engaged in idolatry, which violates the first of the Ten Commandments but also is violating the series of commandments having to do with social interactions: stealing, murdering, committing adultery, swearing falsely. Jeremiah's thinking reflects the logic of the Ten Commandments, in which the first four commandments have to do with the relationship of humanity to God but are linked with the final six commandments, which are concerned for human relationships. As in the Ten Commandments, Jeremiah connects the need for exclusive devotion to the Lord with God's commands that social interactions respect and honor persons and human relationships.

Jeremiah further develops his accusation against Judah by pointing out that they are engaged in two contradictory behaviors. Judah violates the commandments (v. 9; cf. Exod. 20:3–20) that define obedience of God. At the same time, Judah comes to worship "in this house that is called by my name" and assumes, "We are safe" (Jer. 7:10). Together, these behaviors suggest that Judah views worship as a guarantee of security and well-being apart from exclusive devotion to God and obedience expressed through human relationships. The question that sarcastically begins verse 11 reveals the problem with Judah's worship. In referring to the Temple as "a den of robbers," Jeremiah suggests that the temple has become like one of the caves in the hills outside Jerusalem where thieves fled after they committed a crime, a place of hiding and refuge from punishment. Jeremiah's accusations suggest that Judah exploits the alien, widow, and orphan and then comes to the Temple assuming they will be safe irrespective of their obedience of God. The Temple has become Judah's place to hide after exploiting their weak neighbors, and on God's behalf, Jeremiah says to those who make the Temple "a den of robbers," "Behold, I see" (v. 11; NRSV translates, "You know, I too am watching"). Judah trusts "deceptive words," but God is not fooled. The temple will not protect Judah from God's judgment when they worship other gods and exploit their neighbors.

Because Judah trusts deceptive words and makes the temple a den of robbers, Jeremiah announces the destruction of Jerusalem (vv. 12–15). Shiloh had once been the place where God "made my name dwell," but God destroyed it because of "the wickedness of my people Israel" (v. 12; cf. 1:16). Shiloh was a primary worship center in the former Northern Kingdom, Israel. In the Southern Kingdom of Judah, Shiloh and Jerusalem were often contrasted. It was thought that Shiloh was destroyed but Jerusalem never would be. However, Jeremiah announces that the Jerusalem Temple, "the house that is called by my name, in which you trust" (v. 14), will meet the same fate as Shiloh. The occurrence of the word *trust* echoes the accusation "Here you are, trusting in deceptive words to no avail" (v. 8); further, the judgment to "cast out" (v. 15) contrasts with the possibility that "I will dwell with you in this place" should Judah repent (v. 7; cf. v. 4). Clearly, the analogy between Shiloh and Jerusalem would have been shocking for those portrayed in these verses as trusting deceptive words and assuming themselves to be safe because they worshiped in the Jerusalem Temple.

Verse 11 of this text is used in the Gospels of both Matthew and Luke in the story of Jesus' cleansing of the Temple:

> Then he entered the temple and began to drive out those who were selling things there; and he said, "It is written,
>> 'My house shall be a house of prayer';
>> but you have made it a den of robbers." (Luke 19:45–46; see
>>> Matt. 21:12–13)

The use of Jeremiah 7 in connection with Jesus' cleansing of the Temple suggests the enduring concern to which this text points. There is a constant temptation for the community of faith to allow its worship rituals to be taken as a guarantee of God's favor and protection. The criticism in Jeremiah 7 and in Jesus' cleansing of the Temple is not of worship in and of itself. Rather, it is a criticism of worship that tolerates social injustice, that does not look to the transformation of everyday life, that fails to move communities to tangible concern for the poor and marginalized, who are of particular concern to God.

Jeremiah 7 and its use in the New Testament suggest that worship can easily become a hollow ritual. One can well imagine that in Judah at the time of Jeremiah and in Jerusalem at the time of Jesus, there was considerable social expectation that proper folks would go to the Temple each Sabbath. The danger was that somehow the act of going to the Temple in and of itself would be perceived as the means of sustaining a relationship with God. Jeremiah and Jesus both understood the deep connections between praise of God in worship and obedience to God through one's everyday life and relationships. Jeremiah 7 addresses us still about the false notion that our mere participation in worship secures our relationship with God, that there is magic about "the temple of the Lord."

It is likely that most of us seek to guarantee our own security in many ways—through our employment, through careful financial planning, through attention to our health. While such concerns are prudent and even necessary, worship reminds us that we are ultimately secure because we are cared for by God. Worship, then, becomes an invitation and call to extend God's goodness and care to all people with whom we share the creation. Worship is not, as Jesus and Jeremiah knew, another ritual or activity by which we secure ourselves. Instead, worship is an occasion to discover once more that we are God's alone and called to be God's "ambassadors" in the world (2 Cor. 5:20).

Jeremiah 7:16–20

7:16 **As for you, do not pray for this people, do not raise a cry or prayer on their behalf, and do not intercede with me, for I will not hear you.** [17] **Do you not see what they are doing in the towns of Judah and in the streets of Jerusalem?** [18] **The children gather wood, the fathers kindle fire, and the women knead dough, to make cakes for the queen of heaven; and they pour out drink offerings to other gods, to provoke me to anger.** [19] **Is it I whom they provoke? says the LORD. Is it not themselves, to their own hurt?** [20] **Therefore thus says the Lord GOD: My anger and my wrath shall be poured out on this place, on human beings and animals, on the trees of the field and the fruit of the ground; it will burn and not be quenched.**

In these verses, we hear God address Jeremiah ("As for you . . . ") concerning his prophetic task. Prophets were to be mediators between God and the people. For the most part, when we think of prophets, we imagine them as messengers who spoke the word of the Lord to Israel and Judah. However, they also intervened with God on behalf of Israel and Judah. For example, when shown visions of God's intended judgment of Israel, the prophet Amos interceded, begging God to relent (Amos 7:1–6). The precedent for such an intercessory role seems to predate the prophets. Abraham, for instance, when told about God's intended destruction of Sodom and Gomorrah, dared to intercede on behalf of those cities to inquire if there was a way they could be spared. Abraham even negotiated with God about how many righteous persons would need to be found for the cities to be spared (Gen. 18:16–33). Also Moses, after the incident of the golden calf at Mount Sinai, interceded on behalf of Israel seeking God's mercy and finally persuaded the Lord not to make an end to Israel, as was threatened (Exodus 32–34). In the Old Testament, God, who is clearly sovereign, is also portrayed as willing to enter into conversation with humanity, willing to listen, even willing to be persuaded to act in a way not originally intended (such as refraining to execute a previously announced judgment). In this tradition of God's openness to dialogue with humanity, prophets were to speak the word of the Lord to Israel and Judah; but God also entrusted prophets with the task of interceding on behalf of the people.

However, in this text Jeremiah is told by the Lord that he is no longer to pray, raise a cry, or intercede on behalf of Judah, because God will no longer listen (Jer. 7:16). God has seen and heard enough, and this unwillingness to allow Jeremiah to pray suggests that the Lord has firmly decided what is to happen with Judah. Enough is enough. The reasons for this decision are that Judah has failed to listen to God's word and gone after other gods (vv. 17–20; cf. 7:6, 8), particularly worshiping "the queen of heaven" (v. 18). The queen of heaven was a goddess connected with various fertility religions in the ancient Near East, possibly the Babylonian goddess Astarte or the Canaanite goddess Anat (see Jeremiah 44). Though it is difficult to know precisely which fertility cult is being described here, there is no mistake that a blatant participation in the worship of others gods is referenced. What is described in verse 18 seems to be a family cult ritual that involved the husband, wife, and children in preparing an offering for a fertility goddess.

God's refusal to listen further to Judah mirrors the conclusion of the preceding verses, where Jeremiah declares that God will "cast out" Judah because Judah does not listen to God (7:13–15). Judah has not listened to the word of the Lord, so God is no longer willing to listen to Judah through the prophet. God's conversation with Judah is at an end because

Judah has not and will not listen. As in most relationships, when communication ceases, trouble quickly follows. God threatens "anger" and "wrath" that "will burn and not be quenched" (v. 20; cf. 4:4, 8, 26; 5:14; 6:29). Judah has refused to listen to the word of the Lord spoken by Jeremiah and has gone after other gods. God has had enough and wants to hear no more. There is no indication that Judah has amended their ways and their doings, and Jeremiah is not to bother God about Judah any further.

Jeremiah 7:21–28

7:21 **Thus says the LORD of hosts, the God of Israel: Add your burnt offerings to your sacrifices, and eat the flesh. 22 For in the day that I brought your ancestors out of the land of Egypt, I did not speak to them or command them concerning burnt offerings and sacrifices. 23 But this command I gave them, "Obey my voice, and I will be your God, and you shall be my people; and walk only in the way that I command you, so that it may be well with you." 24 Yet they did not obey or incline their ear, but, in the stubbornness of their evil will, they walked in their own counsels, and looked backward rather than forward. 25 From the day that your ancestors came out of the land of Egypt until this day, I have persistently sent all my servants the prophets to them, day after day; 26 yet they did not listen to me, or pay attention, but they stiffened their necks. They did worse than their ancestors did.**

27 So you shall speak all these words to them, but they will not listen to you. You shall call to them, but they will not answer you. 28 You shall say to them: This is the nation that did not obey the voice of the LORD their God, and did not accept discipline; truth has perished; it is cut off from their lips.

These verses explore concerns already introduced in this chapter. Jeremiah charges that Judah "did not obey or incline their ear" (v. 24), an accusation that is repeated four times: in verses 24, 26, 27, 28. The particular example of Judah's not listening that concerns Jeremiah is that they make "burnt offerings and sacrifices" that God "did not speak to them or command" (v. 22).

Such a charge was surely surprising to Jeremiah's audience and is likely surprising to modern readers as well. We usually assume that God commanded the sacrificial practices of ancient Israel and Judah. It certainly seems so as one reads the account of God's instructions to Israel at Mount Sinai. Regulations about sacrifices, offerings, and other details of worship are found in Exodus 25–31 and 35–40, and still more throughout the first half of the book of Leviticus. It certainly seems that God gave commands about sacrifice. So, how is this text to be understood? Two comments may be helpful:

1. It is widely recognized that much of the material about sacrifices and offerings in the Old Testament was added at a late date, sometime after the exile and thus after the time of Jeremiah. The material in the book of Leviticus and in Exodus 35–40 was developed after the time of Jeremiah as part of the effort to restore Judah's worship after the Babylonian exile. Thus, some of the Old Testament regulations regarding offerings and sacrifices would not have been known during Jeremiah's lifetime. Still, the late date of some Old Testament material about sacrifices does not completely solve the problem of this text, for surely sacrifices were offered in the Temple during the time of Jeremiah.

2. However, a strong case can be made that sacrifices were never understood to be the central or most important aspect of the obedience God demanded from Israel and Judah. If one reads the account of Sinai, regulations about sacrifices do not occupy a central place. The Ten Commandments come first (Exod. 20:1–17), then all sorts of detailed regulations and stipulations governing everyday life (Exodus 21–23). It is only after the covenant is ratified (Exodus 24) that stipulations regarding sacrifices are given. This arrangement of material associated with Sinai suggests that obedience to God was first defined as devotion to God alone (the first four commandments) and then through ways in which relationship with God was to be expressed in human interactions (commandments five through ten). Thus, Jeremiah rightly claims that God had not commanded sacrifices as the essential feature of covenantal obedience. The obedience God commanded required exclusive devotion to God and a just ordering of society; and it would not do to substitute sacrifices as central to God's covenantal commands.

Throughout Jeremiah 7, the prophet makes a forceful case that in the primary matters of obedience, exclusive devotion to God, and a just ordering of society, Judah has failed. In the place of the central demands of obedience, Jeremiah sees that Judah substitutes rituals, worship at the Temple (v. 4), and offering sacrifices (v. 22). For Jeremiah, that Judah makes worship rituals the primary expression of their obedience while ignoring the primary matters of obedience is evidence that (like their ancestors; v. 25) they have not listened to or obeyed God. If they had listened and obeyed, they would not have worshiped other gods or oppressed the alien, widow, and orphan.

In verses 27–28, God again addresses Jeremiah regarding his prophetic vocation. While, in 7:16, God denies Jeremiah his role as intercessor, in verses 7:27–28 God charges Jeremiah to continue as the Lord's messenger: "So you shall speak all these words to them." However, God issues a somber warning: "they will not listen to you." That has been the point of Jeremiah 7. Judah will not listen to Jeremiah, who has spoken the word of the Lord, and such failure to listen and obey will lead to God's judgment and the captivity of Jerusalem (1:3).

Jeremiah 7:29–8:3

7:29 **Cut off your hair and throw it away;**
        raise a lamentation on the bare heights,
        for the LORD has rejected and forsaken
        the generation that provoked his wrath.
   [30] **For the people of Judah have done evil in my sight, says the LORD; they have set their abominations in the house that is called by my name, defiling it.** [31] **And they go on building the high place of Topheth, which is in the valley of the son of Hinnom, to burn their sons and their daughters in the fire— which I did not command, nor did it come into my mind.** [32] **Therefore, the days are surely coming, says the LORD, when it will no more be called Topheth, or the valley of the son of Hinnom, but the valley of Slaughter: for they will bury in Topheth until there is no more room.** [33] **The corpses of this people will be food for the birds of the air, and for the animals of the earth; and no one will frighten them away.** [34] **And I will bring to an end the sound of mirth and gladness, the voice of the bride and bridegroom in the cities of Judah and in the streets of Jerusalem; for the land shall become a waste.**
   8:1 **At that time, says the LORD, the bones of the kings of Judah, the bones of its officials, the bones of the priests, the bones of the prophets, and the bones of the inhabitants of Jerusalem shall be brought out of their tombs;** [2] **and they shall be spread before the sun and the moon and all the host of heaven, which they have loved and served, which they have followed, and which they have inquired of and worshiped; and they shall not be gathered or buried; they shall be like dung on the surface of the ground.** [3] **Death shall be preferred to life by all the remnant that remains of this evil family in all the places where I have driven them, says the LORD of hosts.**

Jeremiah calls for lamentation because God has rejected Judah (7:29; cf. 4:8). Previously in the book, Judah was accused of the evil of forsaking Yahweh (for example, 1:16) and rejecting God's instruction (6:19). Now Jeremiah announces that God is rejecting and forsaking Judah because they have "done evil." This evil is identified as setting "abominations in the house that is called by my name, defiling it" (7:30–31). In verse 30, abomination is identified as idolatrous worship and is connected with the horrifying practice of child sacrifice. What this actually involved in Judah is not certain. There were occasions in Judah's history when, under the influence of worship rituals associated with Baal, child sacrifice apparently was practiced. For instance, there is mention in 2 Kings that prior to the time of Jeremiah, persons in Judah, under the pressure of assault from Assyria, resorted to child sacrifice (2 Kings 16:3; 21:6); it is at least possible that such practices continued in Jeremiah's time with the threat of a Babylonian invasion.

The language of Jeremiah 7:31 suggests that whatever practices Jeremiah had in mind, those who engaged in them thought they were commanded by God. By misinterpreting some well-known Old Testament stories, one might get the notion that God commands the sacrifice of children: for instance, the story of Abraham's sacrifice of Isaac (Genesis 22) or the command that the firstborn be given to God (Exod. 22:29–30; cf. Micah 6:6–8). Jeremiah asserts strongly that child sacrifice is abhorrent to God and a gross misunderstanding of whatever traditions may have been used to justify the practice. However the idea that God demands the sacrifice of children may have entered Judah, Jeremiah rejects the practice in the strongest terms.

Jeremiah's accusations against Judah in 7:30–31 lead to two pronouncements of judgment in 7:32–34 and 8:1–3. The judgment announced in 7:32–34 envisions the cessation of proper burials and of wedding celebrations. The burial grounds are portrayed as filled to overflowing with corpses left unburied for birds and beasts to devour. A similar covenant curse appears in Deuteronomy 28:26:

> Your corpses shall be food for every bird of the air and animal of the earth, and there shall be no one to frighten them away.

Covenant curses such as those found in Deuteronomy 28 (also see Lev. 26:14–39), were understood to be the consequences for violating God's covenant stipulations. Jeremiah 7 repeatedly charges that Judah has violated God's commands or broken covenant stipulations. So, it is not surprising that Jeremiah imagines the consequences of Judah's actions resulting in a covenant curse like the one referred to in 7:32. Further, Jeremiah threatens that God will end "the mirth and gladness" of wedding celebrations (v. 34). The sense is that such celebration will be unthinkable because of God's judgment. However, there is also the implication that without weddings, there will be no new generation, and the community will cease to exist. God has accused Judah of failing to listen to God's word (7:1–15); in verses 32–34, Jeremiah connects this failure with the collapse of the social order and Judah's imminent end.

In Jeremiah 8:1–3, the prophet announces a judgment of God that matchs Judah's sin. Judah had worshiped the gods of heaven (7:18). In 8:1–2, the idolatrous worshipers are presented as lying dishonored in death (7:33) before the gods of heaven. God's judgment will be so severe that, for this "evil family" (8:3) who have "done evil" in God's sight (7:30), "death shall be preferred to life."

The texts in Jeremiah 7 connect religious idolatry with the social and political collapse of Judah. While these texts were surely shaped during the exile to explain why the Babylonian captivity occurred, the connection they make between idolatry and social collapse is well known to us. For example, our century has been scarred with tragic and destructive wars. Often, these wars began when some nation or other identified its national ends with God's will. German soldiers in World War I wore belt buckles inscribed with the slogan "God with us." In the United States, the idolatry of racism by the dominant white culture, or at least the religious justification of discrimination, has resulted in decades of racial tension and, at times, social unrest. We have witnessed repeatedly in our contemporary history how idolatry—nationalism, for instance—has resulted in massive social upheaval and collapse.

Jeremiah 8:4–13

8:4 **You shall say to them, Thus says the LORD:**
  When people fall, do they not get up again?
  If they go astray, do they not turn back?
5 **Why then has this people turned away**
  in perpetual backsliding?
  They have held fast to deceit,
  they have refused to return.
6 **I have given heed and listened,**
  but they do not speak honestly;
  no one repents of wickedness,
  saying, "What have I done!"
  All of them turn to their own course,
  like a horse plunging headlong into battle.
7 **Even the stork in the heavens**
  knows its times;
  and the turtledove, swallow, and crane
  observe the time of their coming;
  but my people do not know
  the ordinance of the LORD.

8 **How can you say, "We are wise,**
  and the law of the LORD is with us,"

when, in fact, the false pen of the scribes
has made it into a lie?
⁹ The wise shall be put to shame,
they shall be dismayed and taken;
since they have rejected the word of the LORD,
what wisdom is in them?
¹⁰ Therefore I will give their wives to others
and their fields to conquerors,
because from the least to the greatest
everyone is greedy for unjust gain;
from prophet to priest
everyone deals falsely.
¹¹ They have treated the wound of my people carelessly,
saying, "Peace, peace,"
when there is no peace.
¹² They acted shamefully, they committed abomination;
yet they were not at all ashamed,
they did not know how to blush.
Therefore they shall fall among those who fall;
at the time when I punish them, they shall be overthrown,
says the LORD.
¹³ When I wanted to gather them, says the LORD,
there are no grapes on the vine,
nor figs on the fig tree;
even the leaves are withered,
and what I gave them has passed away from them.

In Jeremiah 7:1–8:3, Judah is accused of trusting deceptive words and not listening to or obeying the word of the Lord. In Jeremiah 8:4–13, God listens to Judah (8:6) but can discern only deceit (8:5) and lies (8:8). Again, the accusation is that the people reject God's word (8:9).

God has called Judah to "return" (4:1) and to "amend your ways and your doings" (7:3, 5). In 8:4–7, Hebrew words closely related to that for "return" occur six times to show that Judah has failed to respond to God's call to return (italicized words are those translating Hebrew words related to *return*):

If they [people] *go astray*, do they not *turn back?*
Why then has this people [i.e., Judah] *turned away* in *perpetual backsliding?*
. . . they have refused to *return*
All of them *turn* to their own course

As a whole, the prophet's accusation presented in verses 4–7 contrasts the actions of Judah—in turning away and not turning back—with the order observed elsewhere in God's creation. For instance, migratory birds know the order of God (that is, "observe the time of their coming"). However, Jeremiah concludes that God's people do not know the "ordinance of the Lord" (v. 7).

The question Jeremiah poses in verse 8 denies the claim of the people "We are wise, and the law of the Lord is with us." This claim is refuted by the use of a single Hebrew word translated two ways in verse 8b: "in fact, the *false* pen of the scribes has made it into a *lie*." The accusation is that some leaders of Judah intentionally falsify God's law. There is an obvious connection with Jeremiah 7:8–10, which accuses Judah of trusting deceptive words. A clue about what is involved in falsifying God's law is found in 8:10 in the charge that "everyone is greedy for unjust gain." Such an accusation is consistent with the violations of God's commandments cited in Jeremiah 7:6, 9. The scribes were the interpreters of Judah's legal traditions, and their false interpretations, it seems, provided a religious justification for social injustice, particularly the exploitation of the poor (alien, widow, orphan; 7:6) by the well-to-do. Jeremiah 8:9 brings these accusations to their conclusion with the charge that "they have rejected the word of the Lord," an accusation also prominent in Jeremiah 7.

As we would expect after a series of accusations, verses 10–13 announce God's judgment. As is typical of the book of Jeremiah, the pronouncements of judgment in these verses are reinforced by further accusations. Jeremiah 8:10b–12 is identical to Jeremiah 6:13–15, and 8:10a closely resembles 6:12 in imagining Judah's capture and plunder by an enemy. Still, the repetition of material from Jeremiah 6 here in Jeremiah 8 suits the context well. Jeremiah concludes that the Lord will overthrow Judah (8:12; cf. "overthrow" in 1:10).

Jeremiah 8:13 is more difficult. On the one hand, the prophet asserts that Judah has borne no fruit ("no grapes . . . nor figs"). There is no evidence that the relationship Judah claims with God has tangible outcomes. Neither the justice nor the wisdom one would expect of a people grounded in God's law is evident in Judah (see vv. 7–8). On the other hand, in verse 13, God declares that "what I gave them has passed away from them." This vague claim can suggest a number of possibilities about what Judah might lose. In light of Jeremiah's message to this point in the book, he may have intended to imply that God would take from Judah the land and its blessings, God's presence and protection, the Temple, the monarchy, or all these. It is difficult to be more precise, and one suspects that whatever Jeremiah's intent, his audience likely dismissed the prophet's words as doom and gloom and whitewashed over them with a quick assurance of "peace" (v. 11). Still, Jeremiah insists that the Lord's judgment looms and Judah will be "overthrown" (v. 12) by the very God they assume will keep them safe (7:10).

An important problem identified in these verses is Judah's self-deceit. Judah, especially the Jerusalem leadership, imagine themselves as righteous persons who faithfully follow God. Jeremiah has a very different evaluation. The prophet's assessment of Judah should give us today pause about the self-deceit and falseness that can capture us. When we hear of problems of economic inequities, abuse of the environment, or racial or gender biases, it is easy to imagine ourselves, our church, and our community free from any responsibility for such problems. We can, in viewing ourselves, easily conclude that we are righteous and obedient. The danger is that we are joining the Jerusalem leaders of Jeremiah's time in "saying, 'Peace, peace,' when there is no peace" (8:11).

Jeremiah 8:14–9:3

14 **Why do we sit still?**
   Gather together, let us go into the fortified cities
   and perish there;
   for the LORD our God has doomed us to perish,
   and has given us poisoned water to drink,
   because we have sinned against the LORD.
15 **We look for peace, but find no good,**
   for a time of healing, but there is terror instead.

16 **The snorting of their horses is heard from Dan;**
   at the sound of the neighing of their stallions
   the whole land quakes.
   They come and devour the land and all that fills it,
   the city and those who live in it.
17 **See, I am letting snakes loose among you,**
   adders that cannot be charmed,
   and they shall bite you,

                              says the LORD.

18 **My joy is gone, grief is upon me,**
   my heart is sick.
19 **Hark, the cry of my poor people**
   from far and wide in the land:
   "Is the LORD not in Zion?

Is her King not in her?"
("Why have they provoked me to anger with their images,
with their foreign idols?")
20 "The harvest is past, the summer is ended,
and we are not saved."
21 For the hurt of my poor people I am hurt,
I mourn, and dismay has taken hold of me.

22 Is there no balm in Gilead?
Is there no physician there?
Why then has the health of my poor people
not been restored?
9:1 O that my head were a spring of water,
and my eyes a fountain of tears,
so that I might weep day and night
for the slain of my poor people!
2 O that I had in the desert
a traveler's lodging place,
that I might leave my people
and go away from them!
For they are all adulterers,
a band of traitors.
3 They bend their tongues like bows;
they have grown strong in the land for falsehood, and not for truth;
for they proceed from evil to evil,
and they do not know me, says the LORD.

Finally, God's people recognize what is happening to them. Because they have sinned against the Lord, they are to perish. The Lord, "the fountain of living water" (2:13), is poisoning Judah's water (8:14). The people see that even the fortified cities to which they flee (v. 14, cf. 4:5–8) will not protect them, and their hopes for security (8:15, "peace . . . a time of healing"; cf. 8:11) are being met by "terror instead" (cf. 6:25). A sense of impending doom is clear in these verses.

While it is clear that in 8:17, God is announcing judgment on Judah, 8:16 could be spoken by either God or the people. No matter who the speaker, the impact of reintroducing the enemy approaching from Dan (that is, from the north; see 1:11–15; 4:15) strengthens the sense of the imminent and inevitable approach of God's judgment. The terror of God's judgment in these verses is highlighted not only by portraying the approach of horses (that is, an enemy) from Dan but also by God's announcement, "I am letting snakes loose among you" (8:17). In contrast to the visible approach of an enemy on horses, snakes are mostly not visible and approach as an unseen threat. One way or another, God will accomplish judgment on Judah. These portrayals of God's judgment at this point in the book contradict the hopes of the people who cling to "deceptive words."

At verse 18 the speaker shifts again, and we hear a lament of the prophet Jeremiah at the prospect of Judah's punishment. However, since Jeremiah is the spokesperson for God, it is likely that we hear God's own anguish through the lament of the prophet. Verses 18–21 express directly Jeremiah's/God's anguish and dismay "for the hurt of my poor people." The people are quoted twice as they express their dismay and confusion:

> Is the LORD not in Zion?
> Is her King not in her?
>   (v. 19)

> The harvest is past, the summer is ended,
>   and we are not saved.
>   (v. 20)

The expectation of Judah is that because God is sovereign (Yahweh is king in Zion), they will be safe (see 7:10). As an enemy approaches and no deliverance is evident ("the summer is ended, and we are not saved"), these hopes are dashed. Between the two cries of Judah in 8:19–20, God speaks:

> Why have they provoked me to anger with their images,
>   with their foreign idols?
>   (v. 19)

Judah assumes God's sovereignty guarantees their security. However, we who have been reading the book understand why Judah is "not saved" (v. 20). The proper response to the question of verse 22, "Why then has the health of my poor people not been restored?" is that Judah provoked God's anger.

God's anger is understandable. The surprise of these verses is the Lord's anguish and hurt. The angry sovereign is portrayed as sick at heart: "My joy is gone, grief is upon me, my heart is sick" (v. 18). There are insufficient tears to express God's distress, and the Lord wishes to flee from this people who have caused so much pain (9:1–2). We are accustomed to thinking about the Lord's anger and judgment but not so used to thinking about God's grief and tears. We are accustomed to thinking about God's power, the Almighty who can accomplish whatever ends by pure force. Yet, the Bible frequently knows God in a different manner—God whose strength lies in a willingness to take risks, and whose power is suffering love.

So, for example, the Lord takes the risk of entrusting the creation to humankind "to till it and keep it" (Gen. 2:15). God is strong and secure enough to risk the creation to mere creatures. However, God then must suffer disappointment when humankind is not the kind of steward of creation God had hoped (Gen. 3:8–13; 4:8–12). Finally, God sees the situation of humanity for what it is, and what God sees causes distress:

> The LORD saw that the wickedness of humankind was great in the earth, and that every inclination of the thoughts of their hearts was only evil continually. And the LORD was sorry that he had made humankind on the earth, and it grieved him to his heart. (Gen. 6:5–6)

God's strength is in risking the creation to human care, yet the risk finally causes God grief. Again, when God seeks to transform and renew the world, it is through Jesus' death on a cross, suffering love, which the apostle Paul knew was "foolishness" to some but also "the power of God" to save (1 Cor. 1:18). Through Jeremiah we hear of the suffering love of God, who longed for a relationship with Judah and was hurt when shunned. A contemporary theologian, William Placher, reflects on the strength of God's suffering by relating this story:

> In his lament for his son Eric, killed at twenty-five in a mountaineering accident, Nicholas Wolterstorff remarks that it was only in the midst of his own suffering that he saw that God suffers. He reflects on the old belief that no one can behold God's face and live. I always thought, Wolterstorff says, that this meant that no one could see God's splendor and live. A friend said perhaps it means that no one could see God's sorrow and live. Or perhaps, he reflects, the sorrow is the splendor. ("Narratives of a Vulnerable God," 151)

Jeremiah invites us to behold the splendor of God, who loves so deeply as to be grief-stricken over Judah's rejection.

This text stresses the failure of God's people to repent or "return" and the anguish this causes God. Yet, underlying this text is a confidence that God who suffers Judah's rejection intends healing and restoration for them. This confidence is expressed in Jeremiah 8:22, whose two questions are assumed to have a positive response: Yes! There is a balm in Gilead, and a physician there. (Gilead was a region east of the Jordan known for a kind of gum tree whose sap had healing qualities.) Yes! God does intend to save and restore the people. Tragically, the people would not seek the healing God offered. Still, God did intend healing. The African American spiritual grasps well the confidence in God that underlies this portion of the book of Jeremiah:

> There is a balm in Gilead to make the wounded whole.
> There is a balm in Gilead to heal the sin-sick soul.

> Sometimes I feel discouraged, And think my work's in vain
> But then the Holy Spirit Revives my soul again.

> Don't ever feel discouraged, for Jesus is your friend,
> And if you lack for knowledge, He'll not refuse to lend.

> If you can't preach like Peter, If you cannot pray like Paul,
> You can tell the love of Jesus, And say, "He died for all."

God offers wholeness if we will, in ways that Judah would not, receive God's offer of healing balm.

Jeremiah 9:4–11

9:4 **Beware of your neighbors,**
   and put no trust in any of your kin;
   for all your kin are supplanters,
   and every neighbor goes around like a slanderer.
5 **They all deceive their neighbors,**
   and no one speaks the truth;
   they have taught their tongues to speak lies;
   they commit iniquity and are too weary to repent.
6 **Oppression upon oppression, deceit upon deceit!**
   They refuse to know me, says the LORD.

7 **Therefore thus says the LORD of hosts:**
   I will now refine and test them,
   for what else can I do with my sinful people?
8 **Their tongue is a deadly arrow;**
   it speaks deceit through the mouth.
   They all speak friendly words to their neighbors,
   but inwardly are planning to lay an ambush.
9 **Shall I not punish them for these things? says the LORD;**
   and shall I not bring retribution
   on a nation such as this?

10 **Take up weeping and wailing for the mountains,**
    and a lamentation for the pastures of the wilderness,
    because they are laid waste so that no one passes through,
    and the lowing of cattle is not heard;
    both the birds of the air and the animals
    have fled and are gone.

¹¹ **I will make Jerusalem a heap of ruins,**
a lair of jackals;
and I will make the towns of Judah a desolation,
without inhabitant.

The prophet warns neighbors not to trust one another. Jeremiah perceives that "deceit" and "lies" are undermining social relationships. Importantly, Jeremiah understands that the social disintegration he observes has a theological cause: "They refuse to know me, says the Lord" (9:6; cf. 8:7; 9:3). The prophet is clear that just and humane social relationships are not possible apart from a relationship with God. Conversely, to claim that one is in relationship with God while exploiting or oppressing one's neighbors is a deceit.

In this speech, Jeremiah is specifically concerned with the commandment about bearing false witness (Exod. 20:16). The sense of the commandment is a prohibition not merely against lying and slander but against the use of such speech to take advantage of or bring harm on another. For instance, in 1 Kings 21 the false witnesses that Queen Jezebel brings forward allow King Ahab and the queen to have Naboth murdered so they can seize his field (1 Kings 21:10, 13). Jeremiah, with the accusation that Judah refuses to know the Lord, links the commandment against false witness to the first four commandments dealing directly with the God-human relationship. These four commandments lay the foundation for the last six commandments, which concern relationships within the human community. Relationship with God and relationship with our neighbors are closely related. For Judah, this perspective undoubtedly grew out of the experience of the exodus, of the God who delivered oppressed persons from slavery. A community shaped by the concerns of the God of the exodus was not much evident by the time of Jeremiah, who characterizes the life of the community as "oppression upon oppression" (9:6). In the New Testament letter of James, the writer, concerned that the life of faith find expression in "works," was keenly aware of the power and danger of the tongue, which he called "a restless evil, full of deadly poison" (James 3:8). Jeremiah, who points out to Judah the oppressive force of slander and deceit, would have agreed with James about the poisonous potential of human speech, a sure sign of little faith.

There is a tendency today to characterize churches as "liberal" or "conservative." At least according to the stereotype, liberal churches are those that have evident commitments to issues of social justice. Conservative churches are thought to be those that more emphasize the relationship of individuals to God and personal morality. The keen perception of the prophet Jeremiah, consistent with the view of scripture more broadly, is that we in the contemporary church too often separate what belongs together. Jeremiah speaks a word that calls the church to examine itself. Concern for social justice and the relationship of individuals to God are not mutually exclusive options; both are vital to a community that would be faithful to God.

This prophetic speech ends with a pronouncement of judgment. God will "test and refine" (9:7) this sinful and deceitful people (cf. 6:27–29, where Jeremiah was to be the assayer of Judah). We know the answer to the query of 9:9: "Shall I not punish them . . . shall I not bring retribution?" Yet, even expecting God's judgment, the scope of what Jeremiah imagines in verses 10–11 is startling: nothing less than the collapse of creation. The imagery of these verses, which portrays creation becoming chaos (mountains and pastures become like the wilderness where "no one passes through," 9:10; cf. 2:6), carries to a logical conclusion the social disintegration brought about by Judah's deceit and refusal to know God. Jerusalem and all of Judah will be like Shiloh (7:12–15), "a heap of ruins, a lair of jackals; . . . a desolation, without inhabitant" (9:11).

Jeremiah 9:12–16

Through Jeremiah, God asks Judah a series of questions. In the initial question (9:12; cf. 8:8) it is asked, "Who is wise enough to understand this?"—that is, God's judgment, announced in 9:10–11. The second question indicates that having heard the word of the Lord would allow one to comprehend God's decision to ruin the land. The third question, "Why is the land ruined?" is similar. So, Jeremiah's persistent claim is that for Judah to be "wise" is for them to understand God's judgment.

The reasons for the ruin of the land have been well developed by this point in the book. However, in case the point has been missed, God's response in verses 13–16 makes explicit "why" the land is ruined. The land is ruined because Judah has forsaken God's law and refuses to obey the Lord. This accusation has occurred repeatedly and summarizes a major theme of the book of Jeremiah to this point. The nature of God's judgment is summarized in verses 15–16, through God's first-person ("I") statements: "I will send the sword . . . until I have consumed them." When Judah is loyal to God, it is Judah's enemies whom God will consume (see 2:3). Now, in judgment, God threatens to consume Judah.

Jeremiah 9:17–22

9:17 Thus says the LORD of hosts:
Consider, and call for the mourning women to come;
send for the skilled women to come;
18 let them quickly raise a dirge over us,
so that our eyes may run down with tears,
and our eyelids flow with water.
19 For a sound of wailing is heard from Zion:
"How we are ruined!
We are utterly shamed,
because we have left the land,
because they have cast down our dwellings."

20 Hear, O women, the word of the LORD,
and let your ears receive the word of his mouth;
teach to your daughters a dirge,
and each to her neighbor a lament.
21 "Death has come up into our windows,
it has entered our palaces,
to cut off the children from the streets
and the young men from the squares."
22 Speak! Thus says the LORD:
"Human corpses shall fall
like dung upon the open field,
like sheaves behind the reaper,
and no one shall gather them."

With the announcement of God's imminent judgment, the prophet imagines the response of the people should they "consider" (v. 17) their situation. Death approaches like an intruder, a thief (v. 21). The people need to prepare for a funeral—their own—and call the "mourning women to come" and "raise a dirge over us" (vv. 17–18). In the funeral customs of ancient Israel, when death was imminent or had occurred, professional mourning women were employed to lead the mourning of the family and community by their own noisy expressions of grief. In these verses, Judah is likened to a person near death, and mourning women are called to lament because death is overtaking God's people (v. 21). Earlier, when God considers the death of the people, God wishes (9:1):

O that my head were a spring of water,
and my eyes a fountain of tears,
so I might weep day and night
for the slain of my poor people!

Now, with the dirge of the mourning women, God imagines the people's tears and, at last, their shame (vv. 18–19; cf. 6:15; 8:12). In the final scene of this scenario (9:22), the prophet offers a vision of corpses piled like dung on a field, with no one to bury them. It is a scene reminiscent of Jeremiah 8:1–3 (cf. Deut. 28:26); God's judgment on Judah's idolatry is portrayed as a covenant curse.

Jeremiah 9:23–26

9:23 **Thus says the** LORD: **Do not let the wise boast in their wisdom, do not let the mighty boast in their might, do not let the wealthy boast in their wealth;** 24 **but let those who boast boast in this, that they understand and know me, that I am the** LORD; **I act with steadfast love, justice, and righteousness in the earth, for in these things I delight, says the** LORD.

25 **The days are surely coming, says the** LORD, **when I will attend to all those who are circumcised only in the foreskin:** 26 **Egypt, Judah, Edom, the Ammonites, Moab, and all those with shaven temples who live in the desert. For all these nations are uncircumcised, and all the house of Israel is uncircumcised in heart.**

Jeremiah 7 presented Judah two options: to trust deceptive words or to amend their ways and their doings. Here, at the end of chapter 9, Jeremiah again holds before Judah two options. Each, as Walter Brueggemann has observed, is presented as a triad:

> The first triad is the way of wisdom, might and riches. These modes of self-sufficiency are condemned. . . .
>
> The contrasting triad of "steadfast love, justice, and righteousness" (v. 24) reflects a wholly different orientation, congruent with the character of God who delights in these qualities and insists upon them. Yahweh champions and embodies fidelity, equality, and humanness in the community. Thus, Yahweh is contrasted with other gods who seek satiation (might, riches). (Brueggemann, *Jeremiah 1–25*, pp. 95–96)

This accusation against Judah makes clear that Judah is not wise in the ways of God and does not delight in steadfast love, justice, or righteousness—any more than Judah has amended its ways or shunned deceptive words. Again, these verses connect the quality of relationship with God and the quality of community life.

Knowing the ways of Judah, we are not surprised by the verdict of 9:25–26, though the manner of statement is startling. In these verses, God promises "to attend to" the nations, those "circumcised only in the foreskin" or "uncircumcised." Surely, this would have been welcomed and expected by those who trusted deceptive words. The shock is that God here counts Judah as just one nation among many: "all these nations are uncircumcised, and all the house of Israel is uncircumcised in heart" (v. 26; cf. 4:4, 14). To be circumcised was to be part of the covenant community (Gen. 17:9–14), the community of God's people whose commitment was to the steadfast love, justice, and righteousness in which God delighted. However, because Judah has chosen wisdom, might, and wealth, God concludes Judah is "uncircumcised in heart." Circumcision, like the Temple, has become a deception.

There is a clear warning that the Lord expects much more than a formal affiliation with the community of God's people. To be baptized, to be a member of a church, or for a community to call itself Christian means little in itself. God's people are to trust in the Lord alone (faith) and be committed to serve God's concern for a just and humane social order (obedience)—"steadfast love, justice, and righteousness." In other words, our baptism commits us to God's mission in the world.

Jeremiah 10:1–16

10:1 Hear the word that the LORD speaks to you, O house of Israel. ² **Thus says the LORD:**
Do not learn the way of the nations,
or be dismayed at the signs of the heavens;
for the nations are dismayed at them.
³ **For the customs of the peoples are false:**
a tree from the forest is cut down,
and worked with an ax by the hands of an artisan;
⁴ **people deck it with silver and gold;**
they fasten it with hammer and nails
so that it cannot move.
⁵ **Their idols are like scarecrows in a cucumber field,**
and they cannot speak;
they have to be carried,
for they cannot walk.
Do not be afraid of them,
for they cannot do evil,
nor is it in them to do good.

⁶ **There is none like you, O LORD;**
you are great, and your name is great in might.
⁷ **Who would not fear you, O King of the nations?**
For that is your due;

among all the wise ones of the nations
and in all their kingdoms
there is no one like you.
8   They are both stupid and foolish;
the instruction given by idols
is no better than wood!
9   Beaten silver is brought from Tarshish,
and gold from Uphaz.
They are the work of the artisan and of the hands of the goldsmith;
their clothing is blue and purple;
they are all the product of skilled workers.
10 But the LORD is the true God;
he is the living God and the everlasting King.
At his wrath the earth quakes,
and the nations cannot endure his indignation.

11 Thus shall you say to them: The gods who did not make the heavens
and the earth shall perish from the earth and from under the
heavens.
12 It is he who made the earth by his power,
who established the world by his wisdom,
and by his understanding stretched out the heavens.
13 When he utters his voice, there is a tumult of waters in the heavens,
and he makes the mist rise from the ends of the earth.
He makes lightnings for the rain,
and he brings out the wind from his storehouses.
14 Everyone is stupid and without knowledge;
goldsmiths are all put to shame by their idols;
for their images are false,
and there is no breath in them.
15 They are worthless, a work of delusion;
at the time of their punishment they shall perish.
16 Not like these is the LORD, the portion of Jacob,
for he is the one who formed all things,
and Israel is the tribe of his inheritance;
the LORD of hosts is his name.

With the accusation that Israel has become like the nations, Jeremiah urges: "Do not learn the way of the nations. . . . For the customs of the peoples are false" (10:2–3). These verses concern the idols of the nations, which are contrasted with the God of Israel.

Jeremiah's contrast of God and the idols is accomplished by alternating descriptions that stress the passivity and powerlessness of the idols, on the one hand and the power of God to shape the creation and direct the course of history, on the other (cf. Isa. 44:9–20). Among the descriptions of the idols in Jeremiah 10 are these:

> The idols are like scarecrows in a cucumber field.
> They cannot move or speak.
> They have to be carried, for they cannot walk.
> They cannot do evil, nor can they do good.
> They are stupid and foolish.
> Their images are false, and there is no breath in them.
> They are worthless and a work of delusion.

The people are urged not to learn the "way of the nations," yet we know this is exactly what they have done. They live in delusion, expecting powerless and worthless gods to save them. In contrast to the idols, God is portrayed as the powerful sovereign of the whole creation: the king of the nations (v. 7), the "living God" whose wrath the nations cannot endure (v. 10), the God who made the earth and stretched out the heavens (v. 12).

Jeremiah repeatedly accuses Judah of turning to and trusting in idols (for instance, they "went after worthlessness," 2:5; 10:15). This poem summarizes the theological core of Judah's problem, which has been the subject of the book of Jeremiah from the beginning. The people have forsaken the Lord, who directed history's course, and have sought security in other gods, who are powerless and worthless. Because Israel has forsaken the God who gives life, God is directing the course of history toward Judah's death—the captivity of Jerusalem (1:3).

Jeremiah's denunciation of the idols raises the question of why Judah would even consider turning from the Lord to worthless idols. Obviously, if Judah has turned from the Lord to idols, these other gods must not have seemed so worthless. That is undoubtedly the case. The idols, after all, seem to provide a way for Judah to control matters, even to control the gods. It was thought that the gods worshiped at the fertility cults could be influenced and persuaded and even manipulated. That was the point of sacrifices and cult prostitution. The cult rituals were understood as an opportunity for humans to get the gods to do as they wanted. Sacrifices and cult prostitution were especially thought to influence the gods to bring rain and fertility.

The Lord God of Israel, by contrast, is beyond such manipulation. In the book of Jeremiah, God's rejection of the temple rituals as a source of security (7:4, 10), and the marginal status afforded sacrifices (7:21–22) testify to the sovereignty of the Lord beyond human control. What Jeremiah claims in this text, consistent with the Bible as a whole, is that the Lord God is ultimately sovereign, beyond human control and manipulation, concerned for the well-being of creation and humankind, and to be trusted. By contrast, Jeremiah describes the idols, who can be controlled, as sovereign over nothing, worthless, and to be rejected.

Obviously, the problem of idolatry looms large in the book of Jeremiah, and in reading this book we are pressed to ask repeatedly to which false and deceptive idols we may have turned for life and security. Idols ancient and modern lead to death. The book of Jeremiah urges that we trust and serve the God of life, the God of Jesus, whom Jesus commanded that we love with our whole being (Matt. 22:34–40; Luke 10:25–28).

Jeremiah 10:17–25

10:17 Gather up your bundle from the ground,
　　　O you who live under siege!
　　18 For thus says the LORD:
　　　I am going to sling out the inhabitants of the land
　　　at this time,
　　　and I will bring distress on them,
　　　so that they shall feel it.

　　19 Woe is me because of my hurt!
　　　My wound is severe.
　　　But I said, "Truly this is my punishment,
　　　and I must bear it."
　　20 My tent is destroyed,
　　　and all my cords are broken;
　　　my children have gone from me,
　　　and they are no more;
　　　there is no one to spread my tent again,
　　　and to set up my curtains.
　　21 For the shepherds are stupid,
　　　and do not inquire of the LORD;
　　　therefore they have not prospered,
　　　and all their flock is scattered.

　　22 Hear, a noise! Listen, it is coming—
　　　a great commotion from the land of the north
　　　to make the cities of Judah a desolation,
　　　a lair of jackals.
　　23 I know, O LORD, that the way of human beings is not in their control,

that mortals as they walk cannot direct their steps.
24 **Correct me, O LORD, but in just measure;**
    not in your anger, or you will bring me to nothing.

25 **Pour out your wrath on the nations that do not know you,**
    and on the peoples that do not call on your name;
    for they have devoured Jacob;
    they have devoured him and consumed him,
    and have laid waste his habitation.

These concluding verses of Jeremiah 10 further develop the accusation of Judah's misplaced trust. God pronounces a judgment that is expected: God will not "dwell" with this people, but they will instead "live [the same Hebrew word as for 'dwell'] under siege." Further, God will not permit Judah to dwell in the land but announces, "I am going to sling out the inhabitants of the land." The negative outcomes threatened in Jeremiah 7 are to be realized and God's people brought to lamentation (10:19–20; cf. 7:29; 9:19). Children will be mourned (10:20; also see 6:26), as well as the destruction of "my tents" and "my curtains" (10:19–20; see 4:19–22). As previously mentioned, "tents" and "curtains" likely refer to the destruction of the Temple, which occurred with the Babylonian invasion of 587 B.C. These verses, like verses 10:17–18, relate directly to Jeremiah 7 and point toward the destruction of Jerusalem.

Verses 21–22 are spoken by someone other than those who cry woe in verses 19–20, probably the prophet indicating why God's judgment will occur and how. Blame is laid on the "shepherds," Judah's kings, who are characterized as "stupid" and who "do not inquire of the Lord" (10:21; see 2:8). The agent of God's judgment is once more identified as the enemy from the north (1:15), who will destroy the land.

This prophetic speech (10:21–22) leads to another lament by the people in verses 23–25. So the pattern of the text is:

verses 17–18—Speech of God (or the prophet): an announcement of judgment

verses 19–20—Lament of the people

verses 21–22—Speech of God (or the prophet): rationale for and means of judgment

verses 23–25—Lament of the people

What is difficult is how to interpret the tone and intent of the community's lament in verses 23–25 at this point in the book. It is widely recognized that verses 23–25 draw from other scriptural texts: verse 23 from Proverbs 16:9 and 20:24; verse 24 from Psalm 6:1; verse 25 from Psalm 79:6–7. This combination of material develops three thrusts: (1) Verse 23 is a pious recognition that ultimately humans do not set the "way" of their lives, rather God does; (2) verse 24 admits the need for correction but appeals for leniency, for God to act in "justice" (the NRSV translates "in just measure") and not in anger; (3) verse 25 urges that God's wrath be poured out on the nations who "devour" (see Jer. 2:3; 5:17; 9:16) Jacob's habitation.

Verse 25 is particularly interesting in its quotation of Psalm 79, a prayer that sought God's help because the nations had "defiled your holy temple" and "laid Jerusalem in ruins" (Ps. 79:1). The use of this particular psalm, which appeals to God as the guarantor of Jerusalem's security, seems to hark back to Jeremiah 7 (but also see Jer. 8:19–20). The Temple liturgy quoted in Jeremiah 7, "the temple of the Lord," was an expression of confidence that God would guarantee the security of Jerusalem. However, Jeremiah called this liturgy "deceptive" apart from obedience of God. There is nothing in Jeremiah 7–10 to suggest that the people heeded the call to amend their ways. Thus, it seems likely that Judah's prayer in verses 23–25, using Psalm 79, illustrates the kind of "deceptive words" they were trusting "to no avail" (Jer. 7:8). They imagined that God would protect them but failed to amend their ways and doings. They said, "I know . . . " (10:23), but we who have followed the text from Jeremiah 7 know they "do not know [either] the ordinance of the Lord" (8:7) or God ("me," 9:3, 6). They appeal to God's justice for leniency (10:24, "in just measure"), but God charges that they deal falsely and do not know God's ordinance (8:7–10). They urge that God's wrath be poured out on the nations who devoured Jacob but do not realize that God will devour them because they have not obeyed God's voice (9:13–16) and have become like the nations in God's eyes (9:25–26).

Jeremiah 7 presents two options to God's people: Amend your ways and your doings, or trust deceptive words. Judah's words at the end of Jeremiah 10 indicate that they continue to trust in deceptive words. There is no indication that they repent. We are taken another step in understanding why God directed history toward the captivity of Jerusalem.

"Hear the Words of This Covenant"
(Jeremiah 11–12)

Jeremiah 11 begins with the announcement by God "Cursed be anyone who does not heed the words of this covenant" (v. 3). In ancient Israel, covenant was a primary way in which God's relationship with Israel was understood. *Covenant* has different meanings in the Old Testament. For example, God's covenants with Noah (Genesis 9) and Abram (Genesis 15) stress the Lord's promises to Israel. In these instances, covenant is an obligation that God assumes. The covenant with Israel at Sinai (Exodus 20–24), rooted in God's exodus deliverance of Israel (Exod. 20:2), stresses much more the obligation of Israel to God (Exod. 20:3–20). God saved Israel from Egypt, and Israel is to respond by obeying God. The book of Deuteronomy is also concerned with a covenant that stresses obligation and obedience. Jeremiah 11 has in mind a covenant that stresses the obligation of Judah to respond to God in obedience, a covenant like those of Sinai and the book of Deuteronomy.

Exodus 20–24 remembers when Israel entered into a covenant with God. This covenant is finally ratified in Exodus 24. In Exodus 20 is a brief summary of what God had done for Israel: "I am the Lord your God, who brought you out of the land of Egypt, out of the house of slavery" (v. 2). The Ten Commandments, which follow (vv. 3–17), summarize the primary obligations of Israel in response to God's deliverance. The First Commandment is that Israel is to worship no other gods. The obligations outlined in the Ten Commandments are elaborated in Exodus 21–23 before the covenant is finally ratified (Exodus 24).

The consequences of keeping and breaking covenant are called blessings and curses. Blessings are ways in which God will continue to do good for Israel if they respond to God in obedience. One expression of covenant blessings is found in Deuteronomy 28:1–14. Covenant curses are the consequences should God's people fail to keep covenant.

Deuteronomy 28:15–68 expresses one way in which Israel understood covenant curses. (For another example of covenant blessings and curses, see Leviticus 26.)

Joshua 24:1–28 is a good example of Israel affirming their Sinai covenant relationship with God. This is the story of a gathering of Israel at Shechem after entering the promised land. The purpose of the gathering is to reaffirm the covenant between God and Israel (24:25) originally established at Sinai. The basis for the covenant is the memory of what God did for Israel, so a long recital of God's deeds is found in verses 1–13. However, because the Lord delivered Israel from slavery, God has expectations of Israel; likewise, Israel's memory of God's deeds creates a sense of obligation. So, when the recital of God's deeds concludes, the next verse commands that Israel "revere" and "serve" God (v. 14). The primary covenant obligation is to serve God only and to have nothing to do with other gods (vv. 14–18). There is a warning that if the covenant is violated, especially by worshiping other gods, then God will "turn and do you harm, and consume you, after having done you good" (v. 20); that is, God threatens covenant curse. As the conclusion of this account in Joshua 24 suggests, covenants were understood as legal documents, to which there were witnesses and of which there was a written record (vv. 22–28).

Jeremiah 11:1–8 introduces covenant curse, a theme that is prominent not only in Jeremiah 11–12 but through chapter 20, in which the prophet speaks of his own life as cursed. Frequent references to Deuteronomy 28 sustain the theme of covenant curse through Jeremiah 11–20. This theme is developed in Jeremiah 11–12 by bringing the charge that the people have failed to listen to or obey (in Hebrew, "listen" and "obey" are expressed by the same word) the words of God's covenant.

Jeremiah 11–12 also includes two prophetic laments (11:18–20; 12:1–4), and several more appear before the conclusion of Jeremiah 20. In these laments, Jeremiah cries out in complaint to God about what has befallen him as a result of his service to God. The laments of Jeremiah closely resemble the lament psalms (for instance, Psalms 10, 31, 43) in their language and tone. Lament psalms express to God the petitioner's physical, emotional, or social distress. Those who prayed these psalms pleaded that God act to set their situation right. Typically, the lament psalms end with an expression of confidence that God will hear the prayer and act to deliver the one who prays. In the book of Jeremiah, the laments of the prophet are frequently followed by God's response, sometimes offering assurance, sometimes rebuking Jeremiah.

Jeremiah 11:1–8

11:1 **The word that came to Jeremiah from the LORD:** 2 **Hear the words of this covenant, and speak to the people of Judah and the inhabitants of Jerusalem.** 3 **You shall say to them, Thus says the LORD, the God of Israel: Cursed be anyone who does not heed the words of this covenant,** 4 **which I commanded your ancestors when I brought them out of the land of Egypt, from the iron-smelter, saying, Listen to my voice, and do all that I command you. So shall you be my people, and I will be your God,** 5 **that I may perform the oath that I swore to your ancestors, to give them a land flowing with milk and honey, as at this day. Then I answered, "So be it, LORD."**

6 **And the LORD said to me: Proclaim all these words in the cities of Judah, and in the streets of Jerusalem: Hear the words of this covenant and do them.** 7 **For I solemnly warned your ancestors when I brought them up out of the land of Egypt, warning them persistently, even to this day, saying, Obey my voice.** 8 **Yet they did not obey or incline their ear, but everyone walked in the stubbornness of an evil will. So I brought upon them all the words of this covenant, which I commanded them to do, but they did not.**

Verses 1–5 are closely related to Deuteronomy 27:14–26. Jeremiah 11:3, along with the end of 11:5, is a paraphrase of Deuteronomy 27:26:

"Cursed be anyone who does not uphold the words of this law by observing them."

All the people shall say, "Amen!"

Deuteronomy 27:14–26 reflects a worship ritual of ancient Israel. The presiding priest would indicate that should one violate some stipulation of God's covenant, then one would be cursed—be punished by God in some way. In response to the warning about incurring covenant curse, the people were to respond "Amen," that is, they affirmed, "So be it." This worship ritual or litany was a way to express commitment to God's covenant by public recognition that one deserved "curse," God's punishment, should one violate the covenant.

While Jeremiah 11:1–5 is based on Deuteronomy 27:26, it is not identical to it. Deuteronomy 27 speaks of God's *law*, and Jeremiah 11 speaks of *covenant*, a broader term. Jeremiah 11:4–5 expands on the Deuteronomy 27 by directly relating the Sinai covenant to (1) God's deliverance of Israel from Egypt (Jer. 11:4): and (2) the promise of land to the ancestors (11:5). This is an important point in the book of Jeremiah, which understands that the exodus and God's gift of land are the basis for God's relationship with Israel and Judah (for instance, Jer. 2:6–7). Because the Lord had delivered Israel from Egypt, God's people are obligated to "listen to my voice, and do all that I command you" (11:4). The book is clear that possession of the land of milk and honey and Israel's continued relationship with God are conditional on listening to and obeying God.

Unlike Deuteronomy 27, it is not the people who respond to God's warning of curse in Jeremiah 11 but the prophet who says, "Amen." That is, the prophet is presented as standing in the role of the people, responding as they should have. Jeremiah understands that continued relationship with God and life in the land depends on covenant obedience, on listening and obeying. Given what we know of Judah from the first ten chapters of the book, it is not surprising that the people do not respond.

Verses 6–8 build on God's call for covenantal listening and obedience. The verses reaffirm Jeremiah's call to be a prophet (cf. Jer. 1:4–10; 6:27). The prophetic role is understood in relationship to God's Sinai covenant. Jeremiah is to announce the central covenantal requirement, that Judah "hear the words of this covenant and do them" (11:6). The reason the Lord gives this charge to Jeremiah is God's memory of Israel's "ancestors," whom God warned "persistently" to "obey my voice" (v. 7). Yet, this older generation followed their "evil will" and did not listen or obey. Thus, God brought about "all the words of the covenant" (v. 8; see v. 3)—a way of saying curse or judgment. While it is not clear which occasion of God's judgment on the ancestral generation this text has in mind (cf. Exodus 32; Numbers 14; Joshua 7; Judges 6), this text stresses that covenant disobedience was a long-standing problem with God's people.

Jeremiah 11:9–13

These verses move from the generation of the ancestors to the time of Jeremiah. God makes the accusation that, like their ancestors, the present generation has also "refused to heed my words" (9:10). This refusal to listen is made more specific by the charge "they have gone after other gods to serve them" (v. 10). The first and most important covenant stipulation demanded that God alone be worshiped: "You shall have no other gods before me" (Exod. 20:3). Exclusive devotion to God, who had brought Israel out of Egypt, was fundamental to listening to and obeying God, to covenant with God. Rather than the people exclusively devoting themselves to God, Judah's gods are legion, as many as their towns or the streets of Jerusalem (Jer. 11:13). Judah's violation of covenant is massive, and God reaches the obvious conclusion that "the house of Israel and the house of Judah have broken the covenant that I made with their ancestors" (v. 10).

With this announcement that the covenant is broken, we are prepared to hear that there will be covenant curse, the consequence for anyone "who does not heed the words of this covenant" (11:3). For the moment, however, the consequence of having broken covenant is described only generally as "disaster" (v. 11; cf. 1:14). Further, because Judah has refused to listen to the Lord, God will not listen to them (11:11; cf. 7:16–20, where Jeremiah is forbidden to pray for Judah). Having broken covenant, the Lord in effect abandons Judah to the gods to whom they have turned but who cannot save them (11:12).

This text identifies a primary peril of idolatry. If we turn from God to idols, then we are dependent on our new gods to save us. Martin Luther, the great Reformer, said this of God and idols:

> What is it to have a god, or what is God? Answer: A god is that to which we look for all good and where we resort for help in every time of need; to have a god is simply to trust and believe in one with our whole heart. . . . The confidence and faith of the heart alone make both God and an idol. (Luther, *Large Catechism*, p. 44)

To have a god is to entrust ourselves to that god completely for our well-being and security. So, if money has become our god, then we assume that the more money we have, the more secure we will be, and in difficult times we believe money will save us. If our employment has become our god, then we imagine that our job will keep us secure and provide for our well-being, and in difficult times we will count on our employment to pull us through. If technology is our god, then we imagine we are secure because there is technical know-how to keep us well, and in difficult times we are confident that some technological advance will save us.

Jesus told a parable that exposes the peril of idolatry in a powerful manner:

> Someone in the crowd said to him, "Teacher, tell my brother to divide the family inheritance with me." But he said to him, "Friend, who set me to be a judge or arbitrator over you?" And he said to them, "Take care! Be on your guard against all kinds of greed; for one's life does not consist in the abundance of possessions." Then he told them a parable: "The land of a rich man produced abundantly. And he thought to himself, 'What should I do, for I have no place to store my crops?' Then he said, 'I will do this: I will pull down my barns and build larger ones, and there I will store all my grain and my goods. And I will say to my soul, Soul, you have ample goods laid up for many years; relax, eat, drink, be merry.' But God said to him, 'You fool! This very night your life is being demanded of you. And the things you have prepared, whose will they be?' So it is with those who store up treasures for themselves but are not rich toward God." (Luke 12:13–21)

Idols, ancient or modern, cannot keep us secure or save us.

Jeremiah 11:14–17

11:14 **As for you, do not pray for this people, or lift up a cry or prayer on their behalf, for I will not listen when they call to me in the time of their trouble.** [15] **What right has my beloved in my house, when she has done vile deeds? Can vows and sacrificial flesh avert your doom? Can you then exult?** [16] **The LORD once called you, "A green olive tree, fair with goodly fruit"; but with the roar of a great tempest he will set fire to it, and its branches will be consumed.** [17] **The LORD of hosts, who planted you, has pronounced evil against you, because of the evil that the house of Israel and the house of Judah have done, provoking me to anger by making offerings to Baal.**

God's command that Jeremiah not "lift up a cry or prayer" (v. 14) reinforces God's resolve not to listen to the people, because they have refused to listen to God (v. 11). The Lord's edict that Jeremiah no longer pray on Judah's behalf (v. 14) is identical to Jeremiah 7:16 (see comments, pp. 79–81). The relationship between God and Judah depended on listening, on mutual attention of one to the other. The exodus from Egypt began when God "heard their groaning" as the Israelites suffered under Pharaoh's oppression (Exod. 2:24). The Lord's relationship with Israel and Judah was to be sustained as the prophets continued to intercede on their behalf (see the discussion of Jer. 7:16–20, 79–81). However, the relationship between God and Judah portrayed in these verses is in collapse. Judah has not listened to the words of the covenant, and God is determined not to listen to the prophet when he raises before God the cry of the people.

Two images are used in Jeremiah 11:15–17 to underscore the brokenness of the relationship. First, Israel is compared to a bride ("my beloved") who lost the right to her husband's home because of vile deeds (cf. 2:1–3; 3). The reference to "sacrificial flesh" (11:15) suggests these vile deeds involved some kind of fertility worship; the "house" may be the Jerusalem Temple. In the second image, Israel is compared to "a green olive tree" planted by God but about to be consumed in a great tempest (cf. the image of the degenerate vine in 2:21). Listening has ceased, the covenant is broken, the relationship between God and the people is in collapse.

In contemporary church life, the word *covenant* has become very popular. It is used to describe many kinds of relationships: Youth fellowships and confirmation classes develop covenants to express commitments and expectations among those in the group; marriages are described as covenants; in some denominations, the relationships between church agencies and local churches are described as covenantal; churches sometimes describe ecumenical partnerships as covenants; the communion cup is the "cup of the new covenant." This series of texts in Jeremiah 11 reminds the church of the seriousness of covenant with God. Covenant is rooted in God's listening and response to our human groaning (Exod. 2:24). In turn, covenant requires that we heed God's word: "Hear . . . the Lord is our God, the Lord alone" (Deut. 6:4). To be in covenant is to know that God has heard us, saved us, and claimed us for obedient listening. The church can be understood as the covenant people of God only because of God's initiative toward us in Jesus Christ. The communion cup is the "cup of the new covenant" by which we remember how God has reached out for relationship with us, bound us in the church in relationship to God and one another, and called us to be faithful disciples in the world.

Jeremiah 11:18–23

> 11:18 It was the LORD who made it known to me, and I knew;
>   then you showed me their evil deeds.
> 19 But I was like a gentle lamb
>   led to the slaughter.
>   And I did not know it was against me
>   that they devised schemes, saying,
>   "Let us destroy the tree with its fruit,
>   let us cut him off from the land of the living,
>   so that his name will no longer be remembered!"
> 20 But you, O LORD of hosts, who judge righteously,
>   who try the heart and the mind,
>   let me see your retribution upon them,
>   for to you I have committed my cause.
> 21 Therefore thus says the LORD concerning the people of Anathoth, who seek your life, and say, "You shall not prophesy in the name of the LORD, or you will die by our hand"— 22 therefore thus says the LORD of hosts: I am going to punish them; the young men shall die by the sword; their sons and their daughters shall die by famine; 23 and not even a remnant shall be left of them. For I will bring disaster upon the people of Anathoth, the year of their punishment.

This is the first lament or complaint of the prophet in the book of Jeremiah. The most obvious reading of these verses is to hear them as the prayer of the prophet when he discovered that persons were plotting against him because he had spoken God's word of judgment and announced covenant curse. We proceed on this basis for now, though later we need to see other ways in which this prayer might be heard.

Much of the language of this prayer is similar to prayers found in the Psalms. The prayer probably does not tell us as much about the prophet's inner feelings as about how people in this ancient time expressed their concern to God. God showed Jeremiah the evil of the house of Judah and Israel (11:17; cf. 2:13). What Jeremiah did not realize was that he was the object of the "schemes" of persons identified in 11:21 as "people of Anathoth," persons from Jeremiah's hometown. Jeremiah "was like a gentle lamb led to the slaughter" (v. 19; cf. Ps. 44:11, 22), surprised that he himself was a target of plotters. Among the judgments announced by Jeremiah is that Judah will be like a green olive tree destroyed in a tempest (11:16). Similar language is used by those who plot against Jeremiah, who are quoted in verse 19 saying, "Destroy the tree with its fruit." Jeremiah has announced a harsh judgment, covenant curse. Those who plot against Jeremiah intend that he will receive the judgment he announced. His enemies intend not just to end Jeremiah's life ("let us cut him off from the land of the living") but to blot out all memory of him. This plot against Jeremiah, God's spokesperson, illustrates and confirms the central claim of earlier sections of Jeremiah 11 that Judah will not listen to or obey God (vv. 3, 8, 10, 11) and has broken covenant.

Verse 20 expresses Jeremiah's complaint in legal categories. The prophet appeals to God as a judge before whom he argues his "cause," a word that means "case" in a legal sense. Of course, Jeremiah appeals to God because it is Jeremiah's service as God's spokesperson that has led him into difficulty. The prophet prays that God "judge righteously," that is, set his situation right. Jeremiah requests of the divine judge "retribution," judgment on those who plotted evil against him. Such a request is often found in lament psalms (see Pss. 35:1–8; 54:3–5).

The charges against those who plot against Jeremiah are detailed in 11:21–23. God is the speaker. The plotters seek Jeremiah's life because he prophesies judgment (v. 21). Remember that the religious and political establishment in Jerusalem assumed God would guarantee the well-being and security of Judah and Jerusalem (see, for instance, Jeremiah 7), so most in Judah would have heard Jeremiah's announcements of judgment as treasonous and blasphemous. God announces judgment on those who plot against God's prophet: death for those who sought Jeremiah's death, "not even a remnant . . . left" of those who intended that Jeremiah would "no longer be remembered," "disaster" on those who committed "evil deeds" ("disaster" and "evil" are the same Hebrew word). God promises to defend Jeremiah against those who would silence him (f 1:17–19).

Verses 18–23 can be read as part of the drama that involves God, Jeremiah, and Judah. The word of the Lord is spoken through God's prophet, but God's people will not listen or obey. Judah's failure to heed the word of the Lord is quite evident in the plot against Jeremiah. God comes to Jeremiah's defense and threatens covenant curses on those who plot against the prophet. The righteous Judge is directing history toward "the captivity of Jerusalem" (1:3) because Judah has failed to heed the words of God's covenant spoken by Jeremiah.

However, in the book of Jeremiah, which was written and shaped as a reflection on the Babylonian exile for a later generation, these verses have implications beyond the particular circumstances of Jeremiah's life and the Babylonian exile. These verses claim that God is the righteous Judge of history who upholds order in creation. Those who resist God's sovereignty, who are represented in the particular circumstances that shaped the book of Jeremiah by the political and religious establishment in Jerusalem and their supporters who plotted against Jeremiah, will be judged by God. The book claims that God is the righteous Judge, before whom stand persons, nations, and kingdoms. God is sovereign and directs history as God intends: to pluck up and to tear down (1:10) and toward "the captivity of Jerusalem" (1:3); to build and to plant (1:10) and to "restore the fortunes of . . . Israel and Judah" and Jerusalem (30:3). God, the righteous Judge, directs history and upholds the order of creation.

Jeremiah 12:1–6

12:1 **You will be in the right, O LORD,**
        when I lay charges against you;
        but let me put my case to you.
        Why does the way of the guilty prosper?
        Why do all who are treacherous thrive?
   2   **You plant them, and they take root;**
        they grow and bring forth fruit;
        you are near in their mouths
        yet far from their hearts.
   3   **But you, O LORD, know me;**
        You see me and test me—my heart is with you.
        Pull them out like sheep for the slaughter,
        and set them apart for the day of slaughter.
   4   **How long will the land mourn,**
        and the grass of every field wither?
        For the wickedness of those who live in it
        the animals and the birds are swept away,
        and because people said, "He is blind to our ways."

⁵ **If you have raced with foot-runners and they have wearied you,**
how will you compete with horses?
And if in a safe land you fall down,
how will you fare in the thickets of the Jordan?
⁶ **For even your kinsfolk and your own family,**
even they have dealt treacherously with you;
they are in full cry after you;
do not believe them,
though they speak friendly words to you.

Here is the second lament of Jeremiah (12:1–4) and God's response (vv. 5–6). This lament uses some of the same words and ideas as the first, but in different ways. For example, in both laments Jeremiah expresses his concerns as a legal matter, but in the second lament the prophet brings "charges" against God, whereas in the first he commits his "cause" to God (12:1; the Hebrew word for "charges" is the same word translated "cause" in 11:20). In the first lament, Jeremiah appeals to God to "judge righteously"; in this second lament, the prophet acknowledges God will be "right" (the same Hebrew word that is translated "righteously" in 11:20) even though he has brought charges against God. In the first lament, the prophet is positioned with God against those who have plotted against him. In the second lament, the prophet's complaint is that the "treacherous thrive" and God seems to support them (12:1–2). The first lament and God's response confirm a well-ordered moral world in which those who commit evil receive evil (disaster) from God (11:18, 23). In this second lament, the prophet complains because God's well-ordered moral world seems to be in collapse. In the first lament, the prophet is "like a gentle lamb led to the slaughter" (11:19) who has committed his cause to God (11:20), who promises to set things right with the men from Anathoth (11:21–23). In the second lament, Jeremiah appeals to God to set things right with the guilty who prosper (12:1): "Pull them out like sheep for the slaughter" (12:3).

At the conclusion of the second lament or complaint (v. 4), Jeremiah wonders about God's intentions. The prophet, as God's spokesperson, has announced the destruction of the land because of the wickedness of Judah. However, in this lament, the prophet demands to know "how long"—how long God will allow Judah to assume God "is blind to our ways." Jeremiah wants to know if and when God intends to be the righteous Judge and Sovereign of the world.

God's response to the prophet's first lament was supportive and promised to set things right with the Anathoth plotters. God's response to Jeremiah's second lament is different and a surprise. God at once warns and chides the prophet that the worst is yet to come for him. Verse 5 employs two images. First, God uses a racing image to ask how Jeremiah will be able to compete with horses when human opponents have wearied him. Second, God uses a journey image to ask how Jeremiah will fare in the thickets of the Jordan (in ancient times, a near-jungle region inhabited by wild beasts) when he has fallen on much easier terrain. Both images warn and chide the prophet that whatever he has endured in God's service will become much more demanding in the future. The tone of God's response (v. 5) suggests that Jeremiah's complaint is trivial and unjustified, and God and Jeremiah are presented in conflict. The prophet's charge against God (v. 1) and God's rebuke (v. 5) stand in an unresolved tension.

At verse 6, God's rebuke takes the form of a warning to Jeremiah about his own family and kinfolk, who have "dealt treacherously" with the prophet. Remember that Jeremiah was from Anathoth. The treacherous persons who thrive, in this second complaint (v. 1), and the plotters in the first complaint are presented as persons from Anathoth with a relationship to the prophet. Jeremiah's service for God has created conflict on all sides—with God, whom he serves as prophet (12:5); with his own kinfolk (v. 6); and with the populace and their leaders, so harshly condemned by Jeremiah. Nothing in God's response to Jeremiah indicates that his conflicts will ease. Instead, God warns Jeremiah that his prophetic call will require still more of him.

The difficulty of Jeremiah's task is reinforced by a subtle feature of verse 6. The prophet is warned not to "believe" (the Hebrew word used is the basis for the English word *amen*) the "friendly" (the Hebrew word literally means "good") words of his family and kinfolk. That is, Jeremiah is not to believe or say "Amen" to the good words of those closest to him. At the beginning of Jeremiah 11, God announced, "Cursed be anyone who does not heed the words of this covenant" (v. 3), to which the prophet answered, "So be it" (that is, "amen"; v. 5). This phrase uses the same Hebrew word translated in Jeremiah 12:6 as "believe." Thus, while Jeremiah is not to say "amen" to the good words of his relatives and friends, he is to say "amen" to God's announcement of covenant curse. God has called Jeremiah to a ministry that demands single-minded devotion and threatens his relationship with those persons closest to him.

At the seminary where I teach, each school year begins with a service of commitment that invites reflection about service to God. The liturgy includes these words, which say for us in the church what Jeremiah came to know so well:

I am no longer my own, but yours. Put me to what you will, rank me with whom you will; put me to doing, put me to suffering; let me be employed for you or laid aside for you, exalted for you or brought low for you; let me be full, let me be empty; let me have all things, let me have nothing; I freely and heartily yield all things to your pleasure and disposal. (Adapted from *The Book of Common Worship*, The Church of South India, p. 137)

God calls us to serve, but the ministries to which we are called are sometimes difficult and demanding. It could be that such service will cost us much and offer little reward apart from the intrinsic worth of serving God.

Jeremiah 12:7–13

12:7   I have forsaken my house,
      I have abandoned my heritage;
      I have given the beloved of my heart
      into the hands of her enemies.
  8   My heritage has become to me
      like a lion in the forest;
      she has lifted up her voice against me—
      therefore I hate her.
  9   Is the hyena greedy for my heritage at my command?
      Are the birds of prey all around her?
      Go, assemble all the wild animals;
      bring them to devour her.
 10   Many shepherds have destroyed my vineyard,
      they have trampled down my portion,
      they have made my pleasant portion
      a desolate wilderness.
 11   They have made it a desolation;
      desolate, it mourns to me.
      The whole land is made desolate,
      but no one lays it to heart.
 12   Upon all the bare heights in the desert
      spoilers have come;
      for the sword of the LORD devours
      from one end of the land to the other;
      no one shall be safe.
 13   They have sown wheat and have reaped thorns,
      they have tired themselves out but profit nothing.
      They shall be ashamed of their harvests
      because of the fierce anger of the LORD.

The preceding texts in chapters 11 and 12 have presented Jeremiah's difficult position. He is caught between God's charge to speak covenant curse and those who plot against him as a result; between serving God faithfully and seeing the treacherous thrive. In 12:7–13 we hear the Lord's anguished voice. God, the righteous Judge, has pledged to uphold the order of creation against those who plotted against Jeremiah (11:22–23). Further, God has rebuked Jeremiah for not being tough and persistent enough (12:5–6). God seems steeled and in control; so to hear the Lord's anguish is unexpected at this point in the text.

Jeremiah, in complaint, has asked God, "How long will the land mourn . . . because people said, 'He is blind to our ways' " (12:4). Although God's initial response to Jeremiah's complaint (vv. 5–6) was to rebuke the prophet, verses 7–13 suggest that Jeremiah's complaint has more impact on God than is immediately evident. Throughout verses 7–13, God is presented as anguished over the invasion of Judah and concerned about "my heritage" (vv. 7, 8, 9). Heritage has two meanings in the Old Testament. First, heritage refers to God's land. The Lord has given the land to Israel, but not as a possession. The land is God's "heritage," God's precious and valued possession on loan to Israel. Second, Israel is referred to in the Old Testament as God's "heritage" (for instance, Deut. 32:9), precious and valued by God. In Jeremiah 12:7–13, both senses of *heritage* are evident: as God's people and as God's land.

One accusation is that "my heritage"—meaning the people of Judah—has turned against God (v. 8). The righteous Judge cannot ignore Judah's hostility and has to make the difficult decision to abandon "my heritage" (v. 7). Invaders are summoned (v. 9) to trample down and destroy God's "vineyard" and "portion" and to make the "pleasant portion a desolate wilderness (v. 10; cf. 2:7). Here, the references seem to be to the land. What the invaders will do to God's precious heritage—the people of Judah and the land—they will do at God's behest, and ultimately Judah will be devoured by "the sword of the Lord" (v. 12).

As mentioned earlier, there is a connection between verses 7–11 and Jeremiah's complaint in 12:4:

> How long will the land mourn,
>   and the grass of every field wither?
> For the wickedness of those who live in it
>   the animals and birds are swept away,
>   and because people said, "He is blind to our ways."

We now know why the land mourns, and it is not because God is blind to what is occurring in Judah. Quite the contrary: the land mourns (see 12:11) because God's heritage "has become to me like a lion in the forest; she has lifted up her voice against me" (v. 8). The land mourns because God, the righteous Judge, has to render a verdict and make the decision to abandon and forsake God's heritage.

Yet, the righteous Judge is not some unmoved mover. We glimpse in these verses God's anguish at the decision righteousness demands. There is considerable pathos because God must abandon that which is precious. We perhaps have glimpsed the anguish these verses convey if we recall the farm crisis of the 1980s. In those years, on the evening news, we saw the pain of Midwest farm families. They had lived and worked on the same family farm for generations when they had to forsake and abandon those precious and valued farms due to bankruptcy. The anguish of those families was poignant. These verses in Jeremiah 12 present an anguished God who is forced to abandon a precious heritage because Judah has turned against the Lord.

Jeremiah 12:14–17

These verses are connected to the prior material in Jeremiah 12 by the word *heritage* and by reference to the nations that are to invade Judah (v. 14). God, the righteous Judge, is again presented as acting to set the world right. The affirmation of these verses is that beyond judgment, God intends restoration.

These verses use the thematic statement for the book of Jeremiah from 1:10, God's charge to the prophet Jeremiah:

> See, today I appoint you over nations and over kingdoms,
>   to pluck up and to pull down,
>   to destroy and to overthrow,
>   to build and to plant.

God announces what is intended for those nations who would touch the precious "heritage" given Judah and Israel (12:14). God's intentions are announced through a threefold repetition of "pluck up":

1. The Lord announces that those nations—"my evil neighbors"—who harm God's heritage will be plucked up (v. 14a). We have seen repeatedly why and how God intended to pluck up Judah from the land God had given them. Now the Lord announces that the nations who do harm to God's heritage, land and people, will be plucked up.
2. God promises to "pluck up the house of Judah from among them" (v. 14b). This is a different sense of "pluck up," indicating God's deliv-

erance of Judah from the nations. Judah's "evil neighbors" will be plucked up in judgment, but God's judgment of the nations means that Judah will be "plucked up" in deliverance, rescued from the nations. The use of "pluck up" to speak of Judah's deliverance reverses the sense of this word in Jeremiah 1:10.

3. Finally, "pluck up" is used to indicate God's deliverance of the nations, "every one of them" (v. 15). In compassion, God will "pluck up" all the nations and return them to their heritage and land, even as God intends such restoration for Judah.

God, the righteous Judge, will "pluck up" both Judah and Judah's neighbors in judgment. Yet what God ultimately intends is the restoration of Judah and the nations, to pluck them up to restore them to the heritage and land God intends for each. These verses affirm a bold vision of the world rightly ordered under God's sovereign rule.

Verses 16–17 present the conditions under which the nations might experience well-being or woe. The nations who have taught Judah the ways of Baal must submit to God if they are to be "built up" (v. 16). By contrast, "if any nation will not listen," God will "uproot it and destroy it." Jeremiah 11:1–8 announces that Judah is under covenant curse because they have failed to listen and obey God. Central to covenantal obedience is devotion to God (Exod. 20:3; cf. Jer. 11:9–13). What has been demanded of God's people will also be the norm for the nations. In submission to God there is well-being; failure to listen and obey God brings covenant curse. God, the righteous Judge, finally intends to set right the world.

The New Testament, too, envisions the righteous Judge calling the nations to account and establishing God's sovereign reign over them:

> When the Son of Man comes in his glory, and all the angels with him, then he will sit on the throne of his glory. All the nations will be gathered before him, and he will separate people one from another as a shepherd separates the sheep from the goats, and he will put the sheep at his right hand and the goats at the left. Then the king will say to those at his right hand, "Come, you that are blessed by my Father, inherit the kingdom prepared for you from the foundation of the world; for I was hungry and you gave me food, I was thirsty and you gave me something to drink, I was a stranger and you welcomed me, I was naked and you gave me clothing, I was sick and you took care of me, I was in prison and you visited me." (Matt. 25:31–36)

The nations and kingdoms are accountable. Matthew, like the book of Jeremiah, understands that care for society's poorest and weakest is essential to obedience (cf. Jer. 7:5–7) to the God of the exodus. It is the standard to which the righteous Judge of the world holds all peoples and nations.

"I Will Ruin the Pride of Judah"
(Jeremiah 13–16)

Jeremiah 13 begins with the announcement of God's intention to "ruin the pride" of Judah and Jerusalem because they have refused "to hear my words" (13:9–10; cf. 12:17). Jeremiah 13–16 develops through an overlapping of themes. In Jeremiah 13, the theme of Judah's pride and God's intention to bring shame to Judah is introduced. Toward the end of Jeremiah 13, the "iniquity" of the people becomes a theme that overlaps with concern for Judah's pride. God threatens judgment by sword, famine, and pestilence in Jeremiah 14, and this theme continues through Jeremiah 16. Like Jeremiah 11–12, Jeremiah 13–16 stresses God's judgment and covenant curse, the result of Judah's iniquity; but also, beyond judgment, this section of the book affirms God's intention to restore Judah and the nations.

Jeremiah 13:1–11

13:1 Thus said the LORD to me, "Go and buy yourself a linen loincloth, and put it on your loins, but do not dip it in water." ² So I bought a loincloth according to the word of the LORD, and put it on my loins. ³ And the word of the LORD came to me a second time, saying, ⁴ "Take the loincloth that you bought and are wearing, and go now to the Euphrates, and hide it there in a cleft of the rock." ⁵ So I went, and hid it by the Euphrates, as the LORD commanded me. ⁶ And after many days the LORD said to me, "Go now to the Euphrates, and take from there the loincloth that I commanded you to hide there." ⁷ Then I went to the Euphrates, and dug, and I took the loincloth from the place where I had hidden it. But now the loincloth was ruined; it was good for nothing.

⁸ Then the word of the LORD came to me: ⁹ Thus says the LORD: Just so I will ruin the pride of Judah and the great pride of Jerusalem. ¹⁰ This evil people, who refuse to hear my words, who stubbornly follow their own will and have gone after other gods to serve them and worship them, shall be like this loincloth, which is good for nothing. ¹¹ For as the loincloth clings to one's

loins, so I made the whole house of Israel and the whole house of Judah cling to me, says the LORD, in order that they might be for me a people, a name, a praise, and a glory. But they would not listen.

These verses report a prophetic sign-act. Prophets were at times commanded by God to undertake some action that was then interpreted as part of the prophet's message to Israel or Judah. The prophet Ezekiel, for instance, was commanded by God to pack his baggage as if being forced to go into exile to a foreign land; then he was to dig through the Jerusalem city wall (that is, create a breach in the wall, as an invading army might do) and carry his baggage through the breached wall (Ezekiel 12; cf. Ezekiel 4–5; Hosea 1). This sign-act was to dramatize Ezekiel's message that God intended to send Judah into exile.

In Jeremiah 13, God commands the prophet to purchase and wear a new linen loincloth, a widely used undergarment (vv. 1–2). Then God commands the prophet ("the word of the Lord came to me a second time") to bury the loincloth in a rock cleft in the river Euphrates (vv. 4–5). There has been much debate about the location where this event occurred, since Jeremiah lived in Jerusalem, some four hundred miles from Babylon and the Euphrates River. It seems likely that the reference to the Euphrates River should be understood symbolically, as a way to indicate the role of Babylon in God's judgment of Judah. Finally, "after many days" (the sense is of a long time; v. 6), the Lord commands Jeremiah to retrieve the loincloth from the river where he buried it. Of course, the loincloth is "ruined . . . good for nothing" (v. 7).

Verses 8–11 interpret this sign-act, though in two different ways. The first interpretation, the most obvious, builds on the fact that the loincloth is ruined and good for nothing. God announces, "I will ruin the pride of Judah and . . . Jerusalem" (vv. 8–10). Judah's pride, the cause of God's judgment, is identified with two primary ways in which the people have disobeyed God and echo often-repeated charges against Judah in the book of Jeremiah. Judah's pride is evident in that they (1) refuse to hear God's words and instead have followed their own will; and they (2) worshiped other gods. Concern with Judah's failure to listen to God and their worship of other gods is prominent at the end of Jeremiah 12 and functions as a link between the chapters. God promised that the nations will be restored if they turn from the Baals, but they will be destroyed if they do not listen to God (12:16–17). The sign-act of these verses announces that Judah, too, will be ruined if in their pride they refuse to listen to God and worship other gods.

The sign-act of the prophet is interpreted a second way in verse 11. This interpretation builds on the way in which a loincloth "clings to one's loins." God intends that "the whole house of Israel and the whole house of Judah cling to me." The word *cling* is used in the Old Testament to suggest loyalty and obedience to God. Second Kings 18:5ff. describes King Hezekiah of Judah:

> He trusted in the LORD the God of Israel. . . . For he held fast [the same word as "cling" in Jer. 13:11] to the LORD; he did not depart from following him but kept the commandments that the LORD commanded Moses. The LORD was with him; wherever he went, he prospered.

God seeks covenant loyalty and obedience. As a result God hopes that Judah and Israel will be "a people, a name, a praise, and a glory" (Jer. 13:11). This phrase indicates covenant blessings as in Deuteronomy 28:10: "All the peoples of the earth shall see that you are called by the name of the Lord." Covenant obedience, clinging to God, means covenant blessing. Yet God's conclusion is "they would not listen." The sign-act points to covenant disobedience and builds the case for the ruin of God's people, for covenant curse.

One final dimension of this text needs to be noted. The central indictment of Judah and Jerusalem through this sign-act is that they did not listen, that is, they did not obey God. In contrast to Judah, the prophet Jeremiah is commanded three times to do something as this sign-act unfolds, and each time he obeys: "Buy yourself a loincloth. . . . So I bought a loincloth" (vv. 1–2); "Take the loincloth . . . and hide it. . . . So I went, and hid it" (vv. 3–4); "Go now to the Euphrates, and take from there the loincloth. . . . Then I went to the Euphrates" (vv. 6–7). The prophet hears God's word and obeys it as Judah should have but did not. Jeremiah embodies the obedience God seeks from Judah.

Jeremiah 13:12–14

13:12 **You shall speak to them this word: Thus says the LORD, the God of Israel: Every wine-jar should be filled with wine. And they will say to you, "Do you think we do not know that every wine-jar should be filled with wine?"** 13 **Then you shall say to them: Thus says the LORD: I am about to fill all the inhabitants of this land—the kings who sit on David's throne, the priests, the prophets, and all the inhabitants of Jerusalem—with drunkenness.** 14 **And I will dash them one against another, parents and children together, says the LORD. I will not pity or spare or have compassion when I destroy them.**

These verses are based on the proverb that is quoted in verse 12: "Every wine-jar should be filled with wine." God instructs Jeremiah to quote the proverb with the anticipation that those who hear will respond by saying, in effect, "Of course, don't you think we know that?" What is not clear is what this proverb might have meant. Many ideas have been suggested, among the most prominent that the proverb expresses a truism: What else would you do with a wine jar but fill it with wine? It may be something such as one might hear where I live: Of course it's hot and humid, it's summer in St. Louis. Others have suggested that the proverb expresses confidence that God will always provide abundance: Of course the wine jars are filled; we are blessed by God, who will always keep them full. The last sense of the proverb seems to lend itself to the interpretation of it in verses 13–14.

Three actions that God intends are announced. God announces to the inhabitants of the land who assume God's blessing: "I am about to fill the inhabitants of this land . . . with drunkenness" (v. 13); "I will dash them against one another"; "I [will] destroy them" (v. 14). The inhabitants of the land will lose control, stumble around, experience impaired judgment, and ultimately injure and destroy one another. The prophet's warning portrays the abuse of a good thing. One wonders if the self-destructive drunkenness described in verses 13–14 might be an allusion to "confusion of mind," a covenant curse in Deuteronomy 28:28 (especially since the verses to follow seem to allude to nearby verses in Deuteronomy 28; see comments to follow on Jer. 13:16–17).

As readers, we are reminded of ideas we have already encountered in the book of Jeremiah: (1) The connection of these verses with 13:1–11 is signaled by the use of the same Hebrew word for "ruin" (in 13:7, 9) and "destroy" (13:14). The sign-act of the prior verses pointed to the ruin or destruction of the loincloth and God's intention to ruin Judah's pride. In verses 12–14, the ruin God intends is specifically identified as the ruin or destruction of the inhabitants of the land. Further, in verses 12–14 we have Judah, proud and confident of God's blessing, presented as a self-destructive drunk without pride, disgraced and shamed. (2) In the wider context of the book, we have encountered the smug self-assurance of the people, so confident of divine protection that they are blind to their accountability to God (for instance, Jeremiah 7). In 13:12–14, God turns the confidence of Judah that God will bless them—every wine jar should be filled—into judgment: God makes them self-destructively drunk. Judah has impaired judgment about God's blessing of them, and this drunkenness will result in Judah's destruction.

Out-of-control drunks, if they are not to do harm to themselves or to others, need to be saved by someone ("Don't let friends drive drunk"). At the same time, families and friends who constantly rescue an alcoholic allow that person to avoid confronting his or her illness. Only God is capable of saving the hopelessly drunk and disoriented inhabitants of the land of Judah from destruction (ruin). In the unfolding drama of the book of Jeremiah, God gives Judah numerous chances to "return," but to no avail. God finally declares, "I will not pity or spare or have compassion" (13:14). God's decision is clear: Judah's problem can no longer be denied, and God declares that there must be judgment.

Jeremiah 13:15–27

There are three sections in these verses (13:15–17, 18–19, 20–27), each of which may have been an independent unit before they were placed together in the final form of the book. The themes of these verses have close connections to material with which we are already familiar in Jeremiah. Particularly, the theme of pride and shame unifies verses 15–27 and connects them to God's announcement in Jeremiah 13:9, "I will ruin the pride of Judah." Closely associated with the theme of pride and shame is the repeated declaration that God intends to exile Judah. These two themes occur in all three sections: (1) in verses 15–17, Jeremiah admonishes, "Do not be haughty" (v. 15) and mourns because "the Lord's flock has been taken captive" (v. 17); (2) in verses 18–19, the king and the queen mother are told, "Take a lowly seat" (v.18), and it is twice announced, "Judah is taken into exile" (v. 19); and (3) in verses 20–27, God announces, "I myself will lift up your skirts . . . and your shame will be seen" (v. 26; cf. v. 22) and "I will scatter you like chaff" (v. 24). The poem in verses 15–27 is about the ways in which God will "ruin the pride of Judah" by sending them into exile.

Verses 15–17 are a call to repentance, expressed through a positive and a negative command. The positive command is that Judah "hear." Having threatened to ruin the pride of Judah, the Lord cites as a first example of Judah's pride their refusal to hear God's words (13:9–10). The negative command is that Judah "not be haughty"—in the context of Jeremiah 13, an admonition that must be heard as a complement to God's command that Judah "hear and give ear." The exhortation in verse 16, "Give glory to the Lord," complements the two admonitions of the prior verse. God will be given glory when Judah hears the Lord and is not haughty. The pride of Judah is that Judah refuses to hear God's word and follows after other gods (13:10).

The call for Judah to repent is urgent; the people must repent soon, before God acts to bring darkness and gloom (v. 17). The imagery of verse 17—God changing light to darkness, the reference to twilight, and the threat of stumbling in the gloom—may echo a covenant curse from Deuteronomy 28:29: "you shall grope around at noon as blind people grope in darkness, but you will be unable to find your way." The imagery may also reflect the collapse of creation we have encountered previously in Jeremiah (for instance, Jer. 4:23–26). The urgency of repentance is reinforced a second way in 13:17. God calls Judah "to hear and give ear" (v. 15), but this call to repent recognizes the consequences if Judah will not listen: They will be taken captive (v. 17; cf.1:3).

The placement of this call to repent after God's declaration of no pity or compassion (v. 14) is surprising. We have been led to believe that the time for Judah's repentance is past and judgment inevitable. There may be no explanation for the placement of this text, except perhaps these verses reflect Jeremiah's message from a time when he thought Judah might yet repent. Or the placement of the verses at this point in the final form of the book may reflect careless editing or a logic we cannot understand. However, an explanation for the placement of this surprising call for Judah to repent may be found in verse 17, where it is reported that the prophet weeps at the prospect of Judah's captivity. Jeremiah is God's spokesperson, so the grief of the prophet reflects God's grief as well. The thought of "the Lord's flock" being taken captive causes God anguish, which we hear expressed through Jeremiah. Perhaps it is the Lord's anguish that, beyond all that we have been led to expect, allows God to offer Judah a final chance to repent of their pride.

Jeremiah 14:1–10

14:1 **The word of the Lord that came to Jeremiah concerning the drought:**
 2 **Judah mourns**
 and her gates languish;
 they lie in gloom on the ground,
 and the cry of Jerusalem goes up.
 3 **Her nobles send their servants for water;**
 they come to the cisterns,
 they find no water,
 they return with their vessels empty.
 They are ashamed and dismayed
 and cover their heads,
 4 **because the ground is cracked.**
 Because there has been no rain on the land

> the farmers are dismayed;
> they cover their heads.
> 5 Even the doe in the field forsakes her newborn fawn
> because there is no grass.
> 6 The wild asses stand on the bare heights,
> they pant for air like jackals;
> their eyes fail
> because there is no herbage.
>
> 7 Although our iniquities testify against us,
> act, O LORD, for your name's sake;
> our apostasies indeed are many,
> and we have sinned against you.
> 8 O hope of Israel,
> its savior in time of trouble,
> why should you be like a stranger in the land,
> like a traveler turning aside for the night?
> 9 Why should you be like someone confused,
> like a mighty warrior who cannot give help?
> Yet you, O LORD, are in the midst of us,
> and we are called by your name;
> do not forsake us!
> 10 Thus says the LORD concerning this people:
> Truly they have loved to wander,
> they have not restrained their feet;
> therefore the LORD does not accept them,
> now he will remember their iniquity
> and punish their sins.

These verses concern a drought and divide into three sections. Verses 1–6 describe the consequences of the drought; verses 7–9 include a lament by the people occasioned by the drought; and verse 10 reports God's response to the people's lament. The themes of Judah's shame and their iniquity are further developed. A conversation among God, Jeremiah, and Judah begins here and continues through Jeremiah 15:9.

Droughts were understood in ancient Israel as God's judgment and as a covenant curse. In Deuteronomy 28:23–24, one form of covenant curse is described in this way:

> The sky over your head shall be bronze, and the earth under you iron. The LORD will change the rain of your land into powder, and only dust shall come down upon you from the sky until you are destroyed.

Several centuries before Jeremiah, the prophet Elijah announced God's judgment on Israel by declaring, "As the Lord the God of Israel lives, . . . there shall be neither dew nor rain these years, except by my word" (1 Kings 17:1). Though today we attempt to understand droughts through the science of meteorology, in the Old Testament droughts were understood as God's punishment for violating covenant.

It is not possible to identify historically the date of the drought described in Jeremiah 4:1–6. (Droughts were not uncommon.) However, the severity of the drought these verses describe is emphasized by a series of negative statements: "no water" (v. 3) and "no rain" (v. 4) result in "no grass" (v. 5) and "no herbage" (v. 6). Obviously, the farmers who depended on the rain for their crops and livestock were "dismayed" (v. 4). Even the "nobles," economically privileged and often having access to resources that poor farmers lacked, could find no water when they sent their servants out. God threatened to "ruin the pride of Judah" (13:9), and with this drought, rich and poor, peasant farmer and nobility alike experience shame. The order of creation is near collapse. The doe has to forsake her fawn, and the wild asses pant near death (vv. 5–6). In ancient Israel, this drought would have been understood as God's judgment, as a covenant curse.

So, in verses 7–9 the people pray to God. The prayer is typical of prayers found in the Psalms that are directed to God by persons in difficulty (for instance, Psalms 3, 4, 5, 35). The prayer in Jeremiah 14:7–9 begins like a confession through which the people admit their "iniquities," "apostasies," and "sins." Yet, while there is admission of fault by God's people, the central urging of the prayer is for God to "act . . . for your name's sake" (v. 7; also see v. 9). The questions addressed to God in verses 8 and 9 attempt to spur God to action by challenging God's character and integrity. The petitioners ask why God, known as Israel's hope and savior in time of trouble, is acting like a stranger (v. 8), and why God the mighty warrior is confused and appears unable to give help (v. 9). Judah has sinned, but through this prayer they suggest that inaction is making God look bad. Those who pray want it clear that if Judah is shamed, then God, too, is shamed. The prayer's final petition is a plea, "do not forsake us!" (v. 9).

When the Lord responds to this prayer, God vows to "remember their iniquity and punish their sins." Specifically, what God remembers is how Judah "loved to wander" (v. 10a, which echoes 2:23–25). Judah's prayer in 14:7–9 accuses God of desertion and powerlessness and asks God to alleviate the drought despite Judah's sin and iniquity. God's response takes a counterview of the situation. The drought is not a sign that God is forsaking Judah or is powerless. Rather, the drought is a covenant curse, the judgment on Judah, who have forsaken God. It is not God but Judah that needs to change.

This text, which associates a drought with God's judgment, incorporates a perspective about which we need to exercise great care. It is neither helpful nor possible for us to claim that we understand God's intentions through a natural disaster and so equate the destruction caused by a drought, flood, or hurricane with some human sin. For instance, just because a house or a town is destroyed by a flood or by a tornado, we cannot conclude that the persons afflicted are morally deficient or more sinful than others. (See Jesus' reflection in Luke 13:1–5 about those on whom a tower fell.) Even if writers in the Old Testament were willing to associate natural disasters and illnesses with God's judgment, such conclusions in specific cases are dangerous and, when made, place us in a position of claiming to understand much more about God than we creatures possibly can. Central to what we can know and understand is that God gave God's only Son for the sake of the world (John 3:16). Can we imagine this God snuffing out life in a fit of anger or frustration? Certainly, we need to take seriously how human sin might contribute to natural disasters: for instance, the overuse of fossil fuels that may cause global warming and increase the frequency and severity of hurricanes, or the development of wetlands that may make periodic flooding more severe by restricting river channels. Mostly, we need to admit that destructive natural disasters are a tragic mystery we cannot readily explain or easily blame on a loving God.

Jeremiah 14:11–12

14:11 **The LORD said to me: Do not pray for the welfare of this people.** [12] **Although they fast, I do not hear their cry, and although they offer burnt offering and grain offering, I do not accept them; but by the sword, by famine, and by pestilence I consume them.**

The command that the prophet cease to pray for the "welfare" of Judah (v. 11) indicates that God is now ready to give up on relationship with Judah. The Hebrew for the word "welfare" is *tov*, the word translated as "good" in the Genesis 1 creation story: "And God saw that it was good" (Gen. 1:4, 10, and so forth). The word indicates God's blessing and so the well-being of the creation. God intended "good" for all the creation and for Israel and Judah. The just-voiced prayer of the community (14:7–9) suggests, however, that Judah intends no change and continues in a false assurance that the Lord will overlook their iniquity to uphold God's own name. In this circumstance, neither prayer nor offerings will be of any help. Instead of welfare (good), God announces that the community is to be consumed "by sword, by famine, and by pestilence." Welfare signals God's blessing. Sword, famine, and pestilence are used in the book of Jeremiah to signal covenant curse.

Jeremiah 14:13–16

At several points in the book of Jeremiah, he is presented confronting prophets who offer a more reassuring word than his. This is the first such encounter. Jeremiah appeals to God because there are prophets directly contradicting the judgment God has had him announce. At this point in the book, this text disrupts the sustained conversation between God and Judah that began in Jeremiah 14:1 and resumes in verse 17. But perhaps the point of placing this incident here is to indicate that "lying" prophets disrupt the encounter between God and Judah for which Jeremiah is the mediator. Worse than disruptive, these prophets are deceptive. Jeremiah has been forbidden by God to pray for the "welfare" of Judah and has announced God's judgment by sword, famine, and pestilence (vv. 11–12). These other prophets announce just the opposite: "You shall not see the sword, nor shall you have famine, but I will give you true peace in this place" (v. 13).

In response to God's spokesperson, the Lord stresses that the prophets who oppose Jeremiah do not speak with divine authority. They were not commissioned (v. 14). So, God pronounces judgment on them (vv. 15–16), charging that they have misrepresented themselves as God's spokespersons and are "lying." In God's denial of any connection with these lying prophets, we hear echoes of God's call to Jeremiah to be a prophet (1:4–10). God says of the lying prophets, "I did not send them [cf. God's command to Jeremiah "for you shall go to all to whom I send you," 1:7], nor did I command them [cf. "you shall speak whatever I command you," 1:7] or speak to them [cf. 1:4, 9, where God's word comes to Jeremiah and is placed in Jeremiah's mouth]." God sent, commanded, and has spoken to Jeremiah, but not to these lying prophets.

God's judgment on the lying prophets continues the theme of sword, famine, and pestilence (vv. 15–16). This covenant curse is announced by Jeremiah as God's judgment on Judah but is denied by the prophets who oppose Jeremiah. God's judgment on the lying prophets is that they and those in Judah who support them will be consumed by sword and famine. In other words, the prophets will suffer the covenant curse they have denied. Lack of proper burial (v. 16) is a covenant curse explicitly mentioned in Deuteronomy 28:26.

The problem of prophets whose message is more reassuring than Jeremiah's recurs later in the book, especially in Jeremiah's encounter with Hananiah in Jeremiah 28. After 587 B.C., it was easy to see that Jeremiah was correct and those who said there would be no judgment were wrong. Yet, it would have been much more difficult for the contemporaries of Jeremiah to make a judgment between Jeremiah and the prophets who said all would be well.

It remains difficult in our time, too, to distinguish who speaks for God and who is a "lying" prophet. Perhaps we can learn from the book of Jeremiah. In Jeremiah 14, it seems that those who deny the possibility of covenant curse—famine, sword and pestilence—are those who imagine that God guarantees security and well-being. Sin and iniquity are recognized, but it is assumed that God will overlook these. By contrast, Jeremiah takes sin and iniquity seriously and understands that Judah will be held accountable by God. Jeremiah knows that covenant curse is a real possibility. Dietrich Bonhoeffer's notion of "cheap grace" is helpful:

> Cheap grace is the preaching of forgiveness without requiring repentance, baptism without confession, absolution without personal confession. Cheap grace is grace without discipleship, grace without the cross, grace without Jesus Christ living and incarnate. (*The Cost of Discipleship*, p. 47)

The lying prophets among us offer cheap grace. The Jeremiahs among us call us to the costly discipleship of the cross, of surrendering our lives in obedience to God.

Jeremiah 14:17–18

14:17 **You shall say to them this word:**
Let my eyes run down with tears night and day,
and let them not cease,
for the virgin daughter—my people—is struck down with a crushing blow,
with a very grievous wound.
18 **If I go out into the field,**
look—those killed by the sword!
And if I enter the city,
look—those sick with famine!
For both prophet and priest ply their trade throughout the land,
and have no knowledge.

God's course seems certain from prior sections of the book of Jeremiah. For the iniquity of Judah, God is going to send sword, famine, and pestilence. There is no possibility of peace, only of covenant curse. So it is surprising that in verses 17–18 we hear of God's hurt and anguish. God speaks of Judah in intimate, relational language, "the virgin daughter—my people" (v. 17). Their judgment is described graphically as "a crushing blow" and "a very grievous wound." It is as if a member of the family were seriously injured in an accident or taken unexpectedly and gravely ill. God cries and cannot cease (v. 17). The horror of the situation is evident everywhere: in the field, those killed by the sword, and in the city, those sick from the famine (v. 18). God insists on covenant curse, but it is painful for God, who is in agony over what takes place. God is portrayed much like a pained parent who knows a child must be punished but who suffers the punishment more than the child.

Only in the last phrases of verse 18 does God's anguished tone recede. God has to punish Judah, but it is the priests and prophets who have brought covenant curse on Judah (cf. 14:13–16; also 2:8) because they have "no knowledge." We know that the lying prophets assume that all is well and that God will give "true peace in this place" (14:13ff.). The Jerusalem leadership had no knowledge of Judah's guilt or of the possibility of covenant curse, and they did not know of God's anguish over Judah, which was about to be dealt a "crushing blow" (v. 17).

Jeremiah 14:19–22

14:19 **Have you completely rejected Judah?**
　　　 Does your heart loathe Zion?
　　　 Why have you struck us down
　　　 so that there is no healing for us?
　　　 We look for peace, but find no good;
　　　 for a time of healing, but there is terror instead.
　20 **We acknowledge our wickedness, O LORD,**
　　　 the iniquity of our ancestors,
　　　 for we have sinned against you.
　21 **Do not spurn us, for your name's sake;**
　　　 do not dishonor your glorious throne;
　　　 remember and do not break your covenant with us.
　22 **Can any idols of the nations bring rain?**
　　　 Or can the heavens give showers?
　　　 Is it not you, O LORD our God?
　　　 We set our hope on you,
　　　 for it is you who do all this.

At verse 19, the conversation among God, Jeremiah, and Judah resumes. Since the text that follows this one reports God's response to Jeremiah (15:1–4), it is likely that the prophet speaks the intercession of these verses on behalf of the people. The prophet asks three questions about God's intentions to continue in relationship with Judah: Has God "completely rejected Judah"? Does God "loathe Zion"? Why no healing? As the prophet prays on behalf of Judah, he expresses hope for "healing," as well as the people's disappointment that there has been "terror instead" (v. 19). Jeremiah voices a confession on behalf of Judah for their wickedness, iniquity, and sin (v. 20). Finally, the prophet petitions God, "for your name's sake," to sustain relationship with Judah (vv. 21; cf. v. 7).

Jeremiah's prayer focuses on the issue: Has God rejected Judah? The petition that God "remember" and "not break your covenant with us" (v. 21) is the heart of the matter. Yet, we have earlier heard God's resolve to "remember their iniquity" (v. 10). These two possible ways in which God might remember Judah—to remember (and keep) covenant or to remember (and judge) iniquity—stand in tension. Jeremiah's prayer in verses 19–22 pleads that God remember covenant and not Judah's sin and iniquity. The prayer concludes with the hope that God, who alone can bring the blessing of rain, will "do all this." With the petition that God give rain, the conversation begun at Jeremiah 14:1 comes full circle. When God remembered Judah's sin and iniquity, there was covenant curse, "no rain" (v. 4). Should God remember covenant, then there will be the hope of blessing, and the rains will return.

As Jeremiah's prayer concludes, the tension between the two ways in which God might remember is not resolved. Judah lived where persons and communities always live before God, in the tension between God whose mercy is long-suffering and who keeps covenant and God who holds humanity accountable for sin and iniquity. Still, Jeremiah 14 indicates that for too long Judah has denied accountability before God. We need to read further to hear God's response to Jeremiah's prayer.

Jeremiah 15:1–4

15:1 Then the LORD said to me: Though Moses and Samuel stood before me, yet my heart would not turn toward this people. Send them out of my sight, and let them go! [2] And when they say to you, "Where shall we go?" you shall say to them: Thus says the LORD:

Those destined for pestilence, to pestilence,
and those destined for the sword, to the sword;
those destined for famine, to famine,
and those destined for captivity, to captivity.

³ **And I will appoint over them four kinds of destroyers, says the LORD: the sword to kill, the dogs to drag away, and the birds of the air and the wild animals of the earth to devour and destroy.** ⁴ **I will make them a horror to all the kingdoms of the earth because of what King Manasseh son of Hezekiah of Judah did in Jerusalem.**

God responds to Jeremiah's prayer (14:19–22) by referring to Moses and Samuel, two figures from the history of Israel who were notable intercessors between God and Israel. Moses was the mediator between God and Israel during the exodus from Egypt. Because the preceding material has concerned Judah's sin and iniquity and God's threatened judgment, Moses' role in pleading with God to spare Israel after the incident with the golden calf (Exodus 32–34) comes to mind. In part, Moses' mediation is recounted this way in Exodus 32:30–34:

> On the next day Moses said to the people, "You have sinned a great sin. But now I will go up to the LORD; perhaps I can make atonement for your sin." So Moses returned to the LORD and said, "Alas, this people has sinned a great sin; they have made for themselves gods of gold. But now, if you will only forgive their sin—but if not, blot me out of the book that you have written." But the LORD said to Moses, "Whoever has sinned against me I will blot out of my book. But now go, lead the people to the place about which I have spoken to you; see, my angel shall go in front of you. Nevertheless, when the day comes for punishment, I will punish them for their sin."

While God rejected this initial request, Moses was eventually able to persuade God to continue to journey with Israel through the wilderness (Exod. 33:12–17). Samuel, too, was mediator between God and Israel when Israel, for instance, sought God's help when attacked by the Philistines. Samuel's mediation resulted in Israel's deliverance (1 Sam. 7:7–11; cf. 1 Sam. 8:4–22):

> When the Philistines heard that the people of Israel had gathered at Mizpah, the lords of the Philistines went up against Israel. And when the people of Israel heard of it they were afraid of the Philistines. The people of Israel said to Samuel, "Do not cease to cry out to the LORD our God for us, and pray that he may save us from the hand of the Philistines." So Samuel took a sucking lamb and offered it as a whole burnt offering to the LORD; Samuel cried out to the LORD for Israel, and the LORD answered him. As Samuel was offering up the burnt offering, the Philistines drew near to attack Israel; but the LORD thundered with a mighty voice that day against the Philistines and threw them into confusion; and they were routed before

Israel. And the men of Israel went out of Mizpah and pursued the Philistines, and struck them down as far as beyond Beth-car.

Regarding Judah, however, God declares that even if Moses or Samuel himself were to interene it would do no good. God rejects any intercession from Jeremiah. Judah will not turn to God (see Jer. 3:11–4:2 and God's repeated calls to "return"), so God will "not turn toward this people" (15:1). Rather, the Lord orders that Judah be sent away and finally sent into exile (vv. 2–3). The judgments described in verses 2–3 include many references to the covenant curses of Deuteronomy: "captivity" seems related to Deut. 28:36, 60–65; "the sword to kill, the dogs to drag away, and the birds of the air and the wild animals of the earth to devour and destroy" seems related to Deut. 28:26; and "I will make them a horror" seems related to Deut. 28:25, 37. Jeremiah 14 suggests two ways in which God may remember: God may remember the covenant and the Lord's commitment to Israel, or God may remember Judah's sin and iniquity. These verses in Jeremiah 15 suggest that God chooses to remember both the sin and iniquity of Judah and the covenant, so that God will inflict covenant curses on Judah (see Jer. 11:1–5).

These verses conclude with a reference to Manasseh, who was king of Judah from 687–642 B.C. Manasseh ruled during a time when Assyria dominated Judah. From the perspective of the writers of the books of Kings, Manasseh was among the worst of all Judah's kings because he promoted the worship of other gods (2 Kings 21). The primary stipulation of covenant was that God alone be worshiped (Exod. 20:3). The book of Jeremiah repeatedly has made the point that God's people worship other gods. From Jeremiah 11 on, the book has claimed that God will bring covenant curse because of the sin and iniquity of Judah. Manasseh was the primary illustration of Judah's sin and the reason God chose to inflict covenant curses on them.

Jeremiah 15:5–9

15:5 Who will have pity on you, O Jerusalem,
or who will bemoan you?
Who will turn aside
to ask about your welfare?
6 You have rejected me, says the LORD,
you are going backward;
so I have stretched out my hand against you and destroyed you—
I am weary of relenting.
7 I have winnowed them with a winnowing fork

in the gates of the land;
I have bereaved them, I have destroyed my people;
they did not turn from their ways.

8   Their widows became more numerous
than the sand of the seas;
I have brought against the mothers of youths
a destroyer at noonday;
I have made anguish and terror
fall upon her suddenly.

9   She who bore seven has languished;
she has swooned away;
her sun went down while it was yet day;
she has been shamed and disgraced.
And the rest of them I will give to the sword
before their enemies,

says the LORD.

God's speech in these verses echoes material from previous verses. For example, in 15:1 it is indicated that God would "not turn toward" Judah even if Moses and Samuel were to intercede on their behalf. These verses continue the theme of turning. First, God asks, "Who will turn aside to ask of your welfare?" (15:5). It is a question whose implied answer is "No one." Because Judah has rejected God and even turned backward (v. 6), the Lord will not turn toward Judah, and neither will anyone else, such as Judah's political and military allies. An earlier prayer of Jeremiah indicated Judah's puzzlement about why there was no "peace" (14:19). God's question (v. 5) suggests no one will care about the "welfare" (the same Hebrew word as for "peace" in 14:19) of Judah. On the contrary, God is resolved to destroy Judah (vv. 6, 7, 8). Further delay of judgment is unlikely, for God declares, "I am weary of relenting" (v. 6). Judah has chosen curse rather than blessing, death rather than life (cf. Deut. 30:15–20).

Paul, in reflecting on the human condition, concludes that "there is no one who is righteous, not even one" (Rom. 3:10, a paraphrase of Eccl. 7:20). Paul's conclusion well summarizes the thrust of this section of the book of Jeremiah. In Judah, Jeremiah finds no one who is righteous, or worse, no one who recognizes that they are not righteous. However, bleak as Paul's conclusion is, he does not despair, for Paul knows "since all have sinned and fall short of the glory of God, they are now justified by his grace as a gift" (Rom. 3:23). Finally, too, the book of Jeremiah affirms that God's grace as a gift prevails over Judah's rebellion. But first, the book makes unmistakably clear the depth of Judah's rebellion and the serious-ness of the fracture between God and the people.

Until we have confronted the depth of our sin and rebellion, we are likely to think that we somehow deserve something from God, even as Judah assumed they deserved God's protection and care. Only when "shamed and disgraced" could Judah possibly be restored again to rela-tionship with God. So, as we worship weekly, the prayer of confession opens the way for us to renewed relationship with God. It is our chance to "turn back" to God and receive God's grace as a gift.

Jeremiah 15:10–14

15:10 **Woe is me, my mother, that you ever bore me, a man of strife and contention to the whole land! I have not lent, nor have I borrowed, yet all of them curse me. ¹¹ The LORD said: Surely I have intervened in your life for good, surely I have imposed enemies on you in a time of trouble and in a time of distress. ¹² Can iron and bronze break iron from the north?**

¹³ Your wealth and your treasures I will give as plunder, without price, for all your sins, throughout all your territory. ¹⁴ I will make you serve your ene-mies in a land that you do not know, for in my anger a fire is kindled that shall burn forever.

Verse 10 is another complaint or lament of Jeremiah, which is followed by God's response in verses 11–14. Jeremiah laments his birth because his life has become one of contention. Jeremiah, like Judah, experiences "curse"; but Jeremiah claims that, unlike Judah, he is innocent of exploit-ing persons (v. 10; cf. for instance, 9:4–6) and suffers unjustly. Ironically, Jeremiah frequently intervenes with God on behalf of the very people by whom he is now cursed (the sense of the Hebrew word for "curse" here is more like "abuse").

God's response to Jeremiah's complaint in verses 11–14 is in two parts. First, in verse 11, the Lord characterizes as "for good" the interventions in Jeremiah's life, even in sending enemies to oppose him (v. 11). It is difficult to fathom how the abuse Jeremiah has suffered at the hands of enemies might be thought "for good," but perhaps this is understandable from God's perspective. God called Jeremiah as spokesperson to announce to Judah a word of plucking up and tearing down (1:10). An indication that Jeremiah has served well God's intention for him is that Jeremiah has enemies among those who reject God (12:6). Thus, God's interventions in Jeremiah's life and "for good" in that they allow the prophet to serve God's purposes.

God's second response to Jeremiah's complaint is reported in 15:12–14. At the time of Jeremiah's call, God indicated that Jeremiah would be "an iron pillar, and a bronze wall" so the inhabitants of the land, Jeremiah's enemies, could not prevail against him (1:18–19). In this situation, God's response moves in another direction. God declares that Jeremiah—iron and bronze—will not be able to break "iron from the north" (15:12), a reference to the enemy from the north that God is sending to destroy Judah (see 1:15; 4:6; 6:22). Frequently, Jeremiah has been presented in the book as interceding on behalf of Judah to persuade God not to "pluck up and tear down" (for instance, see 7:16; 11:14–15; 14:11–12; 15:1) as the enemy from the north will surely do. God's response to Jeremiah in verse 12 suggests that while enemies have not prevailed against him personally, neither has Jeremiah prevailed through his intercessions against God's intention to use the foe from the north to pluck up and tear down.

Though the NRSV divides a paragraph to separate verses 13–14 from verse 12, these two verses actually complete the thought of verse 12. The intercessions of Jeremiah—iron and bronze—will not break "iron from the north," the foe God will send to destroy Judah. So Judah, including the prophet Jeremiah, will serve enemies in a foreign land. God will see that the prophet's enemies do not prevail against him; but the prophet's words of intercession will not prevail against God's "anger" (v. 14). God's resolve to pluck up and tear down is unswerving.

Yet, God's response to Jeremiah's complaint mostly ignores the prophet's concern, his own innocent suffering. So, Jeremiah again voices his complaint to God in the verses that follow.

Jeremiah 15:15–21

15:15 **O LORD, you know;**
      remember me and visit me,
      and bring down retribution for me on my persecutors.
      In your forbearance do not take me away;
      know that on your account I suffer insult.
16 **Your words were found, and I ate them,**
      and your words became to me a joy
      and the delight of my heart;
      for I am called by your name,
      O LORD, God of hosts.
17 **I did not sit in the company of merrymakers,**
      nor did I rejoice;
      under the weight of your hand I sat alone,
      for you had filled me with indignation.
18 **Why is my pain unceasing,**
      my wound incurable,

refusing to be healed?
Truly, you are to me like a deceitful brook,
like waters that fail.

¹⁹ Therefore thus says the LORD:
If you turn back, I will take you back,
and you shall stand before me.
If you utter what is precious, and not what is worthless,
you shall serve as my mouth.
It is they who will turn to you,
not you who will turn to them.
²⁰ And I will make you to this people
a fortified wall of bronze;
they will fight against you,
but they shall not prevail over you,
for I am with you
to save you and deliver you,

says the LORD.
²¹ I will deliver you out of the hand of the wicked,
and redeem you from the grasp of the ruthless.

These verses follow the pattern of this section of the book of Jeremiah: A prophetic complaint to God (vv. 15–18) is followed by God's response (vv. 19–21). The cost to Jeremiah of his prophetic service is again the focus of his complaint.

Jeremiah addresses God, "O Lord, you know; remember me and visit me" (v. 15); yet, Jeremiah's prayer suggests that the prophet is not so sure God knows, remembers, or will visit. Indeed, Jeremiah fears that in "forbearance," God may wait too long to act on his behalf (cf. the claim of God in the previous section, "I have intervened in your life for good," v. 11), and his life will be lost ("do not take me away," v. 15). Jeremiah addresses his prayer to God, yet Jeremiah is clear that the God to whom he prays is really the cause of his trouble: "know that on your account I suffer insult" (v. 15). The God to whom Jeremiah must turn for comfort is also the cause of his suffering.

Verses 16–17 recall the relationship between God and Jeremiah. The prophet is the messenger of the Lord's word, God's spokesperson. The prophet remembers his call (1:4–10; cf. Ezek. 3:1–3) and his close association with God (Jer. 15:16, "I am called by your name"). Jeremiah is God's faithful spokesperson, but this service has been costly. We have seen that the word of the Lord spoken by Jeremiah has been a word of unrelenting judgment. The consequence for the prophet is isolation (v. 17).

The prophet's complaint to God ends with two images, one of himself and one of God (v. 18). Regarding himself, Jeremiah offers that he is in unceasing pain and incurably wounded. Although Jeremiah uses language about physical affliction, the prophet's complaints suggest that the suffering his prophetic service has caused him is primarily social and spiritual. Jeremiah suffers social rejection and, he fears, abandonment by God. Still, the language of wound and illness, when related to how illness was regarded in ancient Israel and Judah, adds depth to Jeremiah's complaint. Illness was regarded to be the result of sin, an indication of covenant curse. In fact, in Jeremiah 8:11, Judah's covenant disobedience itself is referred to as a "wound," as God charges that Judah's prophets have "treated the wound of my people carelessly." Jeremiah is experiencing covenant curse, but he was faithful to God, and his condition is undeserved.

Thus, it is not surprising that Jeremiah believes God has abandoned him. To make this charge, the prophet uses the image of a "deceitful brook" (15:18). Ironically, God has accused Judah of forsaking the Lord, "the fountain of living water" (2:13). Jeremiah now turns this image against God. The image of a fountain of living water presents God as the source of blessing and life (cf. 2:6–7, which recalls how the Lord led Israel through the wilderness, "a land of drought," to the plenty of the promised land). God is a fountain of living water even to Judah, which has turned from God. Jeremiah, unlike Judah, is faithful to God. However, Jeremiah's service to God results in ridicule, plots, and social isolation, and the prophet blames his situtaion on God. Jeremiah's experience does not indicate that God is a source of life and blessing, and so he levels the charge that the Lord is not keeping the commitments made to Jeremiah. In other words, for Jeremiah, God is a deceitful brook and not the fountain of living water God claimed to be. God has been the prophet's only comfort, but for now, it seems that the Comforter has wounded him.

To this point, we have followed the convention of attributing this prayer to Jeremiah. However, as we have seen, Jeremiah often gives voice to the concerns of Judah. In the final form of the book of Jeremiah, another way to hear this prayer is as the complaint of the people voiced through the prophet. Those who experienced the Babylonian captivity may well have felt as if they, like Jeremiah, had served the Lord in costly ways, had been called by God's name, but were finally wounded by God and deserted. When heard in this way, this prayer of Jeremiah becomes the prayer of people who, in many times and places, have responded to God's call, served the Lord in costly ways, but in the end seem to be abandoned by God. So, with Jeremiah, the church listens for the Lord's response.

Initially, at least, the response is more a rebuke than an assurance (15:19). God calls Judah to return (for instance, 3:22; 4:1) and now calls Jeremiah to return or repent (15:19). God characterizes Jeremiah's prayer as "worthless," unworthy of one who is God's spokesperson. In effect, Jeremiah is told, "Get your act together if you want to continue as my prophet." At the end of verse 19, a play on the word *turn* demands that Judah repent ("turn to you") and the prophet not give in to the people ("turn to them") who persecute him for speaking the word of the Lord.

The second part of God's response (vv. 20–21) offers Jeremiah at least some assurance. The image of the prophet as a "fortified wall of bronze" is used again (cf. 1:18; 15:12) to assure Jeremiah of God's continuing protection of him from those who seek his life. Still, there is the recognition that "they will fight against you." It is not quite clear what God's promises of presence, deliverance, and redemption may mean for Jeremiah except that "they shall not prevail over you." If Jeremiah hopes that God will in some way ease the burden of his service or end the conflict that surrounds him, then God's assurance is at best partial. Further, there is no hint that God intends to relent in judging Judah, and the threat of "iron from the north" still looms. The prophetic complaint and God's response conclude with an evident tension between the Lord and Jeremiah. Jeremiah expected more of God, and God expected more of the prophet. This dialogue between God and Jeremiah leaves significant issues unresolved between them.

For the church, this text finally speaks to the tension between God and those who have served God in costly ways through long centuries. Partially, this text speaks that word all of us in the church are eager to hear: "I am with you . . . I will deliver you . . . redeem you." We affirm in the church that God is our only comfort, who is present with us to protect us:

> Question 1: What is your only comfort in life and in death? That I belong body and soul, in life and in death not to myself but to my faithful Savior, Jesus Christ who . . . has completely freed me from the dominion of the devil; that he protects me so well that without the will of my Father in heaven not a hair can fall from my head; indeed, that everything must fit his purpose for my salvation. (*Heidelberg Catechism*)

Yet alongside this word of comfort, Jeremiah 15:15–21 also reminds us that the purpose of God's comfort is so we can serve God fully and freely, even if the cost is high. Prophets and apostles and martyrs and Jesus himself have witnessed in word and deed to the Comforter's call to costly service:

Blessed are those who are persecuted for righteousness' sake, for theirs is the kingdom of heaven.

Blessed are you when people revile you and persecute you and utter all kinds of evil against you falsely on my account. Rejoice and be glad, for your reward is great in heaven, for in the same way they persecuted the prophets who were before you. (Matt. 5:10–12)

Like Jeremiah before us, the Comforter calls us to costly service; and in our costly service, God is our only Comforter.

Jeremiah 16:1–13

16:1 **The word of the LORD came to me:** 2 **You shall not take a wife, nor shall you have sons or daughters in this place.** 3 **For thus says the LORD concerning the sons and daughters who are born in this place, and concerning the mothers who bear them and the fathers who beget them in this land:** 4 **They shall die of deadly diseases. They shall not be lamented, nor shall they be buried; they shall become like dung on the surface of the ground. They shall perish by the sword and by famine, and their dead bodies shall become food for the birds of the air and for the wild animals of the earth.**

5 **For thus says the LORD: Do not enter the house of mourning, or go to lament, or bemoan them; for I have taken away my peace from this people, says the LORD, my steadfast love and mercy.** 6 **Both great and small shall die in this land; they shall not be buried, and no one shall lament for them; there shall be no gashing, no shaving of the head for them.** 7 **No one shall break bread for the mourner, to offer comfort for the dead; nor shall anyone give them the cup of consolation to drink for their fathers or their mothers.** 8 **You shall not go into the house of feasting to sit with them, to eat and drink.** 9 **For thus says the LORD of hosts, the God of Israel: I am going to banish from this place, in your days and before your eyes, the voice of mirth and the voice of gladness, the voice of the bridegroom and the voice of the bride.**

10 **And when you tell this people all these words, and they say to you, "Why has the LORD pronounced all this great evil against us? What is our iniquity? What is the sin that we have committed against the LORD our God?"** 11 **then you shall say to them: It is because your ancestors have forsaken me, says the LORD, and have gone after other gods and have served and worshiped them, and have forsaken me and have not kept my law;** 12 **and because you have behaved worse than your ancestors, for here you are, every one of you, following your stubborn evil will, refusing to listen to me.** 13 **Therefore I will hurl you out of this land into a land that neither you nor your ancestors have known, and there you shall serve other gods day and night, for I will show you no favor.**

In Jeremiah 16:1–13, God continues to address Jeremiah, though the issues in these verses concern mostly God's judgment of Judah in ways with which we are now familiar. As the chapter begins, God commands Jeremiah not to marry or have children. This stipulation continues the themes of the preceding chapter that stress the loneliness and isolation of Jeremiah as a result of his service to God. Unlike chapter 15, however, the reason for Jeremiah's celibacy is not related to God's demands on Jeremiah. Instead, celibacy is linked to God's imminent judgment of Judah, which will result in the death of mothers and fathers, sons and daughters. Particularly the death of children emphasizes the horror of what is to occur. We know all too well from our own experiences how children suffer in social upheaval: the children burned by napalm in Vietnam, the children of Northern Ireland who have been the physical or psychological victims of terrorists attacks, the preschool victims of the Oklahoma City Federal Building bombing in 1995. What will happen to Judah will be horrible, and it is no time to marry or have children. The judgment God intends is linked in these verses and throughout this chapter to the kind of covenant curses indicated in Deuteronomy: for instance, deadly diseases (Jer. 16:4; cf. Deut. 28:22) and bodies left unburied to be devoured by the birds and beasts (Jer. 16:4, cf. Deut. 28:26). The theme of death by sword, famine, and pestilence (see 14:12; 15:2) also is present here. The concern of chapter 16 with covenant curse and God's judgment picks up themes central to the book of Jeremiah.

The themes reintroduced at the beginning of Jeremiah 16 are expanded in verses 5–9. Another sign-act is commanded by God (see Jer. 13:1–11). When the destruction God intends finally occurs, Jeremiah is not to participate in the usual mourning rituals. He is not to marry; he is not to have children; and he is not to participate in the burial of the dead. This chapter communicates the end of the community of God's people. God imagines the cessation of the social rituals that sustain life for another generation, an image reinforced by God's pronouncement in verse 9. God intends an end from which there will be no turning back.

God's resolve to bring an end to Judah is given particular force in verse 5. After the exodus, when Israel worshiped the golden calf, Moses interceded on Israel's behalf to spare them the destruction God intended (Exodus 32–34). After a long time, God finally forgave the people's iniquity and reconfirmed commitment to Israel in these words:

> The LORD, the LORD,
> a God merciful and gracious,
> slow to anger,
> and abounding in steadfast love and faithfulness . . .
> forgiving iniquity and transgression and sin.
>
> (Exod. 34:6–7)

God here resolves to take away "steadfast love and mercy," by which relationship with God's people had been sustained in the most difficult of circumstances. Without steadfast love and mercy, the relationship between God and Judah cannot endure, and the community cannot be sustained. That is the point of Jeremiah 16: to declare that the relationship between God and Judah is at an end and life for Judah is over.

Verses 10–13 summarize the chapter and, more broadly, the material in Jeremiah 13–16. Jeremiah 13 begins with a sign-act that concludes Judah and Jerusalem are "good for nothing" (13:7, 10) because they "follow their own will . . . have gone after other gods to serve them" (13:10) and "would not listen" (13:11). The same accusations are restated in Jeremiah 16:11–12 concluding, as does Jeremiah 13, with the charge that God's people have not listened. Judah has brought about the end that is now inevitable by not listening to the word brought by Jeremiah. The connection between not listening and Judah's end is made explicit in verse 13. The verse begins with the word *therefore*, linking in a cause-and-effect relationship "refusing to listen" and God's judgment to "hurl you out of the land." The exile to Babylon will occur because Judah has not listened to God and "therefore" God will "hurl" them out. The finality of God's judgment is underscored in one further way in verse 13. God declares at the end of the verse, "I will show you no favor"; the Hebrew word translated "favor" here is used in Exodus 34:6 to speak of God's "mercy." Judah will not listen, so God's favor (mercy) will no longer sustain the relationship between God and Judah.

At this point, the book of Jeremiah holds before the church a frightening possibility, that the church as the community of God's people can refuse to listen to God for so long that God might cut the church off. On the one hand, if we in the church fail to take seriously this section of the book of Jeremiah, with its audacious realism that recognizes the possibility that God can end relationship with God's people, we are likely to fall into the prideful self-security that afflicted the leaders of ancient Judah and Jerusalem. They were so confident of God's favor they could not imagine God's judgment. On the other hand, if we in the church think we might cut ourselves off from God's grace by our actions, that seems to deny the gospel that affirms God's mercy to us "while we were yet sinners." The problem is one with which Paul wrestled:

> What then are we to say? Should we continue in sin in order that grace may abound? By no means! How can we who died to sin go on living in it? Do you not know that all of us who have been baptized into Christ Jesus were baptized into his death? Therefore, we have been buried with him by bap-

tism into death, so that, just as Christ was raised from the dead by the glory of the Father, so we too might walk in newness of life. (Rom. 6:1–4)

God's mercy, God's favor, God's grace do not excuse iniquity, but they are God's power that make possible listening and obedience by God's people.

Jeremiah 16:14–21

16:14 **Therefore, the days are surely coming, says the LORD, when it shall no longer be said, "As the LORD lives who brought the people of Israel up out of the land of Egypt," 15 but "As the LORD lives who brought the people of Israel up out of the land of the north and out of all the lands where he had driven them." For I will bring them back to their own land that I gave to their ancestors.**

16 **I am now sending for many fishermen, says the LORD, and they shall catch them; and afterward I will send for many hunters, and they shall hunt them from every mountain and every hill, and out of the clefts of the rocks.** 17 **For my eyes are on all their ways; they are not hidden from my presence, nor is their iniquity concealed from my sight.** 18 **And I will doubly repay their iniquity and their sin, because they have polluted my land with the carcasses of their detestable idols, and have filled my inheritance with their abominations.**

> 19 **O LORD, my strength and my stronghold,**
> **my refuge in the day of trouble,**
> **to you shall the nations come**
> **from the ends of the earth and say:**
> **Our ancestors have inherited nothing but lies,**
> **worthless things in which there is no profit.**
> 20 **Can mortals make for themselves gods?**
> **Such are no gods!**
> 21 **"Therefore I am surely going to teach them, this time I am going to teach them my power and my might, and they shall know that my name is the LORD."**

The usual interpretation is that these verses are the addition of a later editor of the book of Jeremiah, who added this material after the Babylonian exile had occurred. While there is no reason to doubt such a conclusion, the challenge is to understand how the promises of these verses might be heard as consistent with the threats of judgment that precede them in the book. The danger is that these promises will somehow be heard as a denial of the judgment God has announced. However, such a possibility is undercut by the clear future orientation of the promises, indicated by the phrase at the beginning of verse 14. The promises are for "the days [that] are surely coming" and in no way negate God's judgment that has just been so definitively announced. God intends the end of Judah, but this intention of God does not rule out a new beginning in the days that "are surely coming." Similarly, the promise of a new beginning in some future time does not lessen the "great evil" (v. 10) of the end God intends for Judah.

The nature of God's promises in verses 14–21 is confusing and likely reflects a complicated process by which these verses came to the form in which we find them. The material in these verses is in three parts:

1. In verses 14–15, God promises a new exodus. God's people once made oaths remembering how God "brought the people of Israel up out of the land of Egypt." In swearing such oaths, people were making a commitment to do what they promised, and they invoked the Lord, who brought Israel out of Egypt, as the guarantor of their promise. (See 5:2, where Judah is accused of swearing oaths in the Lord's name that they did not keep.) It is imagined that in the future oaths will no longer be sworn invoking the God of the exodus from Egypt but rather invoking the name of the God who will deliver God's people from the "north" (v. 15). God will one day begin anew with this people with a new act of deliverance, a new exodus so impressive that the former exodus will be supplanted in Israel's memory.

2. Verses 16–18 are difficult to interpret and were probably once a continuation from verse 13. Likely, these verses announce God's judgment that fishermen and hunters—an enemy—will seek Judah out for their sin and iniquity. However, set in the midst of material that looks to Judah's restoration, the sense of these verses is difficult to determine. Who are the fisherman and hunters and who is their prey? Perhaps the emphasis should fall on verse 18 and the phrase "I will doubly repay their iniquity and their sin," an idea common in the period of exile (cf. Isa. 40:2). Read this way, the verses indicate that God's restoration will occur when Judah has paid double for their sins. Another possibility is that Jeremiah 16:18 refers to the nations who have polluted "my land" and whom God will expel. These verses are very difficult to understand because they are not specific about who the fishers, the hunters, and the sinners who pollute God's land are. However, the next verses may provide some indication about how these verses should be read.

3. Verses 19–21 are a prayer addressed to God, who is called "my strength and my stronghold, my refuge . . . " (cf. Ps. 46:1). The confidence that is expressed through this prayer is that the nations will turn from their

idols to the God of Israel. Finally, the nations will "know that my name is the Lord" (v. 21). This hope that the nations will turn to God is common to other Old Testament prophetic books that come from the time of Israel's exile (for instance, Ezek. 28:24; 29:16; and also see Isa. 2:1–5).

A common pattern in the prophetic books of the Old Testament sees as related God's restoration of Israel, God's judgment of the nations, and the conversion of the nations to God. That may be the pattern intended in Jeremiah 16: Verses 14–15 present the restoration of Judah; verses 16–18 envision the judgment of the nations; verses 19–21 imagine the conversion of the nations (thus suggesting that verses 16–18 be read with stress on the Lord's judgment of the nations).

Jeremiah 16, as the conclusion of a section that began in Jeremiah 13, moves from a strong reaffirmation of God's intention to judge Judah to a surprising announcement of God's intention to restore Judah and to transform the nations. In reading this material, the tendency is to negate God's resolve to hold Judah accountable by stressing God's resolve to restore Judah and transform the nations. Care needs to be taken to hold together both of God's resolves. The gospel is not fully expressed either by the cross, God's suffering with and anguish over God's broken world, or by the resurrection, God's powerful transformation and renewal of the hopelessly broken world. The gospel is expressed fully when cross and resurrection are held together: God's anguish over the world opens the way for God's transformation of the world. In the book of Jeremiah, God's plucking up and tearing down do not preclude God's building and planting, but neither does God's intent to build and plant negate the need for God to pluck up and tear down.

"Cursed Are Those Who Trust in Mere Mortals"
(Jeremiah 17–20)

These chapters are again concerned with covenant blessing and curse. This theme is introduced in Jeremiah 17:5–8, which reflects on who is blessed and who is cursed. The section concludes in Jeremiah 20:14–18 as the prophet curses the day of his birth. If the overarching theme is covenant blessing and curse, other themes are also evident: a concern for the "heart" or "will" of God's people, for riches and wealth, for heeding or listening to God's word. However, there is no neat organization to the material in these chapters.

Jeremiah 17:1–4

17:1 **The sin of Judah is written with an iron pen; with a diamond point it is engraved on the tablet of their hearts, and on the horns of their altars,** 2 **while their children remember their altars and their sacred poles, beside every green tree, and on the high hills,** 3 **on the mountains in the open country. Your wealth and all your treasures I will give for spoil as the price of your sin throughout all your territory.** 4 **By your own act you shall lose the heritage that I gave you, and I will make you serve your enemies in a land that you do not know, for in my anger a fire is kindled that shall burn forever.**

The prophet assesses the cause of Judah's difficulties by declaring that "sin" is etched on their "hearts." In the Old Testament, the heart is not, as in our modern Western and American tradition, the seat of feelings or emotions. Rather, the heart is connected with human will or volition. The problem with Judah is that they have a defective heart, that is, their will is dominated by sin. Søren Kierkegaard, the nineteenth-century Danish theologian, spoke of "purity of heart," which is to will one thing: the obedience of God. The heart of Judah is not, to borrow from Kierkegaard, "pure" but rather etched with sin.

The recognition that Judah's problem is with their heart, a will or volition dominated by sin, is important in the book of Jeremiah. This insight anticipates the famous passage about God's new covenant, which is to be written on the heart (31:31–34). Ultimately, God's restoration of Israel will need to address the "heart" of their problem. The prophet connects Judah's defective heart with their defective worship. We can hear in this reflection about Judah's heart the apostle Paul's understanding of the power of sin. Under the power of sin, Paul sees that "I do not understand my own actions. For I do not do what I want, but I do the very thing I hate" (Rom. 7:15). God in Jesus Christ had to overcome the power of sin that Paul understands held humanity captive. So, too, the book of Jeremiah understands that God must correct Judah's heart problem if they are to live faithfully in relationship with God.

The worship practices that are described (17:2) are associated with idols; but then, what would one expect from a people who cannot or will not will what they ought. The consequences of Judah's idolatry are then elaborated (vv. 3–4). The pattern and the content here are familiar. God through Jeremiah accuses the people of disobedience and then pronounces judgment on them. Judah's idolatry sparks God's fierce anger, which will result in loss of the promised land to an enemy whom Judah will serve. What is of note is that though Judah's problem is the sin etched on their heart—a problem with their will—God nonetheless holds Judah accountable. An analogy may be the way we view addictions to drugs or alcohol. These may have power over persons, but persons with addictions are still held accountable for their behavior. Judah has a heart problem, but God still holds Judah accountable for idolatry and the broken relationship with God.

Jeremiah 17:5–8

17:5 **Thus says the LORD:**
Cursed are those who trust in mere mortals
and make mere flesh their strength,
whose hearts turn away from the LORD.
6 **They shall be like a shrub in the desert,**
and shall not see when relief comes.
They shall live in the parched places of the wilderness,
in an uninhabited salt land.

7 **Blessed are those who trust in the LORD,**
whose trust is the LORD.
8 **They shall be like a tree planted by water,**

sending out its roots by the stream.
It shall not fear when heat comes,
and its leaves shall stay green;
in the year of drought it is not anxious,
and it does not cease to bear fruit.

This poem, which much resembles Psalm 1, is linked to verses 1–4 by verse 5 and its concern for persons whose "hearts turn away from the Lord." The focus of this poem is with persons who do or do not "trust" in the Lord. To trust the Lord is to be blessed (vv. 7–8), while failure to trust the Lord results in curse (vv. 5–6). The word *trust* as used in these verses means what is meant by "faith" in the New Testament. Faith is not about having right ideas or espousing correct doctrines but about trusting God.

In this poem Jeremiah uses comparisons to plants to draw a sharp distinction between persons who do and do not trust God, or as we might say it, between those who do and do not have faith. Those who do not trust God are called "cursed" and are compared to desert shrubs struggling to survive in a parched wilderness (v. 6). By contrast, those who trust the Lord are called "blessed" and are compared to a deep-rooted tree planted by a stream, which remains green and bears fruit even during a drought. Without using the phrase, this poem describes God as "the fountain of living water" (2:13). So, to trust God is to be blessed and to live; to "trust in mere mortals" is to be cursed and to die.

The implications for Judah are clear. Judah has come to trust mere mortals, and their hearts are turned away from God. In particular, Jeremiah cites Judah's worship of the fertility deities in order to secure themselves (17:2). The fertility images in this poem are quite important. The fertility cults to which Judah has turned as a source of blessing and well-being bring only curse and death; the prophet affirms that trust in the Lord alone can lead to life for Judah. The prophet's words still challenge us in the church to discern if we trust God alone or trust "mere mortals."

Jeremiah 17:9–11

17:9 The heart is devious above all else;
　　it is perverse—
　　who can understand it?
　10 I the LORD test the mind
　　and search the heart,
　　to give to all according to their ways,
　　according to the fruit of their doings.

¹¹ **Like the partridge hatching what it did not lay,**
so are all who amass wealth unjustly;
in mid-life it will leave them,
and at their end they will prove to be fools.

The two sayings in these verses are like proverbs and were likely well known during the time of Jeremiah. It is not possible to tell if Jeremiah used these sayings or if they were added to the book as it later developed.

The saying in verses 9–10 is included at this point in the book because it concerns the "heart." Jeremiah has asserted that Judah's heart is engraved with sin (17:1) and that the heart that "turns away from the Lord" is cursed (v. 5). This saying affirms that "the Lord . . . search[es] the heart, to give to all according to their ways, . . . the fruit of their doings" (v. 10). Human beings may deceive themselves about their motives and actions, but God knows the human heart and responds accordingly. In the context of Jeremiah 17, the claim of these verses is that blessing and curse, life and death, Judah's political ruin and the loss of the land are not accidents but the consequence of human actions and God's response to Judah.

The saying in verse 11 further illustrates the point that God will "give to all according to their ways." Those who amass wealth are compared to partridges who take over other birds' nests. Jeremiah accuses God's people of amassing "wealth" that is not theirs (2:34; 8:10). This verse announces that Judah's ill-gotten "wealth" will be lost (cf. 17:2). The Lord gives to all "according to their ways" (17:10).

Jeremiah's condemnation of those who have become wealthy by taking advantage of others echoes the concern of many Old Testament prophets. Jeremiah's predecessor Amos comes to mind:

> Hear this, you that trample on the needy,
>   and bring to ruin the poor of the land,
> saying, "When will the new moon be over
>   so that we may sell grain;
> and the sabbath,
>   so that we may offer wheat for sale?
> We will make the ephah small and the shekel great,
>   and practice deceit with false balances,
> buying the poor for silver
>   and the needy for a pair of sandals,
>   and selling the sweepings of the wheat.
>   (Amos. 8:4–6; cf. Isa. 10:1–4)

The words of these prophets should give us pause in our society, which readily assumes that those with wealth have "earned it" and "pulled themselves up by their bootstraps" and just as quickly assumes that poverty is the fault of the poor because they are lazy and refuse to work.

Jeremiah 17:12–13

17:12 **O glorious throne, exalted from the beginning,**
    shrine of our sanctuary!
13 **O hope of Israel! O LORD!**
    All who forsake you shall be put to shame;
    those who turn away from you shall be recorded in the underworld,
    for they have forsaken the fountain of living water, the LORD.

The theme of Jeremiah 17 is that God knows the will or motives of Judah, their heart, and will bring on Judah the curse and death they have chosen for themselves. These verses summarize this theme by emphasizing God's sovereign reign. In verse 12, we hear God addressed in the Temple (cf. Isaiah 6). It seems likely that Jeremiah was quoting what he heard in the Temple in Jerusalem. However, verse 13 points to how Judah failed to acknowledge God's sovereignty. The final phrase of verse 13, "they have forsaken the fountain of living water," is identical to Jeremiah 2:13, God's initial accusation against the people. The "living water" image is quite appropriate in this setting, where water imagery has just been used to speak of God's blessing (17:7–8). The Lord is to Judah the source of life and blessing, eager to continue to sustain Judah. However, Judah, rather than trusting the Lord, has turned away. In forsaking God, Judah is like "a shrub in the desert" rather than "a tree planted by water" (17:6, 8). The Lord offers to be the source of life for Judah, but they turn away.

Jeremiah 17:14–18

17:14 **Heal me, O LORD, and I shall be healed;**
    save me, and I shall be saved;
    for you are my praise.
15 **See how they say to me,**
    "Where is the word of the LORD?
    Let it come!"
16 **But I have not run away from being a shepherd in your service,**
    nor have I desired the fatal day.
    You know what came from my lips;
    it was before your face.
17 **Do not become a terror to me;**

> you are my refuge in the day of disaster;
> 18 Let my persecutors be shamed,
> but do not let me be shamed;
> let them be dismayed,
> but do not let me be dismayed;
> bring on them the day of disaster;
> destroy them with double destruction!

Jeremiah is presented in the book as undertaking a terrible task. Among his own people, he must announce God's word of judgment. In these verses, Jeremiah again voices his own concerns to God. Unlike the persons described earlier in Jeremiah 17, the prophet trusts God, to whom he turns, confident that he will be saved. The prophet is taunted by enemies. Persons say to him, "Where is the word of the Lord? Let it come!" (v. 15). Jeremiah announces God's judgment, the advance of a foe from the north, exile. Yet nothing happens, so Jeremiah pleads with God: (1) He is faithful in God's service (v. 16a); (2) in proclaiming judgment, he announces what God has told him (v. 16b); and (3) God needs to act against the prophet's persecutors (v. 17).

This is a difficult prayer for most of us because it offends principles about love of enemies that we affirm in the Christian tradition. There is no denying that the prophet's attitude toward his persecutors is less than charitable, but three matters are worth noting. First, the context of the prayer is one in which the prophet has risked a great deal and suffered much in God's service. It expresses the sense that perhaps God has forgotten Jeremiah. Second, this prayer is absolutely honest. It gives expression to what Jeremiah feels about his persecutors and in wondering where God is. Jeremiah feels abandoned by God and dares to say so. Third, though the prayer expresses hostility toward enemies, it leaves to God whatever might be done. The prophet asks God to set things right, but the prophet does not himself act to take revenge. The prophet forthrightly pours himself out before the Lord, and we as readers wait for God's response. But God is silent, there is no immediate response. The prophet and Judah and we readers must wait to see what God will do next—as often happens when we pray in moments of despair.

Jeremiah 17:19–28

Sabbath observance was central to the life of ancient Israel and stipulated in the Ten Commandments (Exod. 20:8–11). Through these verses, Jeremiah stresses that on the Sabbath, daily activities and normal business should be curtailed (Jer. 17:21–22, 24; cf. Neh. 13:15–22; Amos 8:5).

Jeremiah's speech is in two parts. In the first part, the prophet concludes that Judah has failed to observe the Sabbath and will not hear or receive instruction (17:19–23). In the second part (vv. 24–27), the prophet offers both a promise and a threat. If the Sabbath is obeyed, then it is promised that it will be well with Judah and Jerusalem: A Davidic king will sit on the throne surrounded by court officials; the land and city will be inhabited forever; and people from all of Judah will come to the city with their offerings (vv. 25–26). However, if God's people fail to observe the Sabbath, then God will destroy Jerusalem (v. 27). Obedience of God will lead to blessing and life, disobedience to curse and death (cf. 11:1–15; 17:5–8). In this second part of the speech in 17:19–27, Jeremiah seems to ignore the conclusion reached in verse 24 that God's people will not listen and continue to violate the Sabbath.

It is difficult to know whether Jeremiah spoke these words or whether they were added later by those who gave the book its final form. There is no reason why Jeremiah may not have accused Judah of failing to observe the Sabbath (vv. 19–23). However, the strict observance of the Sabbath became especially important after 587 B.C. during the Babylonian exile (see Neh. 13:15–22). Even if Jeremiah himself accused Judah of failing to observe the Sabbath, it is likely that this passage as we now have it, which offers Judah the option to observe the Sabbath, came from a time after the exile to urge that the Sabbath be strictly observed, lest another disaster befall God's people.

The placement of this passage at this location in the book is difficult to understand. From Jeremiah 11 forward, the inevitability of God's judgment has been stressed (for example, 13:15–19). It has seemed too late for Judah to repent (17:19–23). The "if . . . then" character of the last half of this passage suggests that repentance may still be possible. The tone would be better suited for a time after the exile when efforts were underway to reestablish order in Judah.

As Christians, we no longer observe the Sabbath, the seventh day, but instead devote the first day of the week, Sunday, to celebrate the resurrection of Jesus. Still, there is something for us to learn from a passage such as this one that demands careful observance of the Sabbath. The point of carefully observing the Sabbath was to devote a day to God's praise. To cease normal activities was an act of faith ("trust"; cf. 17:7). One ceased to try to keep life ordered and secure through one's own efforts and entrusted oneself to God. Sabbath observance was not a way to "earn" God's favor but a response to God's goodness.

The Christian celebration of the Lord's day is a joyous occasion when we can affirm God's goodness. The days that have come before and that will follow may be difficult, chaotic, and troubled. However, on the Lord's day the church is reminded that God who raised Jesus from the dead continues to work to overcome death and chaos in our lives and in our world. To observe the Lord's day is an act of faith, expressing our trust that we do not need to secure ourselves but are held in God's care. So the church gathers to worship God and to sing its praise.

Jeremiah 18:1–12

18:1 **The word that came to Jeremiah from the LORD:** [2] **"Come, go down to the potter's house, and there I will let you hear my words."** [3] **So I went down to the potter's house, and there he was working at his wheel.** [4] **The vessel he was making of clay was spoiled in the potter's hand, and he reworked it into another vessel, as seemed good to him.**

[5] **Then the word of the LORD came to me:** [6] **Can I not do with you, O house of Israel, just as this potter has done? says the LORD. Just like the clay in the potter's hand, so are you in my hand, O house of Israel.** [7] **At one moment I may declare concerning a nation or a kingdom, that I will pluck up and break down and destroy it,** [8] **but if that nation, concerning which I have spoken, turns from its evil, I will change my mind about the disaster that I intended to bring on it.** [9] **And at another moment I may declare concerning a nation or a kingdom that I will build and plant it,** [10] **but if it does evil in my sight, not listening to my voice, then I will change my mind about the good that I had intended to do to it.** [11] **Now, therefore, say to the people of Judah and the inhabitants of Jerusalem: Thus says the LORD: Look, I am a potter shaping evil against you and devising a plan against you. Turn now, all of you from your evil way, and amend your ways and your doings.**

[12] **But they say, "It is no use! We will follow our own plans, and each of us will act according to the stubbornness of our evil will."**

The prophet is commanded to visit a potter's house. Like the vision of the almond tree (1:11–13) or the incident when the prophet buried a loincloth (13:1–11), Jeremiah's visit is the basis of a sign-act. That is, in what God has the prophet see and do is a deeper meaning. Central to these verses are the words from Jeremiah 1:10, "pluck up and break down," "build and plant."

God instructs the prophet to visit the house of a potter and observe the potter at work. As the potter works, he sometimes decides that the emerging vessel is unsatisfactory and destroys it to begin again. The work of the potter serves as a point of departure for God's word to the prophet. The image of God as a potter is common in the Bible, for instance, in Genesis 2:7; Isaiah 29:16; 64:8; and Romans 9:20–24. Jeremiah's use of the image in this speech affirms the Lord's sovereignty over the nations. Various decisions that God might make about the nations are described. For instance, God might decide to "pluck up and break down and destroy," but then, if that nation "turns from its evil," there might be a change of mind (18:7–8). Similarly, the Lord might decide to "build and plant," but if the nation subsequently "does evil," then God might decide differently about the good intended (vv. 9–10). The comparison between the potter and the Lord is obvious. Like the potter with clay, God is sovereign over the nations, free to pluck up and tear down or build and plant as God sees fit.

Jeremiah then applies the image of God the potter directly to Judah. The prophet seems to hold out the possibility (described in v. 8) that though God has devised a plan against Judah, there is still opportunity for Judah to "turn . . . amend your ways and your doings" (v. 11; cf. 7:3, 5). Such an opportunity to repent and avoid disaster echoes the tone of the preceding passage regarding the Sabbath. However, in verse 18:12 we hear Judah reject God's offer and declare their intention to "act according to the stubbornness of our evil will." (The Hebrew word for "will" in verse 12 is the same Hebrew word translated "hearts" in Jeremiah 17:1.) The situation described is absurd, the pot resisting the intention of the potter (cf. Isa. 45:9). God's people are incapable of repentance, and God has little choice but to "pluck up and break down and destroy." God's judgment is as certain as the potter's decision to destroy a pot when the clay will not work.

Jeremiah 18:13–17

18:13 **Therefore thus says the LORD:**
     Ask among the nations:
     Who has heard the like of this?
     The virgin Israel has done
     a most horrible thing.
  14 **Does the snow of Lebanon leave**
     the crags of Sirion?
     Do the mountain waters run dry,
     the cold flowing streams?
  15 **But my people have forgotten me,**
     they burn offerings to a delusion;
     they have stumbled in their ways,
     in the ancient roads,
     and have gone into bypaths,
     not the highway,

¹⁶ **making their land a horror,**
a thing to be hissed at forever.
All who pass by it are horrified
and shake their heads.
¹⁷ **Like the wind from the east,**
I will scatter them before the enemy.
I will show them my back, not my face,
in the day of their calamity.

This passage presents a court trial in which God is the judge, God's people are the accused, and the nations are prosecution witnesses. The nations are asked if they have ever seen a thing as "horrible" as that which Judah has done (v. 13; cf. 2:9–11).

The case God brings against Judah is developed (18:14) through two questions concerned with the order of creation. God's first question asks if the snow on the mountains to Israel's north in Lebanon ever left those mountains. (The snow-capped peak of Mount Hermon, called "Sirion" in this passage, is visible from many points in northern Israel.) The second question asks if the mountain streams ever dried up. Clearly, the answer to both questions is no. The snow and the mountain streams observe the order of God's creation (cf. 8:7) and stay where they belong. The Lord presses the analogy to the Judahites, whom God charges have "forgotten me, . . . have stumbled in their ways, . . . and have gone into bypaths, not the highway" (18:15). The mountain snow and streams know where they belong, but God's people do not. The "virgin Israel" is portrayed as a prostitute hanging out on a side street. The charge is that Judah has committed idolatry by bringing offerings to "a delusion," to the fertility gods.

It seems likely that some parallel is intended with the preceding passage. The snow and streams do not dispute where they belong any more than a pot argues with the potter about its destiny. Yet, the people resist their Sovereign and wander after idols, hopelessly lost as they act "according to the stubbornness of [their] evil will" (v. 12). Judah belongs with God but refuses that relationship.

At the conclusion of this speech (vv. 16–17), God announces the sentence that is to be executed. The use of the word *horror* (v. 16) echoes the covenant curses of Deuteronomy 28:25 and 37. God's judgment is also presented as an east wind. (An east wind in Judah came from the desert and brought harsh conditions.) At the exodus, it was through an east wind that God delivered Israel from Egypt (Exod. 14:21). It will be different this time, for by an east wind God threatens to "scatter them [Judah] before the enemy." Finally, God declares, "I will show them my back, not my face"

(Jer. 18:17). In ancient Israel, God's face was associated with God's gracious presence and saving help (see Num. 6:24–26; Ps. 27:8–9), but when God's face was hidden, trouble followed (see Pss. 13:1; 30:7; 44:24; 88:14). God intends life for Judah, but they have chosen death by acting "according to the stubbornness of [their] evil will" (Jer. 18:12). The curse and death of exile loom.

The section of the book of Jeremiah that began at chapter 17 holds together different dimensions of being human before God. One dimension of the human situation recognized in these verses is the power of sin, how the human will is engraved with sin and we humans are held as slaves to sin (17:1–2; 18:12; cf. Gal. 4:3, 8). As persons enslaved to sin, we in the church need God to act to set us free as we affirm what God has done in Jesus Christ (see Gal. 4:4–7; cf. Jer. 31:31–34). The other dimension of the human situation, particularly evident in the verses just discussed, is that humans are responsible for their actions and held accountable by God. As Christians freed from sin's power, we are responsible for our actions and accountable before God when we choose to "follow our own plans" (Jer. 18:12). Having been freed from the power of sin, we are free to embrace the blessing and life God intends for us, free for fresh obedience to God:

> For you were called to freedom, brothers and sisters; only do not use your freedom as an opportunity for self-indulgence, but through love become slaves to one another. (Gal. 5:13–14)

Jeremiah 18:18–23

As the book unfolds, Jeremiah's announcement of God's harsh and seemingly irrevocable judgment is connected to a plot against the prophet's life (v. 18; but see v. 23). The plotters described in verse 18 represent the Jerusalem leadership of Judah with their various functions: the priests who were responsible for instructing Judah in what it meant to be God's people; the wise who gave counsel to the political leadership; and prophets who interpreted God's will for the present day, though surely the prophets meant here did so with a much more optimistic message than Jeremiah's (see comment on Jeremiah 28, pp. 216–20). Those in power in Jerusalem are presented in verse 18 as working together against Jeremiah. In Hebrew, the phrase translated by the NRSV as "bring charges against him" is actually more harsh, something like "strike him with the tongue." His adversaries plan a public repudiation of Jeremiah that will discredit him.

In response to this plot, Jeremiah again turns to God. Verse 20 is the heart of his complaint. Jeremiah argues that he sought "good" (used twice in this verse) for Judah and attempted to turn away God's wrath. His "rec-ompense" is a plot against his life, total rejection. To hear these verses as the prophet's complaint is the obvious way to read them. Yet, we need to remember that when Jeremiah speaks, he speaks for God; so it is possible that in this complaint we hear not only Jeremiah's distress but also God's. It is quite possible that God wonders, too, "Is evil recompense for good?" (v. 20; cf. 15:11). God, too, tries to find a way around "wrath," but the invi-tation for Judah to "turn" (18:11) is met with the response, "It is no use!" (18:12). The plot and prayer of these verses can apply equally to God and the prophet. The plot signals a rejection of the prophet and the Lord who sent him. The prayer expresses the prophet's despair but likewise can express the despair of God, for whom the prophet speaks.

God's response to this situation is indicated toward the end of this prayer. The expression "famine . . . sword . . . pestilence," which occurs in verse 21, echoes a theme introduced earlier (14:11). These verses express how Jeremiah hopes God will deal with those who plot against him. They have rejected God and God's prophet, and the Lord should reject them; they have sought the death of God's prophet, and they should die. Yet, whatever is to occur with the plotters is left to God. The prophet does not act to revenge himself on those who have plotted against him.

Chapter 18 begins with God's plan for Judah's judgment and ends with Judah's plot against Jeremiah. God has a "plan for evil" against Judah but is willing to forgo the plan if Judah will "turn" (v. 11). God's people respond by rejecting the possibility that God might yet build and plant as they say, "We will follow our own plans" (v. 12). At the end of the chap-ter, we glimpse the kind of plan Judah has in mind, as they "make plots" against Jeremiah (vv. 18ff.). The judgments urged at the conclusion of Jeremiah's prayer (vv. 21–23) provide a vision of God's plucking up and breaking down (v. 7). Once more, Judah is portrayed as rejecting an oppor-tunity to repent, rejecting God's prophet, rejecting God. The plot against Jeremiah moves Judah closer to curse, death, and exile.

Jeremiah 19:1–15

19:1 **Thus said the LORD: Go and buy a potter's earthenware jug. Take with you some of the elders of the people and some of the senior priests, ² and go out to the valley of the son of Hinnom at the entry of the Potsherd Gate, and proclaim there the words that I tell you. ³ You shall say: Hear the word of the LORD, O kings of Judah and inhabitants of Jerusalem. Thus says the LORD of hosts, the God of Israel: I am going to bring such disaster upon this** place that the ears of everyone who hears of it will tingle. ⁴ Because the people have forsaken me, and have profaned this place by making offerings in it to other gods whom neither they nor their ancestors nor the kings of Judah have known; and because they have filled this place with the blood of the innocent, ⁵ and gone on building the high places of Baal to burn their children in the fire as burnt offerings to Baal, which I did not command or decree, nor did it enter my mind; ⁶ Therefore the days are surely coming, says the LORD, when this place shall no more be called Topheth, or the valley of the son of Hinnom, but the valley of Slaughter. ⁷ And in this place I will make void the plans of Judah and Jerusalem, and will make them fall by the sword before their enemies, and by the hand of those who seek their life. I will give their dead bodies for food to the birds of the air and to the wild animals of the earth. ⁸ And I will make this city a horror, a thing to be hissed at; everyone who passes by it will be horrified and will hiss because of all its disasters. ⁹ And I will make them eat the flesh of their sons and the flesh of their daughters, and all shall eat the flesh of their neighbors in the siege, and in the distress with which their enemies and those who seek their life afflict them.

¹⁰ Then you shall break the jug in the sight of those who go with you, ¹¹ and shall say to them: Thus says the LORD of hosts: So will I break this people and this city, as one breaks a potter's vessel, so that it can never be mended. In Topheth they shall bury until there is no more room to bury. ¹² Thus will I do to this place, says the LORD, and to its inhabitants, making this city like Topheth. ¹³ And the houses of Jerusalem and the houses of the kings of Judah shall be defiled like the place of Topheth—all the houses upon whose roofs offerings have been made to the whole host of heaven, and libations have been poured out to other gods.

¹⁴ When Jeremiah came from Topheth, where the LORD had sent him to prophesy, he stood in the court of the LORD's house and said to all the people: ¹⁵ Thus says the LORD of hosts, the God of Israel: I am now bringing upon this city and upon all its towns all the disaster that I have pronounced against it, because they have stiffened their necks, refusing to hear my words.

God commands Jeremiah to perform another symbolic action. He is to shatter an earthenware jug. Most of this chapter contains a long series of accusations by God against Judah that interpret the symbolic action of breaking the jug. The themes of the chapter are familiar by this point in our reading. If one reads this chapter as a contribution to the unfolding drama of the book of Jeremiah, it strengthens the case for God's judgment of Judah. If one reads this chapter in the historical setting in which it was likely written, during the time of the Babylonian exile, one can hear a reflection about why the exile occurred, as well as a warning to future generations about the need for exclusive devotion to God.

The chapter falls into several sections. Jeremiah is instructed to buy from a potter an earthenware jug, then to take some of the priests and elders with him and go out of Jerusalem through the Potsherd Gate (probably a south gate to Jerusalem also known as the Dung Gate because it was used to haul garbage from the city) into Hinnom Valley. This valley, along with the Kidron Valley, was used as the garbage dump of ancient Jerusalem. The garbage would have included the ancient equivalent of our broken dishes, broken earthenware jugs and bowls. God then instructs the prophet to bring accusations against Judah. (The significance of the earthenware jug is picked up at verse 10.) These accusations begin and end with the charge of idolatry (vv. 4–5), and in between Jeremiah charges that "they have filled this place with the blood of the innocent" (v. 4b), an accusation of social injustice of an unspecified nature. Thus, God will bring disaster on Judah (v. 3).

These verses closely resemble Jeremiah 7 in relating social injustice and idolatry (see 7:5–9). In the ancient Near East, the power of kings came from the perception that kings were the earthly representatives of the gods. Kings, along with the priests who served them, controlled the religious rites and rituals of a society that were thought to be necessary for social well-being and security. For instance, the sacrificial rituals that priests and kings controlled were thought to appease the gods and ensure that the gods would provide rain and food. Naturally, when a king was thought to be a god's earthly envoy who was indispensable for the well-being of a society, the king's power to exploit others as he saw fit had religious justification.

By contrast, the God of Israel, known as Yahweh, was the God who freed slaves from Egypt. Yahweh opposes the power of kings to exploit the poor and marginal in society (see 1 Sam. 8:10–21). Even when Israel and Judah eventually had a king, Yahweh held kings responsible for the care of the poor (see Psalms 72, 82). Prophets like Jeremiah voiced God's concern for the poor and warned kings against exploitative actions. However, when Judah and Israel turned from Yahweh to the idols, the check on the exploitative power of kings was lost. In the common religion of the ancient Near Eastern world, gods permitted kings almost unlimited power. So, it is not surprising that Jeremiah 19, as in Jeremiah 7, idolatry is linked to the exploitation of the poor.

While our political and religious systems are no longer like those of the ancient Near Eastern world, there is a caution for us in this material. Any effort to justify political power by an appeal to religion is potentially dangerous. If a political system, party, or leader imagines that it is somehow a god's earthly agent, indispensable to the well-being and order of the world, grandiose notions of power are likely to follow. A despot such as Adolf Hitler was eager to enlist the church for his cause. Yet the exploitative possibilities when politics and religion are linked should give us caution about speaking of America as a Christian nation or the common practice of American presidents to end their speeches with a phrase like "God bless the United States of America." Religious justification for any political scheme is potentially dangerous.

In Jeremiah 19, God's accusation against Judah is developed a step further when the word *therefore* is used to specify the consequences of Judah's idolatry and social exploitation. God's speech is given in the first person ("I"). A frightening litany of the punishments God intends is presented. Many of the details of these verses reflect the covenant curses of Deuteronomy 28. (Remember that Jeremiah 11 began by announcing covenant curse, and that theme has continued through the intervening chapters.) For instance, the latter half of verse 7 reflects Deuteronomy 28:26; verse 8 reflects Deuteronomy 28:25, 37; and verse 9, Deuteronomy 28:53–54. In worshiping idols and exploiting the innocent, Judah has broken covenant with God and chosen curse, death, and exile. These verses underscore the point in horrifying detail.

Verses 10–13 interpret what it means that the prophet broke the jug as God directed. The action reflects the intention of God to "break this people and this city . . . so that it can never be mended" (v. 11). The subsequent verses elaborate this judgment. Covenant curses are evident ("they shall bury until there is no room to bury," v. 11b; cf. Deut. 28:25), though the important point is defilement (Jer. 19:13). Just as God's people have defiled the land by their worship of idols, so God will defile them. In the world of ancient Judah, the garbage heap would have been a defiled place, unclean and filled with taboo material. God announces that the land, the people, and even Jerusalem will become a defiled garbage heap (v. 12). But then, the people have already made it such by their idolatry. The chapter ends with a brief report that the prophet, unlike Judah, did and said as God commanded him (vv. 14–15).

Jeremiah 19 develops the plot of the book one more step. It is noteworthy that in this chapter there is no longer any call for repentance. It is too late for that. God has determined that the only course left is to break Judah and crush any idea they may have had that their plans (v. 7; cf. 18:12) might prevail against God. Judah chose to break covenant with God, and God intends curse, death, and exile.

Jeremiah 20:1–6

20:1 Now the priest Pashhur son of Immer, who was chief officer in the house of the LORD, heard Jeremiah prophesying these things. 2 Then Pashhur struck the prophet Jeremiah, and put him in the stocks that were in the upper Benjamin Gate of the house of the LORD. 3 The next morning when Pashhur released Jeremiah from the stocks, Jeremiah said to him, The LORD has named you not Pashhur but "Terror-all-around." 4 For thus says the LORD: I am making you a terror to yourself and to all your friends; and they shall fall by the sword of their enemies while you look on. And I will give all Judah into the hand of the king of Babylon; he shall carry them captive to Babylon, and shall kill them with the sword. 5 I will give all the wealth of this city, all its gains, all its prized belongings, and all the treasures of the kings of Judah into the hand of their enemies, who shall plunder them, and seize them, and carry them to Babylon. 6 And you, Pashhur, and all who live in your house, shall go into captivity, and to Babylon you shall go; there you shall die, and there you shall be buried, you and all your friends, to whom you have prophesied falsely.

Verse 1 links this report of the confrontation between Pashhur and Jeremiah with the prior event, the breaking of the earthenware jar, which some elders and priests were invited to witness (19:1). As the plot of the book develops from Jeremiah 19 to Jeremiah 20, Pashhur first strikes and then imprisons Jeremiah (20:2) as a result of the prophet's words and actions reported in the preceding chapter. Whether or not this sequence of events is historically accurate is difficult to know. In any case, the actions of Pashhur escalate the resistance to the prophet, and beyond the ostracism and plots reported thus far in our reading (for instance, 11:18–23, 15:10–18; 18:18–23), this chapter concerns actions taken by those in power in Judah to silence Jeremiah. Thus, the chapter contributes to the theme of Judah's unwillingness to heed God's word and gives further support to God's decision, by this point irrevocable, to exile Judah.

Jeremiah is far from silenced by Pashhur. Verses 3–6 report Jeremiah's response to Pashhur in three parts:

1. Jeremiah gives Pashhur a new name (v. 3). In the Old Testament, names and the giving of them were important in at least two ways. First, the name itself often characterized the person named or gave some clue about her or his destiny. For example, Sarah named her long-promised son Isaac, a name that played on the Hebrew word for laughter, remembering the words of Sarah at his birth, "God has brought laughter for me" (Gen. 21:6). Jacob, who stole his older brother Esau's birthright, bore a name that meant "supplanter" (Gen. 25:26). Second, the giving of names was a sign of power

and sovereignty. God's charge to the human in the garden to name the creatures of creation (Gen. 2:19–20) reflects this understanding of naming. It is likely that the Genesis 2 creation story reflected the political reality of the ancient Near Eastern world, where a conquering king would rename a sitting monarch as a sign of sovereignty (for instance, 2 Kings 23:34).

Jeremiah's renaming of Pashhur is a daring action. First, Jeremiah's action makes the claim that he has power over Pashhur, a claim that would have been clear to Pashhur but disputed by him. Jeremiah is insisting that as God's spokesperson he has authority, whether Pashhur and those in the Jerusalem establishment recognize it or not. Second, the name Jeremiah gives to Pashhur is a signal about his character. As a priest, Pashhur would have been recognized as a person important to the well-being and security of Judah. Jeremiah views Pashhur very differently. He names Pashhur "Terror-all-around," a person who will be responsible for the disaster about to befall Judah. If Pashhur hoped to silence Jeremiah, he does not succeed at all!

2. As harsh as the confrontation is between Jeremiah and Pashhur, the prophet's real interest is not in Pashhur as an individual but in how all of Judah, led by the Jerusalem leadership, has forsaken God. Verses 4–5 expand Jeremiah's condemnation of Pashhur to these wider circles: to Pashhur's friends, the Jerusalem leadership; to Jerusalem with its treasures, thought to be inviolable to foreign attack; to the whole land of Judah. Jeremiah announces that God will deliver all of these to the king of Babylon, who will dominate Judah even as Jeremiah dominates Pashhur.

3. Finally, verse 6 is again concerned with Pashhur, whose personal destiny, Jeremiah claims, will be death in exile. The priest who was to bring blessing to Judah will himself experience covenant curse, death, and exile. Interestingly, this narrative about Jeremiah and Pashhur ends with Jeremiah's accusation that Pashhur has "prophesied falsely" (v. 6; cf. the uses of "false" in Jeremiah 7 especially). Pashhur threw Jeremiah in the stocks because he judged Jeremiah's prophecy, with its threats of a Babylonian invasion, to be false and, undoubtedly, treasonous. Pashhur acts as one with authority over Jeremiah and surely thinks himself to be God's representative. Jeremiah's speech (20:3–6) counters Pashhur's claims with an alternative view. Pashhur, claims Jeremiah, is the one who is false. His optimistic prophecy about the future and security of Judah apart from covenant obedience is false. His personal authority as a priest, apart from demanding covenant obedience, is false. The entire Jerusalem-centered worldview held by Pashhur, apart from demands for covenant obedience, is false. Pashhur and those whom he represents, the leadership of Jerusalem and the people of Judah, are false. They have chosen covenant curse,

death, and exile. So, the destiny of Pashhur, "Terror-all-around," will be the destiny of all Judah.

Jeremiah 20:7–13

> 20:7 O LORD, you have enticed me,
> and I was enticed;
> you have overpowered me,
> and you have prevailed.
> I have become a laughingstock all day long;
> everyone mocks me.
> [8] For whenever I speak, I must cry out,
> I must shout, "Violence and destruction!"
> For the word of the LORD has become for me
> a reproach and derision all day long.
> [9] If I say, "I will not mention him,
> or speak any more in his name,"
> then within me there is something like a burning fire
> shut up in my bones;
> I am weary with holding it in,
> and I cannot.
> [10] For I hear many whispering:
> "Terror is all around!
> Denounce him! Let us denounce him!"
> All my close friends
> are watching for me to stumble.
> "Perhaps he can be enticed,
> and we can prevail against him,
> and take our revenge on him."
> [11] But the LORD is with me like a dread warrior;
> therefore my persecutors will stumble,
> and they will not prevail.
> They will be greatly shamed,
> for they will not succeed.
> Their eternal dishonor
> will never be forgotten.
> [12] O LORD of hosts, you test the righteous,
> you see the heart and the mind;
> let me see your retribution upon them,
> for to you I have committed my cause.
> [13] Sing to the LORD;
> praise the LORD!
> For he has delivered the life of the needy
> from the hands of evildoers.

Jeremiah's bold confrontation with Pashhur results not in a celebration by the prophet but in another lament. In Jeremiah 11–20 we gain a deep sense of the cost of prophetic service. The language through which Jeremiah addresses God in this lament (20:7) is particularly harsh and suggests deep despair.

The word *entice*, which occurs twice in the first line of Jeremiah's prayer, has two important meanings in the Old Testament. One sense of the word implies deception; that is, to be enticed is to be naive, inexperienced, and easily misled. The word is used in Deuteronomy to speak of being "deceived" or misled to worship other gods (11:16); in 1 Kings, a speech that misleads King Ahab to engage in a foolish battle is called "enticing" (22:20–21); and in Proverbs the word for "entice" is used to describe a person who leads others astray (Prov. 16:29). One charge that Jeremiah brings against God in this prayer is that God has deceived him, misled him, or taken advantage of Jeremiah's naïveté. He was, after all, only a "boy" when God called him to be a prophet (1:6–7; cf. Jeremiah's response to the plots against him in 11:19).

Entice has a second, more ominous sense in the Old Testament: to seduce. In the legal code in Exodus, the word is used to describe the seduction of a virgin (Exod. 22:16–17; cf. Job 31:9). A woman may seduce or entice a man by her beauty (Judg. 14:15). In Hosea, this word, translated as "allure," is used to speak of God's approach to Israel (2:14). In Jeremiah 20:7, the word *entice* is used with the word *overpower*, which has a more violent connotation and suggests rape (see Deut. 22:25–27; 2 Sam. 13:14).

The sense of Jeremiah's address to God is that God has taken advantage of him. Called to God's service while still a "boy," Jeremiah charges that God took advantage of his innocence. He did not know what he was in for. More ominously, Jeremiah charges that God seduced him or "overpowered" him (20:7). The issue Jeremiah raises is the condition under which he serves God. His accusation is that he is no longer serving as God's spokesperson of his own will but is forced by God into service. Concern for Jeremiah's call or vocation is an important issue in the remainder of this chapter.

The overall theme of these verses is carried by a word from verse 7, *prevailed*. In Jeremiah's address to God, the prophet acknowledges that God has "prevailed" over him. The manner in which God has "prevailed" over the prophet is specified in verses 8–9. God compels Jeremiah to speak a word of "violence and destruction" (v. 8), which causes the prophet to become a "laughingstock" whom everyone mocks (v. 7). Further, whenever Jeremiah decides he will not speak God's word anymore, something burns within him; he concludes, "I am weary with holding it in, and I cannot" (v. 9). The word translated "cannot" in the NRSV is the same Hebrew word translated as "prevail" in verse 7. Jeremiah cannot prevail against God.

Because God has prevailed over Jeremiah and the prophet constantly speaks of destruction and violence, he has become an object of derision in the community. Jeremiah hears "whispering" against him: "Perhaps he can be enticed, and we can prevail against him" (v. 10). On the one side, God entices and prevails over the prophet; on the other side, the community to which Jeremiah announces God's word also hopes to entice and prevail over him. This prayer of Jeremiah brings to painful expression how Jeremiah is caught in the middle between God and the people of Judah. The weight of the prophetic office for Jeremiah is profound.

Yet, in recognizing Jeremiah's anguish over his circumstances, we are led to hear in these verses more than a painful human biography. In the anguish of Jeremiah, God's spokesperson, we also hear God's anguish over Judah. If Jeremiah is mocked because of his message of doom, then God's resolve to judge Judah is also mocked. If the community believes that they can prevail against Jeremiah, then the community also believes that they can prevail against God's decision to hold Judah accountable. If Judah denounces Jeremiah, they also denounce God. The plot of the book of Jeremiah has taken us to a low moment in the prophet's life, but also to a low moment in God's relationship with Judah.

The tone of Jeremiah's prayer becomes more confident at verse 11. A shift in tone from despair to confidence is typical of prayers of complaint or lament in the Old Testament (note, for example, the shift in Psalm 22 between verses 8 and 9). The prophet expresses confidence that God, "like a dread warrior," will protect him, and his persecutors will "not prevail" (v. 11). The claim that God sees "the heart and the mind" develops the concern of the book for the heart of Judah that was noted in earlier material (20:12; see 17:1, 5, 9–10; 18:12; cf. 4:4, 14). Jeremiah 20:11–13 strongly affirms God's sovereignty. Jeremiah prays to express ultimate confidence about his own well-being. Finally, in verse 13 the prayer becomes a song of praise to God. The past-tense verb in the second half of verse 13 ("he has delivered the life of the needy") is a way to express confidence; the Lord's future action is spoken of as if it has already happened. However, the affirmation of God's sovereignty needs to be understood more broadly than just applying to the protection of Jeremiah. In the unfolding plot of the book, the affirmation of God's sovereignty in verses 11–13 counters Judah's mockery of God through the prophet. Judah may doubt that

God will bring "violence and destruction," but God, the dread warrior who knows Judah's heart and mind, will surely prevail.

Jeremiah 20:14–18

20:14 **Cursed be the day**
on which I was born!
The day when my mother bore me,
let it not be blessed!

15 **Cursed be the man**
who brought the news to my father, saying,
"A child is born to you, a son,"
making him very glad.

16 **Let that man be like the cities**
that the LORD overthrew without pity;
let him hear a cry in the morning
and an alarm at noon,

17 **because he did not kill me in the womb;**
so my mother would have been my grave,
and her womb forever great.

18 **Why did I come forth from the womb**
to see toil and sorrow,
and spend my days in shame?

After Jeremiah's bold expression of confidence in verses 11–13, verse 14 shifts again to a tone of deep despair. The prophet curses the day of his birth, that is, his very existence (see 15:10, where there is a similar concern). At issue is the prophet's call to serve God, which was recounted in 1:4–10. Jeremiah was "consecrated" and "appointed" a prophet by God "in the womb" (1:5). But having experienced the cost of God's prophetic service, Jeremiah wishes that his mother's womb had been his grave. These verses express a troubling notion. Jeremiah imagines that it would have been better if he had never lived.

In his despair, Jeremiah raises the question about the "why" of his life: "Why did I come forth from the womb?" (20:18). The options Jeremiah proposes are pessimistic and reflect what he experiences as God's spokesperson: "toil and sorrow, . . . shame." However, the narrative in Jeremiah 1 about the prophet's call remembers why he had "come forth from the womb" differently. Jeremiah was to be "a prophet to the nations" (1:5). He was to go where God sent him and speak what God told him, confident that God would deliver him (1:7–8). He was to be the spokesperson for God, announcing the Lord's word of plucking up and pulling down, building and planting (1:9–10). The question with which Jeremiah concludes his prayer draws us deep into the tensions the prophet experiences. To "come forth from the womb" to be God's spokesperson is also to "come forth from the womb" to experience toil, sorrow, and shame.

Jeremiah's assessment is that his life is "cursed" and the messenger of his birth should also be "cursed" (20:14, 15). In Jeremiah 11, God announces that anyone who does not "heed the word of this covenant" will be cursed, and subsequent chapters have given numerous indications that Judah has violated covenant and chosen covenant curse. In Jeremiah 17, the theme of blessing and curse is again evident. Those who "trust in mere mortals" are pronounced "cursed," whereas those "whose trust is the Lord" are called "blessed" (17:5–8). Again, subsequent material emphasizes that Judah has trusted in "mere mortals" and chosen curse, death, and exile. In the verses before us, Jeremiah views himself as "cursed." That is, Jeremiah fully identifies with Judah and shares the destiny of Judah: curse and, eventually, exile (cf. 15:13–14).

In Jeremiah 20, verses 7–13 and 14–18 are complementary and present the two-sided character of Jeremiah's prophetic vocation. Verses 7–13 stress Jeremiah's relationship with God. On the one hand, the prophet is mocked by Judah because he speaks the word of the Lord; on the other hand, Jeremiah trusts God to deliver him. Verses 14–18 stress Jeremiah's identity with God's people as one who shares with them the covenant curse and the sorrow and shame that Judah will experience with God's judgment.

Jeremiah 20 gives anyone who aspires to a "prophetic ministry" much to consider. Often in the church today, ministry that is called prophetic is carried out by persons who position themselves outside or even above those *against* whom their ministry is directed. Thus, these modern prophets, in their critique of church and society, identify themselves as the voice and personification of God's righteous will over against persons who have forsaken God. Quite properly, prophetic ministry does involve a critique of the church for sharing too much in the values of the broader culture. For instance, the church is called to account for being too concerned with financial security, for being too invested in beautiful buildings, for being too much an exclusive club for people who are much alike. Similarly, prophetic ministry properly involves a critique of the church for having too little concern for social justice. A more faithful church, those who would be modern prophets argue, would be more concerned than is presently the case for the poor, for economic relations between first- and third-world countries, with issues such as ageism, racism, or sexism. Such critiques of church and society are integral to the prophetic task, and we have seen how Jeremiah engaged in such critique.

However, what we learn about being a prophet from the book of Jeremiah, and from Jeremiah 20 in particular, are the complex relationships and tensions in which a prophet lives. Jeremiah identifies with God's righteous will but also with God's anguish at being rejected and mocked. Prophetic ministry for Jeremiah is to voice and personify not only God's righteous will but God's deep pain at being rejected by the people. As a Jewish scholar has noted of Jeremiah, "What convulsed the prophet's whole being was God. His condition was a state of suffering in sympathy with the divine pathos" (Heschel, *Prophets*, p. 118). Further, Jeremiah relates to Judah not as some outside critic but as one of God's people who himself struggles to trust God, who dislikes announcing "violence and destruction," who intercedes with God on behalf of Judah, and who finally knows he will share Judah's destiny of curse and exile. Prophetic ministry is about more than critique. It also knows that one has "come forth from the womb" to bear with God and the people sorrow, toil, and shame. Prophets in the tradition of Jeremiah are recognized not just by the sharpness of their critiques but by the depth of their suffering with God and for God's people.

"I Am Setting Before You the Way of Life and the Way of Death"
(Jeremiah 21–25)

Judah has chosen covenant curse, death, and exile. Jeremiah 11–20 presents the prophet making this accusation in a variety of ways, but always to the same point: Judah has broken covenant, so God is directing Judah's history toward the exile. Jeremiah 21–25 continues the theme of covenant curse. Jeremiah is portrayed speaking for God to offer Judah the choice of life and death (21:8). Of course, this is the choice that is always before God's people. The book of Deuteronomy remembers Moses saying to Israel at the edge of the promised land:

> See, I have set before you today life and prosperity, death and adversity. If you obey the commandments of the LORD your God that I am commanding you today, . . . then you shall live and become numerous, and the LORD your God will bless you in the land that you are entering to possess. But if your heart turns away and you do not hear, but are led astray to bow down to other gods and serve them, I declare to you today that you shall perish; you shall not live long in the land that you are crossing the Jordan to enter and possess. I call heaven and earth to witness against you today that I have set before you life and death, blessings and curses. Choose life . . . so that you may live in the land that the LORD swore to give to your ancestors, to Abraham, to Isaac, and to Jacob. (Deut. 30:15–20)

In this passage, life obviously does not just refer to biological life but is about being in relationship with God. Life in relationship with God leads to "prosperity," blessing, and well-being, which for Israel are connected with the promised land. Israel understood life to be a gift from God, but life also involved the human choice of obeying God. By contrast, death was the result of a broken relationship with God and resulted in "adversity," particularly the loss of the land. Death was not merely the biological cessation of life but was to be cut off from God by having chosen to worship other gods.

With Babylon looming on the horizon, Jeremiah holds before Judah once again the challenge of Moses: Choose life, God's blessing, long life in the land. In Jeremiah 21–25, Jeremiah confronts Judah, its kings, and its prophets with the choice of life or death. However, in these chapters the choice between life and death is confusing for Judah. Judah thinks they are choosing life by resisting Babylon, but Jeremiah calls this choice death. Jeremiah claims that to surrender to Babylon is life; but such a choice seems like death to most in Judah (Jeremiah 21). The luxury in which Judah's kings live seems like blessing and life to them; Jeremiah sees the unjust ways of kings as the reason for their wealth that will lead to their death (Jer. 22:13–19). Those who escaped the exile to Babylon surely thought themselves good and blessed by God, but Jeremiah calls those exiled "good figs" (Jeremiah 24). Finally, Jeremiah concludes, "Because you have not obeyed my words, I am going to send for all the tribes of the north . . . even King Nebuchadrezzar of Babylon" (Jer. 25:8–9). Judah chooses death, so God directs Judah's history toward captivity in Babylon (1:3).

The conclusion of Jeremiah 25 concerns God's judgment of the nations. Jeremiah is God's prophet to the nations (1:10). God is sovereign not only over Judah but over all the nations, which are held accountable by God.

Jeremiah 21:1–10

21:1 **This is the word that came to Jeremiah from the LORD, when King Zedekiah sent to him Pashhur son of Malchiah and the priest Zephaniah son of Maaseiah, saying,** 2 **"Please inquire of the LORD on our behalf, for King Nebuchadrezzar of Babylon is making war against us; perhaps the LORD will perform a wonderful deed for us, as he has often done, and will make him withdraw from us."**

3 **Then Jeremiah said to them:** 4 **Thus you shall say to Zedekiah: Thus says the LORD, the God of Israel: I am going to turn back the weapons of war that are in your hands and with which you are fighting against the king of Babylon and against the Chaldeans who are besieging you outside the walls; and I will bring them together into the center of this city.** 5 **I myself will fight against you with outstretched hand and mighty arm, in anger, in fury, and in great wrath.** 6 **And I will strike down the inhabitants of this city, both human beings and animals; they shall die of a great pestilence.** 7 **Afterward, says the LORD, I will give King Zedekiah of Judah, and his servants, and the people in this city—those who survive the pestilence, sword, and famine—into the hands of King Nebuchadrezzar of Babylon, into the hands of their enemies, into the hands of those who seek their lives. He shall strike them down with the edge of the sword; he shall not pity them, or spare them, or have compassion.**

> [8] And to this people you shall say: Thus says the LORD: See, I am setting before you the way of life and the way of death. [9] Those who stay in this city shall die by the sword, by famine, and by pestilence; but those who go out and surrender to the Chaldeans who are besieging you shall live and shall have their lives as a prize of war. [10] For I have set my face against this city for evil and not for good, says the LORD: it shall be given into the hands of the king of Babylon, and he shall burn it with fire.

This story about Zedekiah and Jeremiah introduces the next several chapters and illustrates Judah's confusion about what it means to choose life or death. What Jeremiah calls life, the people see as death, and vice versa.

Verses 1–2 indicate the occasion for the speeches of Jeremiah that follow. King Zedekiah sends a young prince named Pashhur (who happens to have the same name as the priest who imprisoned Jeremiah in the prior chapter 20) and a priest, Zephaniah, to visit Jeremiah. These two are to "inquire" of the Lord through Jeremiah, that is, to seek guidance through the prophet (v. 2). There are clues that allow us to date this event. Zedekiah was made king of Judah after Babylon had looted Jerusalem and taken an initial group of captives to Babylon in 597 B.C. These verses indicate that Babylon was again besieging Jerusalem, so this event must have occurred just before the final fall of Jerusalem in 587 B.C.

Zedekiah instructs his envoys to ask Jeremiah about God's intentions for Judah at the hands of Babylon. He hopes the Lord will "perform a wonderful deed" and make Nebuchadrezzar withdraw (v. 2). Zedekiah's reference to God's wonderful deeds is a way to speak of how God acted throughout the history of Judah and Israel to save or deliver the people from peril. Particularly, God's deliverance of Israel from Egypt is remembered as one of God's "wonders" (Exod. 3:20; 15:11). However, the numerous references to God's wonders in the Psalms suggest the term was broadly used to describe God's unexpected rescue of persons (Pss. 9:1; 26:7; 86:10). Zedekiah hopes that Jeremiah will announce God's rescue of Judah from Babylon, which threatens at the walls of Jerusalem.

The initial response to Zedekiah's inquiry is reported in verses 3–7. Through Jeremiah, God dashes the hopes of Zedekiah. Instead of a "wonderful deed" of rescue, Jeremiah announces, God will turn Judah's weapons against them, and God will "bring together into the center of this city" the Babylonians. The idea that the Babylonians will invade Judah counters a central belief of the leaders of Judah, who think that God established Jerusalem and thereby guaranteed its security forever (remember Jeremiah 7; cf. 2 Samuel 7). With Jerusalem threatened, King Zedekiah expects God's help, and it is shocking to hear Jeremiah announce that rather than protecting Jerusalem, God is giving the city to the Babylonians.

The phrase "outstretched hand and mighty arm" (v. 6) is used in the Old Testament, especially in the book of Deuteronomy, to describe how God acted to free Israel from slavery in Egypt: Exod. 6:6; Deut. 4:34; 5:15; 7:19; 9:29; 11:2; 26:8; Ps. 136:12. Jeremiah's response to Zedekiah indicates that God's "outstretched hand and mighty arm," once used to perform the "wonderful deed" of exodus deliverance, will be outstretched to bring judgment on Judah. The Lord used an outstretched hand and a mighty arm that Israel might have life and blessing in the promised land. However, they have chosen curse and death, so God's outstretched hand and mighty arm will be used to effect the loss of the land.

God's response to Zedekiah concludes in verses 8–10. Throughout the history of Judah and Israel, and in the present situation, too, God has set before Israel "the way of life and the way of death" (v. 8; cf. Deut. 30:15–20, quoted above). However, with Babylon besieging Jerusalem, Jeremiah and Zedekiah understand differently what the choice of "life" or "death" entails. Zedekiah's inquiry to Jeremiah indicates that he thinks life will mean deliverance from Babylon and that surrender to Babylon will mean death. Through Jeremiah God announces that to resist Babylon is death because Babylon is to be the agent of Judah's judgment; life is to surrender to Babylon. God turns Zedekiah's expectations upside down. With Babylon at the gates of Jerusalem, God sets before Judah "the way of life and the way of death," but to Zedekiah, what God calls life seems like death.

Jesus' call to discipleship also involves an upside-down view of life and death:

> He called the crowd with his disciples, and said to them, "If any want to become my followers, let them deny themselves and take up their cross and follow me. For those who want to save their life will lose it, and those who lose their life for my sake, and for the sake of the gospel, will save it. For what will it profit them to gain the whole world and forfeit their life? (Mark 8:34–36)

To be a disciple of Jesus is to surrender to God, to be willing to lose one's life for the sake of Jesus and the gospel. By contrast, those "who want to save their life" risk losing it. Disciples always stand before the Lord like Zedekiah before Jeremiah, needing to learn what it means to choose life or death.

Jeremiah 21:11–14

21:11 To the house of the king of Judah say: Hear the word of the LORD,
   12 O house of David! Thus says the LORD:
   Execute justice in the morning,
   and deliver from the hand of the oppressor
   anyone who has been robbed,
   or else my wrath will go forth like fire,
   and burn, with no one to quench it,
   because of your evil doings.
   13 See, I am against you, O inhabitant of the valley,
   O rock of the plain,

                                                    says the LORD;

   you who say, "Who can come down against us,
   or who can enter our places of refuge?"
   14 I will punish you according to the fruit of your doings,

                                                    says the LORD;

   I will kindle a fire in its forest,
   and it shall devour all that is around it.

These verses are part of a larger section concerned with the kings of Judah (21:11–23:8). Through Jeremiah, God calls Judah's kings, kings of the "house of David," to "execute justice" and deliver from oppressors any who have been robbed (21:12). Robbery did not so much mean an armed holdup as the economic exploitation of the weak by the privileged, a frequent concern of Jeremiah (see 5:26–28; 8:10). Martin Luther interpreted the commandment "You shall not steal" in a manner that captures the sense of "robbery" in Jeremiah 20:12:

> If when you meet a poor man who must live from and to mouth, you act as if everyone must live by your favor, you skin and scrape him right down to the bone, and you arrogantly turn him away whom you ought to give aid, he will cry to heaven. Beware of this, I repeat, as of the devil himself. Such a man's cries will be no joking matter. They will have an effect too heavy for you and all the world to bear, for they will reach God, who watches over the poor, sorrowful hearts, and he will not leave them unavenged. But if you despise and defy this, see whom you have brought upon yourself. (From "Ten Commandments," *Large Catechism*, pp. 397–98)

Ancient Israel's most important memory was that God delivered Israel from the power of an exploitative king, Pharaoh of Egypt (see Exod. 3:7ff.). The kings of Judah and Israel had as one of their primary responsibilities God's concern for the protection of the poor from exploitation:

> Give the king your justice, O God,
>   and your righteousness to a king's son.
> May he judge your people with righteousness,
>   and your poor with justice. . . .
> May he defend the cause of the poor of the people,
>   give deliverance of the needy,
>   and crush the oppressor.
>
> (Ps. 72:1–2, 4, 12–14)

Jeremiah calls Judah's kings to be responsible for justice or face God's wrath (21:12). The choice Jeremiah presents to Judah's kings resembles the choice God offered Judah in Jeremiah 4:1–4: Judah could fulfill God's purpose in calling Abraham, to be a blessing to the nations, or face God's wrath, which would burn like fire. Judah's kings are to be God's agents of justice to protect the poor, or they will face God's judgment.

In 21:13, Jeremiah quotes Judah's kings who said, "Who can come down against us, or who can enter our places of refuge?" The assumption of Judah's kings is that they are guaranteed security by God. The kings of Judah ("the house of David," v. 12) believe that God's promises to King David ensure their well-being and place forever (2 Sam. 7:12–17). Judah's kings have taken God's promise to David of "forever" very seriously. Of course, such open-ended job security can significantly diminish one's sense of responsibility and accountability, and that seems to have happened to Judah's kings. They heard God's "forever" but not God's expectations that kings protect the poor and are accountable before God. Through Jeremiah, God announces a perspective about the responsibilities of Judah's kings that the kings do not share. While Judah's kings perceive that they are secure "forever," God declares, "I will punish you according to the fruit of your doings" (21:14).

Judah's kings are called to be the agents of God's justice in the world, and God announces that they will be judged by the "fruit of their doings." We are reminded of John the Baptist, who, in heralding the advent of God's Messiah (Christ), similarly called those who came to him for baptism to "bear fruits worthy of repentance" (Luke 3:7–14, esp. v. 8). Judah's kings were to be agents of God's justice in Judah just as Christians are called to bear the good fruit of those who have submitted to God's reign. As John the Baptist is remembered in Luke's Gospel (likely reflecting the time and circumstances of Luke's church), he makes specific what it means to "bear good fruit": for the affluent with two coats, it means to share a coat with those who have none; for tax collectors prone to collect too much and enrich themselves, it means to deal fairly in their collections; for soldiers prone to abuse their power, it means to refrain from extortion. The challenge to which we are called in our own time and place by both Jeremiah and John the Baptist is to bear good fruit, to act for the well-being of our brothers and sisters by what we do personally and by how we participate in processes, such as voting, that shape social policy.

Jeremiah 22:1–9

Verses 1–5 reiterate the message to the kings of Judah from the preceding verses. In addition to the admonition to "act with justice and righteousness" and deliver from their oppressors those who have been robbed (v. 3), Jeremiah demands Judah's kings "do no wrong or violence" to widows, aliens, and orphans (v. 3; cf. Jeremiah 7).

The prophet's message to Judah's kings offers conditional terms. "If" they obey God's word, Jeremiah promises, then the kings will continue in power (v. 4). "If" Judah's kings do not obey God's word, however, then "this house" (that is, "the house of David") will become a "desolation" (v. 5). The threat of "desolation" of the land by a "foe from the north" whom God would send occurred earlier in the book of Jeremiah (4:27; 6:8; 9:11; 10:22; 12:11). Verses 7–8 suggest what God's desolation of the house of David will mean.

Both Gilead and "the summit of Lebanon" were heavily wooded areas in Jeremiah's time. In verse 7, "choicest cedars" refers to Jerusalem (the Temple and king's palace), which Solomon built with cedars from Lebanon (1 Kings 5:7–12). God's judgment of Judah's kings will be dire. The house of the kings of Judah (Jerusalem, or more particularly, the king's palace)—built thick with cedar, like the forests of Gilead and Lebanon—will be burned by "destroyers," and the city will become like a desert. Judah's kings heard God's promise to David as unconditional, "forever" (21:13; see discussion above). Through this speech, God's declaration "I will punish you according to the fruit of your doings" (21:14), is reinforced.

This speech concludes with a portrayal of the consequences of God's judgment (22:8–9). The nations will pass by and wonder why the Lord destroyed Jerusalem (cf. the covenant curse of Deut. 28:25, "You shall become an object of horror to all the kingdoms of the earth"), but they will then answer their own question. Even the nations will recognize that Jerusalem's destruction indicates Judah's violation of covenant by worshiping other gods. Judah's kings assume God has promised the house of David life and blessing forever. God announces to Judah's kings that they have broken covenant and chosen curse and death in a way that is so evident even the nations will understand their desolation.

Jeremiah 22:10–12

These three verses illustrate the prophet's point that God will not guarantee the monarchy "forever" and is free to bring it to an end. Though these verses were likely pieced together by later editors of the book of Jeremiah, as they stand in the book, Jeremiah is the speaker. He speaks of the great king Josiah, who died in a battle with Egypt (see pp. 13–14), and of Josiah's son, Shallum (his personal name), who briefly succeeded his father as king. Shallum, whose throne name was Jehoahaz, was king only three months before the Egyptians, who had defeated his father, Josiah, deposed him and took him to Egypt, where he died. In verse 10, Josiah is the king "who is dead"; Shallum (Jehoahaz) is the king "who goes away."

Jeremiah's point is made by the triple repetition of a nearly identical phrase: "he shall return no more" (v. 10); "he shall return here no more" (v. 11); "he shall never see this land again" (v. 12). Jeremiah's "never" contrasts with the assumption that Judah's monarchy is "forever." God can and will allow the end of Judah's monarchy. God can and will impose covenant curse, desolation, and exile. God can and will judge Judah and its monarchs by the fruit of their doings, by their obedience of the covenant. There are no guarantees of "forever."

Jeremiah 22:13–19

22:13 Woe to him who builds his house by unrighteousness,
and his upper rooms by injustice;
who makes his neighbors work for nothing,
and does not give them their wages;
14 who says, "I will build myself a spacious house
with large upper rooms,"
and who cuts out windows for it,
paneling it with cedar,
and painting it with vermilion.
15 Are you a king
because you compete in cedar?
Did not your father eat and drink
and do justice and righteousness?
Then it was well with him.
16 He judged the cause of the poor and needy;
then it was well.
Is not this to know me?
                                        says the LORD.
17 But your eyes and heart
are only on your dishonest gain,

for shedding innocent blood,
and for practicing oppression and violence.
¹⁸ Therefore thus says the LORD concerning King Jehoiakim son of
Josiah of Judah:
They shall not lament for him, saying,
"Alas, my brother!" or "Alas, sister!"
They shall not lament for him, saying,
"Alas, lord!" or "Alas, his majesty!"
¹⁹ With the burial of a donkey he shall be buried—
dragged off and thrown out beyond the gates of Jerusalem.

In this speech, Jeremiah contrasts the reign of Josiah with that of his son Jehoiakim. Jehoiakim was installed by Egypt (after they deposed and exiled Jehoahaz) to succeed Josiah. During Jehoiakim's reign, which began in approximately 609 B.C., Judah was a vassal, first of Egypt, and then of Babylon after 605 B.C. (2 Kings 23:31–35).

Jeremiah uses funeral imagery to condemn Jehoiakim. Prophets often used funeral imagery in speeches of judgment or condemnation (for instance, Isa. 10:5; or Amos 5:1–3). Jeremiah's speech begins with the cry "Woe . . . " (22:13), which announces a death and the beginning of a time of mourning. The prophet concludes his speech by imagining the public rites of mourning for Jehoiakim (vv. 18–19), and again the word for "Woe" is used (translated in v. 18 in the NRSV as "Alas"). In describing Jehoiakim's death, Jeremiah imagines that he will be left unburied and dishonored. However, the core of Jeremiah's speech is concerned with why Jehoiakim will die dishonored.

Jeremiah begins with a description of a royal building project (vv. 13–14). The description suggests that it was a royal palace, perhaps the king's own residence, that was being constructed or renovated. The building was luxurious, even opulent: two-storied, with spacious upper rooms, windows, cedar paneling, and vermilion paint (cf. Solomon's building projects described in 1 Kings 7). It is difficult to overestimate the effort required to build such a residence or the disparity between the residence described and the dwellings of peasants in ancient Judah.

Jeremiah places alongside the description of the grandiose building an assessment of how Jehoiakim deals with the laborers on this project. Jehoiakim "makes his neighbors work for nothing" and "does not give them their wages" (v. 13). Jehoiakim is following a common practice of kings in the ancient Near East in using forced labor to enhance his own affluence and extravagant lifestyle. Solomon, for instance, used forced labor to complete his building projects (1 Kings 5:13–18; 9:15–22). Kings assumed they were vitally important to gods, even indispensable. Thus, they imagined themselves superior to others in society and justified by their gods in using folks "under them" for their own benefit.

However, in Israel and Judah there was a different perspective on kings. God's "wonderful deed" (Jer. 21:2) most remembered by Israel was that the Lord had freed them from forced labor ("the house of slavery") under Pharaoh. Early Israel had no king (see Judg. 8:22ff.) and always remained suspicious of kings and their inclination to oppress persons (1 Sam. 8:10–18). King Jehoiakim's use of forced labor to enhance his own well-being has made Judah much like Egypt (remember Jer. 9:23–26). The kings's exploitation of his "neighbors" violates what it means to be people of God freed by the Lord from slavery in Egypt. Viewing the situation, Jeremiah concludes that Jehoiakim has built by "unrighteousness" and "injustice" (22:13). If kings are to be judged by the fruit of their doings, then it is no wonder that Jeremiah announces over Jehoiakim, "Woe . . . " an unenviable death.

Jeremiah's assessment of Jehoiakim's unrighteous and unjust practices is reinforced by the prophet's comparison of Jehoiakim with his father, King Josiah (vv. 15–17). The question is: What makes a king? Jeremiah argues that Jehoiakim and Josiah provide contrasting answers to this question. Jeremiah charges that Jehoiakim thinks he is a king because he competes in cedar (v. 15). That is, like all the other kings of his ancient Near Eastern world, he lives in considerable comfort and affluence, acquired by the back-breaking labor of his subjects. One can tell by looking that Jehoiakim is a king. By contrast, Jeremiah remembers Josiah, who did "justice and righteousness" (v. 15), who "judged the cause of the poor and needy" (v. 16) and still managed to eat and drink and live "well" (vv. 15–16). Thus, Jeremiah claims that Josiah was blessed because he embodied the values of God, who delivered Israel from slavery and expected of kings that they "defend the cause of the poor of the people, give deliverance to the needy, and crush the oppressor" (Ps. 72:4). Concern for justice, not living in opulence, makes a king. Jeremiah concludes that Jehoiakim, despite all appearances, is not a king because he practices "oppression and violence" (v. 17).

So it is not surprising that Jeremiah pronounces judgment on Jehoiakim, a judgment anticipated from the very first word of this speech, "Woe" (v. 13). Jehoiakim faces death, warns Jeremiah, but not the honorable death of Josiah (2 Kings 23:28–30), killed in battle. Jehoiakim will die, and there will be no one to lament him. Of course! He has oppressed his neighbors (Jer. 22:13), so in death they will not mourn him or honor his royal status (v. 18). Worse, warns Jeremiah, Jehoiakim will be treated like a dead donkey, dumped without burial on the garbage heap (v. 19). To die and not be buried is a covenant curse (see Deut. 28:26). Jehoiakim has acted in unrighteousness and injustice, and God will judge him according to the fruit of his doing. He chose "the way of death" (21:8), so the prophet announces his death. Judah's kings are accountable before God, as Jehoiakim will discover.

Jeremiah bases his condemnation of Jehoiakim for the king's oppressive treatment of his neighbors on an understanding of God that grew out of the exodus. However, from another perspective, Jehoiakim's actions were normal. He was a conformist who, as king of Judah, acted quite normally for a king in the ancient Near East. Regrettably for Jehoiakim, Israel's God, Yahweh, had freed slaves, society's marginalized, and disrupted the normal order of Egypt's king, Pharaoh, for the well-being of persons that ruler had held to be of no account. Israel's God demanded justice for the weakest persons in society, a standard seldom of much concern in royal circles anywhere. Kings in the ancient Near East were much like Jehoiakim in their exploitation of their subjects. Jehoiakim has done nothing out of the ordinary for a king in his time and place, but that is the problem. Jeremiah condemns Jehoiakim for his conformity.

The apostle Paul admonishes, "Do not be conformed to this world, but be transformed by the renewing of your minds, so that you may discern what is the will of God—what is good and acceptable and perfect" (Rom. 12:2). Jeremiah reminds us that we are accountable before God for a too-easy conformity to social norms. God called Jehoiakim and calls us to "break . . . with the prevailing assumptions and idolatries of the present order" and witness to God's victory in history (Wallis, *Agenda for a Biblical People*, p. 36).

Beyond the manner in which this text addresses us in the church, it also raises particular concern for how persons in political leadership are to conduct themselves and the affairs of state. As mentioned, the kings of Israel and Judah were particularly charged by God to work for justice for the poor. We have many expectations of political leaders and public officials. This text, in its wider framework in the Old Testament, suggests that a key criterion by which such political leaders should be judged is their concern for the poorest and weakest in society.

Jeremiah 22:20–23

22:20 Go up to Lebanon, and cry out,
and lift up your voice in Bashan;

> cry out from Abarim,
>   for all your lovers are crushed.
> 21 I spoke to you in your prosperity,
>   but you said, "I will not listen."
>   This has been your way from your youth,
>   for you have not obeyed my voice.
> 22 The wind shall shepherd all your shepherds,
>   and your lovers shall go into captivity;
>   then you will be ashamed and dismayed
>   because of all your wickedness.
> 23 O inhabitant of Lebanon,
>   nested among the cedars,
>   how you will groan when pangs come upon you,
>   pain as of a woman in labor!

The "pain . . . of a woman in labor" (v. 23) is irresistible and unstoppable. Jeremiah uses this image to describe God's judgment of Judah. God decided that Judah would be "ashamed and dismayed" (cf. 14:3), and by this point in Judah's history, God's judgment is irresistible and unstoppable, like a woman's labor. In these verses, Jeremiah personifies Jerusalem and then depicts God calling the city to go to the mountains that surround Jerusalem, to Lebanon, Bashan, and Abarim, to "cry out" because all her "lovers" are crushed or taken captive (22:20, 22). In other words, Jerusalem is portrayed as a lover in mourning. "Lovers" in this speech refers to the foreign allies that Judah trusted for security (see 2:33). The reason for God's judgment is that Judah has at no time (22:21, "from your youth"; cf. 2:2; 3:24) listened to or obeyed God. (Hebrew uses the same word for both "listen" and "obey.") The concerns of these verses, all familiar by this point in the book, emphasize the ways in which Judah has broken covenant and chosen "the way of death" (21:8).

There is little to help us understand the situation that occasioned this speech or the audience to whom it might have been addressed. Three features of these verses may contribute to the placement of them at this point in the book of Jeremiah:

1. In the preceding verses, Jeremiah cries woe to Jehoiakim as he foretells the king's death (22:13–19). In these verses, God orders Jerusalem to cry out over her inevitable judgment. Imagery of death and funerals connect these two speeches.

2. From Jeremiah 21:11, the various texts have concerned God's judgment of individual kings. In these verses, Jeremiah announces that "wind shall shepherd all your shepherds" (22:22). Kings were called "shepherds"

in Judah and Israel (see Ezekiel 34), so Jeremiah imagines Judah's shepherds (kings) scattered. The destiny of the king and the destiny of the people were closely bound. If the kings incurred covenant curse, the community was also cursed (cf. Psalm 72, where the blessing of the king brings blessing to the entire community). If the kings are to be scattered, so will the community be scattered.

3. The reference in 22:23 to "Lebanon, nested among the cedars" refers to Jerusalem, built of cedar by Solomon and his successors (see 21:14). Jehoiakim, remember, has been described as one who thinks he is a king because he competes in cedar (22:15). Proud Jerusalem and its kings, "nested among the cedars," will be "ashamed and dismayed."

Jeremiah 22:24–30

22:24 As I live, says the LORD, even if King Coniah son of Jehoiakim of Judah were the signet ring on my right hand, even from there I would tear you off ²⁵ and give you into the hands of those who seek your life, into the hands of those of whom you are afraid, even into the hands of King Nebuchadrezzar of Babylon and into the hands of the Chaldeans. ²⁶ I will hurl you and the mother who bore you into another country, where you were not born, and there you shall die. ²⁷ But they shall not return to the land to which they long to return.

²⁸ Is this man Coniah a despised broken pot,
a vessel no one wants?
Why are he and his offspring hurled out
and cast away in a land that they do not know?
²⁹ O land, land, land,
hear the word of the LORD!
³⁰ Thus says the LORD:
Record this man as childless,
a man who shall not succeed in his days;
for none of his offspring shall succeed
in sitting on the throne of David,
and ruling again in Judah.

These verses concern Coniah, the son of Judah's king Jehoiakim (v. 24). In Jeremiah 22:10–12, the prophet announces God's judgment on King Jehoiakim, who will be carried away captive and "return no more." Jehoiakim's end was somewhat different from what Jeremiah had imagined. Rather than being taken captive by Babylon, he died in approximately 597 B.C., just as Babylon approached Jerusalem to punish Judah because Jehoiakim had failed to pay tribute to Babylon. While Jehoiakim's last days were surely troubled with the approach of Babylon's army, he was fortunate not to live long enough to experience the judgment Jeremiah had foretold for him. Jehoiakim was succeeded by his son, King Jehoiachin, whose given name was Coniah. Jeremiah predicts for King Jehoiachin (Coniah) the same judgment he announced for his father, exile from which he will "not return" (vv. 26–27).

Many of the details of Jeremiah's speech refute the widely held notion in Judah that the king is indispensable and his place guaranteed "forever" by God. This is the point of verse 24, where the Lord declares that even if Coniah were God's "signet ring on my right hand, even from there I would tear you off." Judah's kings were considered God's earthly envoys or agents, the symbol of God's presence and authority in Judah. Never mind, Jeremiah declares, God does not need King Jehoiachin as a "signet ring"; Coniah is quite dispensable. To claim, as Jeremiah does, that Judah's king will be given into the hands of King Nebuchadrezzar of Babylon (v. 25) would have been considered blasphemous. Yet that is what Jeremiah announces as God's judgment.

In Judah it was widely held that there would always be someone on the throne of David and that the house of David would be secure "forever" (see 2 Sam. 7:16). God's judgment against Coniah is that he will be "childless . . . for none of his offspring shall succeed in sitting on the throne of David and ruling again in Judah" (Jer. 22:30). God can do without not only Coniah but also the house of David. The announcement that God would end the succession of Davidic kings with Jehoiachin would have been an enormous jolt. It would have called into question the very basis of all order and security and would have been unthinkable to most in Judah.

Yet, in this speech, Jeremiah has a larger concern than King Jehoiachin. God's judgment of Jehoiachin signals judgment on Judah as a whole. The king and people are linked. Coniah is "a despised broken pot" (v. 28), and we have already heard that Judah is also a clay pot, to be broken at God's choosing (Jeremiah 19). Further, in the thought of ancient Judah and Israel, the well-being of the land was connected with the king. In Psalm 72, this connection is presented in a positive light: The king's concern for justice will result in fertility and blessing for the land (72:1–7). In Jeremiah 22:28–30, Jehoiachin is declared to be a broken pot and childless, and this is understood to have consequences for the land. Jeremiah gives voice to God's dismay about the land, mourning it: "O land, land, land" (v. 29). The promised land was God's gift to Israel and Judah, the place where the Lord intended life and blessing for them (evident in the phrase "the land of milk and honey"). The land, like the king, was considered indispensable to

Judah. However, the land with the king is to suffer death and be lost, and though God orders the death and loss, God also mourns the land.

One of the ways in which prophets, ancient or modern, can be recognized is that they, like Jeremiah, challenge realities that we think are "givens." Most consider these givens to be indispensable and necessary for the very order of life and the world. However, prophets can perceive these givens to be oppressive realities that stifle God's hopes for well-being in the world. Luther in the sixteenth century dared to ask if the pope was indispensable to the church. Women suffragists in early-twentieth-century America dared to ask if excluding women from voting was indispensable to the country's political system. Mohandas Gandhi dared to ask if the caste system was indispensable for life in India. Peace activists since World War II have dared to ask if the so-called deterrent of massive stores of nuclear weapons among nations is necessary for world peace. Martin Luther King Jr. in the 1960s dared to ask if segregation was necessary to the social order of the United States. Who today can we identify as a contemporary prophet, who dares to ask if the realities many think indispensable for the order of the world may not be demonic, a clay pot God will shatter?

Jeremiah 23:1–8

23:1 **Woe to the shepherds who destroy and scatter the sheep of my pasture! says the LORD.** [2] **Therefore thus says the LORD, the God of Israel, concerning the shepherds who shepherd my people: It is you who have scattered my flock, and have driven them away, and you have not attended to them. So I will attend to you for your evil doings, says the LORD.** [3] **Then I myself will gather the remnant of my flock out of all the lands where I have driven them, and I will bring them back to their fold, and they shall be fruitful and multiply.** [4] **I will raise up shepherds over them who will shepherd them, and they shall not fear any longer, or be dismayed, nor shall any be missing, says the LORD.**

[5] **The days are surely coming, says the LORD, when I will raise up for David a righteous Branch, and he shall reign as king and deal wisely, and shall execute justice and righteousness in the land.** [6] **In his days Judah will be saved and Israel will live in safety. And this is the name by which he will be called: "The LORD is our righteousness."**

[7] **Therefore, the days are surely coming, says the LORD, when it shall no longer be said, "As the LORD lives who brought the people of Israel up out of the land of Egypt,"** [8] **but "As the LORD lives who brought out and led the offspring of the house of Israel out of the land of the north and out of all the lands where he had driven them." Then they shall live in their own land.**

These verses conclude the material about Judah's kings that began at Jeremiah 21:11. Jeremiah is presented as offering one final speech condemning Judah's kings (vv. 1–2) but then, in three different ways, voicing hope for Judah's future (vv. 3–4, 5–6, 7–8). The swing from severe condemnation to expectancy about Judah's future is jarring; but then, we have seen this at several places in the book. For instance, in Jeremiah 16, the prophet announces God's intention to "hurl" Judah from the land for breaking covenant (vv. 11–13). This harsh judgment is followed immediately with a passage that anticipates the days that are "surely coming" (16:14–15), at which time God's people will no longer recount the exodus from Egypt but will remember instead the deliverance from "the land of the north." God's judgment is certain and inevitable, given Judah's disobedience. However, judgment is not God's ultimate intention for Judah. God will "pluck up and break down," but then God will "build and plant" (1:10). In these eight verses opening chapter 23, we hear once more God's certain intention to "pluck up and tear down" Judah, but beyond judgment, God's ultimate intention to "build and plant."

Jeremiah's final condemnation of Judah's kings (vv. 1–2) uses the imagery of shepherds and sheep. Sheep whose shepherds do not "attend" (v. 2) to them become scattered, and the shepherds are to blame. So, Jeremiah argues, Judah will be scattered or driven away (v. 2), exiled, because Judah's kings have not been attentive; and God will hold the shepherds accountable. The judgment that is threatened plays on the word *attend*. The shepherds have "not attended" to the sheep, Judah; but God will "attend" to the shepherds for their "evil doings." While Jeremiah's accusations against Judah's kings are quite general at this point, we know from the series of passages we have just read in Jeremiah 21–22 the specific ways in which Judah's kings have failed as shepherds: They have failed to execute justice and righteousness, to deliver from the oppressor those robbed, the widow, and the alien; they have failed to judge the cause of the poor and needy, all the while seeking their own opulent comfort. Rightly, God charges that the shepherds have destroyed God's sheep (v. 1).

The use of sheep and shepherds to speak of the relationship of God's people to their leaders is common in the Bible. In the Old Testament, Ezekiel condemns Judah's kings, their shepherds, for failing to attend to God's flock in ways very similar to this passage (Ezekiel 34). In the New Testament, in the Gospel according to Mark, Jesus looks at the crowd before him with compassion because "they were like sheep without a shepherd" (6:34). The shepherds in Mark are the Pharisees and Sadducees.

The shepherds in Jeremiah, Judah's kings, scattered the flock, but such scattering is not what God intended. In 23:3–5, Jeremiah imagines a restoration of Judah in which the scattered flock will be gathered and the inattentive shepherds will be replaced. The Lord intends that the people be blessed, "be fruitful and multiply." This is God's intention for all of humanity (Gen. 1:28), but especially for God's people. God also made this promise to Abraham (Gen. 17:1–8), and it was passed from Isaac to Jacob: "May God Almighty bless you and make you fruitful and numerous, that you may become a company of peoples. May he give to you the blessing of Abraham" (Gen. 28:3–4). Despite the sheep being scattered because of inattentive shepherds, Jeremiah declares, the Lord's intention for Israel and the world is blessing, and this intention will be realized.

In Jeremiah 23:5–6, the prophet imagines the future God intends for Judah in another way. Judah's kings, charged to be agents of blessing by practicing justice and righteousness (see 21:12), instead have practiced injustice and unrighteousness (22:1–3, 13). However, in the days that are "surely coming," Jeremiah foresees a king of the house of David who will "execute justice and righteousness in the land," a "righteous Branch" for David. After plucking up and tearing down, God intends building and planting, kings who will be attentive to justice and righteousness. This vision of Judah's future is a play on the name of Judah's last king before the exile, King Zedekiah. Zedekiah's name in Hebrew means "The Lord is righteousness," but it is clear in the book of Jeremiah that the prophet did not think Zedekiah was righteous (21:1–2; cf. 34:1–6; 37–39). However, Jeremiah imagines that day when there will be a king of the house of David who will be what Zedekiah's name falsely claims, an embodiment of the Lord's righteousness.

The third vision of Judah's future that Jeremiah offers is of a new exodus. In Jeremiah 21, Zedekiah hopes that God would "perform a wonderful deed for us" and deliver Judah from Babylon. Jeremiah counters Zedekiah's false hope by indicating that God will fight against Judah with an "outstretched hand and a mighty arm," an allusion to God's exodus deliverance. In these verses in chapter 23 that imagine a time after the Babylonian exile, Jeremiah announces that God, who will scatter Judah in judgment, will also in time gather them. Then the people will no longer remember God as the one who brought Israel up from Egypt but as "the Lord . . . who brought out and led the offspring of the house of Israel out of the land of the north and out of all the lands where he had driven them" (v. 8). The decisive act for which the Lord will be remembered will be a new act of deliverance, a new exodus.

Thus, the prophet Jeremiah—or some would say, those who edited the final version of the book of Jeremiah—imagines that after God's judgment, after Judah's captivity, God will reestablish the monarchy, will rehabilitate the house of David, whose kings have played a large role in leading Judah to captivity. When we examine the history of Judah after the exile in Babylon, it is difficult to identify who might have been "for David a righteous Branch." However, we in the church confess that in the fullness of time, God did raise up a righteous Branch, Jesus of Nazareth. He was the embodiment of God's righteousness, who "has brought down the powerful from their thrones, and lifted up the lowly" (Luke 1:52); he was the one through whom God's promises to David and Abraham were fulfilled, and so the son of David and Abraham (Matt. 1:1, 17); he was, at last, the "good shepherd" who laid down his life for the sheep (John 10:1–18; cf. Matt. 2:6). Jeremiah promised that God would raise up a righteous Branch who would execute justice and righteousness. We confess that we know his name, and it is Jesus.

Jeremiah 23:9–12

23:9 **Concerning the prophets:**
My heart is crushed within me,
all my bones shake;
I have become like a drunkard,
like one overcome by wine,
because of the LORD
and because of his holy words.
10 **For the land is full of adulterers;**
because of the curse the land mourns,
and the pastures of the wilderness are dried up.
Their course has been evil,
and their might is not right.
11 **Both prophet and priest are ungodly;**
even in my house I have found their wickedness,
                                        says the LORD.
12 **Therefore their way shall be to them**
like slippery paths in the darkness,
into which they shall be driven and fall;
for I will bring disaster upon them
in the year of their punishment,
                                        says the LORD.

Jeremiah 23:9–40 focuses on Judah's prophets. However, verses 9–12 are a general indictment of the religious leaders of Judah, "both prophet and priest" (v. 11; cf. 2:8). The accusation Jeremiah makes is quite general:

They are called "ungodly" and accused of "wickedness." Subsequent material clarifies the substance of these charges.

The central point of these verses is that the failure of the religious leaders, prophets and priests, will bring covenant curse on Judah (v. 10). The land is said to be full of "adulterers" (v. 10), an image of idolatry. Jeremiah's accusation is that the prophets and priests did nothing to call Judah back from adultery to a relationship with God. Jeremiah has, of course, called God's people to "return" (see 3:12, 14; 4:1); but in the book, Jeremiah is presented as isolated, estranged, and the object of ridicule because of his prophetic activity, his call for repentance ignored.

The consequence of the adultery in the land is covenant curse so that the land will not yield crops, that is, it will no longer bring blessing. God has entrusted the land to Judah as a place of blessing, a "plentiful land" with "fruits . . . and good things" (2:7; cf. 4:26). However, Judah has chosen curse through adultery, and Jeremiah accuses the prophets and priests of participating in this "wickedness" (23:11). The land mourns because of the curse that has come upon it: Its pastures are dried up (v. 10; cf. 4:23–26; 14:1–6). As part of the flood story in Genesis 6:13, the land (earth) is described as full of violent men, and the consequence is the collapse of God's creation in the Flood. In these verses in Jeremiah 23, the prophets and priests, who should have joined Jeremiah in calling Judah to return to God, are held accountable for the loss of the land. So, Jeremiah announces God's intention to call Judah's religious leadership to account, to "bring disaster upon them" (v. 12; cf. 1:14–16). The general accusations of these verses are elaborated upon in the remainder of Jeremiah 23.

Jeremiah 23:13–15

> 23:13 **In the prophets of Samaria**
> **I saw a disgusting thing:**
> **they prophesied by Baal**
> **and led my people Israel astray.**
> 14 **But in the prophets of Jerusalem**
> **I have seen a more shocking thing:**
> **they commit adultery and walk in lies;**
> **they strengthen the hands of evildoers,**
> **so that no one turns from wickedness;**
> **all of them have become like Sodom to me,**
> **and its inhabitants like Gomorrah.**
> 15 **Therefore thus says the LORD of hosts concerning the prophets:**
> **"I am going to make them eat wormwood,**
> **and give them poisoned water to drink;**

for from the prophets of Jerusalem
ungodliness has spread throughout the land."

"The prophets of Samaria" (v. 13), prophets of the Northern Kingdom, Israel, which fell to Assyria in 722 B.C., are compared to the "prophets of Jerusalem" (v. 14), who are Jeremiah's contemporaries in Judah. The comparison is of bad to worse: In the prophets of Samaria, God saw "a disgusting thing" (v. 13), but in the prophets of Jerusalem, God declares, "I have seen a more shocking thing" (v. 14). The negative comparison of the prophets of Jerusalem with the prophets of Israel by itself leads one to a clear conclusion. God has already directed the history of the Northern Kingdom to captivity by Assyria. If the prophets of Jerusalem are worse than the prophets of Samaria, then God will undoubtedly direct the course of Judah's history to captivity as well (see 1:3). Judgment is inescapable for Judah, which has become to God like Sodom and Gomorrah (Genesis 18–19), so evil that their destruction is God's only option (Jer. 23:12; cf. 20:16; see also Isa. 1:10).

While the role of prophets in Israel and Judah is to be a corrective to the people, God's voice that calls them back to relationship, Jeremiah sees that the prophets of Israel and Judah have led God's people astray and contributed to their doom. Prophets arose in the life of ancient Israel with the institution of kingship. Kings, with their power, were likely to forget that at the core of being God's people was the Lord's gracious offer of relationship ("I am the Lord your God, who brought you out of the land of Egypt," Exod. 20:2) and demand of loyal obedience ("You shall have no other gods before [beside] me," Exod. 20:3). Kings were likely to think they could make it on their own and do as they pleased (remember Jer. 21:11–23:8 and Jeremiah's accusation against Judah's kings). Jeremiah's accusation against the prophets of Jerusalem is that they not only have failed to be the corrective voice of memory in Judah but actually have contributed to Judah's disobedience. Instead of calling the people to loyalty to God alone, they have participated in and encouraged idolatry. Jeremiah charges that Jerusalem's prophets have "prophesied by Baal," "led my people Israel astray" (23:13; cf. 8:10, where prophet and priest are accused of false dealings that contribute to unjust gain), and "strengthen[ed] the hands of evildoers" (v. 14). Read in the context of the previous material detailing the injustice and exploitation practiced by Judah's kings, the strong impression is that Judah's prophets not only have turned away from the God of exodus but have supported Judah's kings ("strengthened the hands of evildoers") in exploiting the weakest persons of Judah (see 21:12;

22:3, 13, 16–17), who were precious to the God who had brought Israel out of slavery. The judgments announced in 23:15 are expected after Jeremiah's harsh accusations.

Jeremiah accuses Judah's prophets of being voices in support of the status quo, persons who strengthen the hands of those whose practice of social and economic exploitation has led God's people astray. Are there faithful prophets among us in the church today who are our conscience and memory, calling us back into relationship with God and to act as agents for God's justice for the poor? The Old Testament scholar Walter Brueggemann has reflected in this way about "prophetic ministry":

> [P]rophetic ministry does not consist of spectacular acts of social crusading or of abrasive measures of indignation. Rather, prophetic ministry consists of offering an alternative perception of reality and in letting people see their own history in light of God's freedom and his will for justice. The issues of God's freedom and will for justice are not always and need not be expressed primarily in the big issues of the day. They can be discerned wherever people try to live together and worry about their future and identity. (*Prophetic Imagination*, p. 110)

Faithful prophets remind the people of who God is, what God has done, and how the people are called to be agents of justice in the world.

Jeremiah 23:16–22

23:16 **Thus says the LORD of hosts: Do not listen to the words of the prophets who prophesy to you; they are deluding you. They speak visions of their own minds, not from the mouth of the LORD.** [17] **They keep saying to those who despise the word of the LORD, "It shall be well with you"; and to all who stubbornly follow their own stubborn hearts, they say, "No calamity shall come upon you."**

> [18] **For who has stood in the council of the LORD**
> **so as to see and to hear his word?**
> **Who has given heed to his word so as to proclaim it?**
> [19] **Look, the storm of the LORD!**
> **Wrath has gone forth,**
> **a whirling tempest;**
> **it will burst upon the head of the wicked.**
> [20] **The anger of the LORD will not turn back**
> **until he has executed and accomplished**
> **the intents of his mind.**
> **In the latter days you will understand it clearly.**

21 **I did not send the prophets,**
    yet they ran;
    I did not speak to them,
    yet they prophesied.
22 **But if they had stood in my council,**
    then they would have proclaimed my words to my people,
    and they would have turned them from their evil way,
    and from the evil of their doings.

There is a conflict between Jeremiah, whose announcement of God's judgment has been widely rejected, and other (unnamed) prophets who promise, "It shall be well with you" and "No calamity shall come upon you" (v. 17). Jeremiah warns that Judah should not listen to these optimistic prophets. At issue is the validity and authority of the message of those prophets who imagine that all will be well for Judah (vv. 18–22).

These optimistic prophets threaten to delude Judah (v. 16). Jeremiah is commanded by God to proclaim that the Lord will "pluck up and tear down" before God will "build and plant" (1:10). The optimistic prophets presented in these verses deny the possibility that God will pluck up and tear down Judah. Earlier in the book, Jeremiah called Judah's perception that the Temple would guarantee their security "deceptive" (7:4, 7). Here, Jeremiah claims that Judah is being deluded by optimistic prophets who announce that all is well. These prophets, rather than calling Judah to return to God, give Judah permission to follow "their own stubborn hearts" (23:17; "hearts" here and "minds" in the preceding verse are translations of the same Hebrew word). The optimistic prophets thus allow to continue Judah's pattern of covenantal disobedience, which the book of Jeremiah has consistently presented and condemned.

Verses 18–22 are concerned with the validity and authority of these optimistic prophets. One of the primary ways prophets were understood was as God's messengers. In the ancient Near Eastern world of Israel and Judah, the gods were imagined to belong to a divine council, a kind of cosmic royal court from which the gods ruled the world. In Israel and Judah, Yahweh was seen as the head of the divine council, and prophets were understood as messengers from the divine council who announced God's will and intention (see 1 Kings 22). The problem with the optimistic prophets Jeremiah identifies is that they are not authorized messengers from the divine council. They have not stood in "the council of the Lord so as to see and hear his word" (23:18). In the ancient world, messengers ran to deliver their message. The optimistic prophets run as if they are messengers from the divine council, but God has not sent them or spoken to them (v. 21). They act like they are God's messengers, but they speak only for themselves (cf. v. 16). By contrast, Jeremiah is "sent" by God as a messenger to speak God's word (1:7), and he is authorized as the optimistic prophets are not.

Not surprisingly, there is a sharp contrast between the message of the "pretend" prophets and the message of Jeremiah (23:18–22). Whereas the optimistic prophets speak the "visions of their own minds" to people who "stubbornly follow their own stubborn hearts [minds]" (vv. 16–17), the authentic prophetic messenger, Jeremiah, announces God's resolve to accomplish "the intents of his [God's] mind" (v. 20). Whereas the optimistic prophets proclaim that all is well and no calamity will come to Judah (vv. 16–17), God's authentic messenger, Jeremiah, announces to Judah the coming wrath and judgment (v. 19). Jeremiah proclaims God's word that seeks to turn Judah from their evil way (v. 22; see 3:14, 22; 4:1) rather than the optimistic message of the prophets that confirms Judah in their rebellion against God (v. 17; cf. 23:13–14). The prophets who only pretend to be God's messengers are unable to offer "an alternative perception of reality" (Brueggemann *Prophetic Imagination*, p. 110) or to speak a word that might turn the course of Judah's history (v. 22) from broken covenant relationship and God's certain judgment.

It is never easy for the church to discern who is God's messenger and who speak only for themselves. However, these verses provide a clue about distinguishing authentic from phony messengers. The phony messengers announce that all will be well and deny that God may be displeased by what is happening or that the Lord expects any change. Phony messengers say what we like to hear, and their message is easy to accept. The authentic messengers of God announce that God may be angered by the attitudes and actions of the people and that the Lord demands change, repentance from our evil doings (v. 22). The word of these prophets challenges and is likely much harder to accept. The people of Judah found the prophets who did not speak for God much easier to take than Jeremiah, and we in the church are probably very like the people of Judah.

Jeremiah 23:23–32

23:23 **Am I a God near by, says the LORD, and not a God far off?** [24] **Who can hide in secret places so that I cannot see them? says the LORD. Do I not fill heaven and earth? says the LORD.** [25] **I have heard what the prophets have said who prophesy lies in my name, saying, "I have dreamed, I have dreamed!"** [26] **How long? Will the hearts of the prophets ever turn back—those who prophesy lies, and who prophesy the deceit of their own heart?** [27] **They plan** to make my people forget my name by their dreams that they tell one another, just as their ancestors forgot my name for Baal. [28] Let the prophet who has a dream tell the dream, but let the one who has my word speak my word faithfully. What has straw in common with wheat? says the LORD. [29] Is not my word like fire, says the LORD, and like a hammer that breaks a rock in pieces? [30] See, therefore, I am against the prophets, says the LORD, who steal my words from one another. [31] See, I am against the prophets, says the LORD, who use their own tongues and say, "Says the LORD." [32] See, I am against those who prophesy lying dreams, says the LORD, and who tell them, and who lead my people astray by their lies and their recklessness, when I did not send them or appoint them; so they do not profit this people at all, says the LORD.

God speaks through Jeremiah and continues the critique of Judah's more popular prophets. The speech divides into three sections:

1. In verses 23–24, God raises questions about what kind of god the prophets imagine they are dealing with. The question "Am I a God near by?" should be answered no, for God is certainly not some kind of local deity who functions as the patron god of Judah. Indeed, God asks, "Do I not fill heaven and earth?" God, whose sovereignty is over nations and kingdoms, is transcendent (1:10; 10:2–16). God's claim to be transcendent counters the perception, popular in Judah, that God is "near by" and concerned only to keep Judah secure (remember Jeremiah 7). However, if God is transcendent and cosmic, does that mean God is so distant as not to notice what is going on with Judah? That is the concern of God's question in verse 24, "Who can hide in secret places so that I cannot see them?" The answer to this question is "No one." So, while God is not the local, patron deity of Judah with a sole commitment to keep Judah secure, that does not mean God is unaware of what Judah is doing.

2. As this speech continues, it is clear that Judah's prophets have not hidden where God could not see (vv. 25–29). Though dreams are hidden to all but those who dream them, God claims to be aware of these prophets' dreams. Prophetic dreams were the visions prophets claimed to have received from God as the basis for their message. Prophets frequently had visions, as we have seen even with Jeremiah—for instance, the vision of an almond tree and a boiling pot (Jer. 1:11–13; cf. Isaiah 6; Ezekiel 37). However, God is severely critical of the dreams of the popular prophets of Judah and the prophecies that follow from them, which God calls "lies" and "the deceit of their own heart" (23:26; also see v. 16). These prophets, God charges, make Judah "forget my name" (v. 27); they turn Judah not to God but to the Baals; they may tell their dreams, but their dreams are not the word

of the sovereign God of all the earth (v. 24), who intends judgment on Judah (vv. 26–29). These prophets misrepresent God, or more accurately, do not represent God at all but only themselves. By their lies, they attempt to present God as nearby in order to serve the narrow purposes of Judah's security, but the God of "heaven and earth" (v. 24) sees through their "plan" (v. 27).

3. The speech concludes as God declares three times about Judah's prophets, "I am against [them]" (vv. 30–32). Jeremiah has been appointed and sent by God (1:7, 10), and God has promised Jeremiah, "I am with you" (1:19). God is against these prophets whom God did not send or appoint (v. 32) and who speak only their own words and not God's, words that are lies that will lead Judah astray.

The problem with Judah's prophets goes beyond the false assurances they give or their failure to call Judah to repent. The fundamental problem with Judah's prophets is that they misrepresent God as Judah's local, patron deity, concerned only to protect Judah's security. In this, there is another clue for the church in distinguishing among those who are and are not God's prophets in our time. Persons who present God as a deity with local concerns to protect the security of a particular people are much like the popular prophets of Judah. Such persons may claim, for instance, that God favors a particular church, denomination, ethnic group, or nationality and seeks the well-being of that group to the exclusion of others. The God of Jeremiah and the church is the God who holds all nations and kingdoms accountable (will pluck up and tear down) but ultimately seeks the well-being of all nations and kingdoms (will build and plant).

Jeremiah 23:33–40

23:33 **When this people, or a prophet, or a priest asks you, "What is the burden of the LORD?" you shall say to them, "You are the burden, and I will cast you off, says the LORD."** [34] **And as for the prophet, priest, or the people who say, "The burden of the LORD," I will punish them and their households.** [35] **Thus shall you say to one another, among yourselves, "What has the LORD answered?" or "What has the LORD spoken?"** [36] **But "the burden of the LORD" you shall mention no more, for the burden is everyone's own word, and so you pervert the words of the living God, the LORD of hosts, our God.** [37] **Thus you shall ask the prophet, "What has the LORD answered you?" or "What has the LORD spoken?"** [38] **But if you say, "the burden of the LORD," thus says the LORD: Because you have said these words, "the burden of the LORD," when I sent to you, saying, You shall not say, "the burden of the LORD,"** [39] **therefore, I will surely lift you up and cast you away from my presence, you and the city that I gave to you and your ancestors.** [40] **And I will bring upon you everlasting disgrace and perpetual shame, which shall not be forgotten.**

These verses, which seem to be an appendix to the material that has condemned Judah's optimistic and popular prophets, are very difficult to interpret. The verses develop by a play on a Hebrew noun translated in the NRSV as "burden." However, the noun has more than one meaning. One sense of the noun is much like the English word *burden*, that is, a heavy object to be carried or an arduous task that leaves one weary. Another sense of the noun in the Old Testament, however, has no English equivalent. It is a technical word meaning an oracle that a prophet or priest has received from God. Finally, to make sense of these verses we need to be aware that the Hebrew noun meaning both "burden" and "oracle" is related to a Hebrew verb that means "to lift or carry."

Initially (v. 33), God instructs Jeremiah how to respond should someone ask him, "What is the burden of the Lord?" that is, what oracle God has given. Perhaps what is imagined here is the kind of request for an oracle (burden) that Zedekiah made to Jeremiah when Babylon was besieging the city in the hope that God would "perform a wonderful deed" (21:1–2). Jeremiah is to respond using the word *burden* in the usual sense, saying on God's behalf, "You are a burden, and I will cast you off." In other words, Jeremiah is to announce that Judah has worn God out, and God will cast them off.

This play on the word *burden* is picked up in verses 38–40, which use the connection between the noun *burden* and the verb *lift up*. Again, if the people asked for a "burden," an oracle, Jeremiah is to respond by saying that Judah is "the burden [in the usual sense] of the Lord" (v. 38), and as a consequence, God will "lift you up and cast you away" (v. 39).

The middle section of this text has a different concern and is more in keeping with the concerns about Judah's prophets developed in the two prior sections of Jeremiah 23. In verses 34–37, the situation imagined is not that Jeremiah is being asked about a burden (oracle) but that the people, prophets, or priests presume to have received "the burden of the Lord" (that is, an oracle, v. 34). In these verses, a burden is characterized as "everyone's own word" used to "pervert the words of the living God" (v. 36). In this sense, "burden" is much like the prophets' "visions of their own minds" (23:16) or their "dreams" (23:25–28).

It is likely that these verses were added late in the development of the book of Jeremiah by someone trying to summarize the critique of Judah's popular prophets that began at Jeremiah 23:9. While the editor who added this material may have helped persons in his time better understand the book, exactly what was being clarified is now difficult to determine.

Jeremiah 24:1–10

24:1 The LORD showed me two baskets of figs placed before the temple of the LORD. This was after King Nebuchadrezzar of Babylon had taken into exile from Jerusalem King Jeconiah son of Jehoiakim of Judah, together with the officials of Judah, the artisans, and the smiths, and had brought them to Babylon. 2 One basket had very good figs, like first-ripe figs, but the other basket had very bad figs, so bad that they could not be eaten. 3 And the LORD said to me, "What do you see, Jeremiah?" I said, "Figs, the good figs very good, and the bad figs very bad, so bad that they cannot be eaten."

4 Then the word of the LORD came to me: 5 Thus says the LORD, the God of Israel: Like these good figs, so I will regard as good the exiles from Judah, whom I have sent away from this place to the land of the Chaldeans. 6 I will set my eyes upon them for good, and I will bring them back to this land. I will build them up, and not tear them down; I will plant them, and not pluck them up. 7 I will give them a heart to know that I am the LORD; and they shall be my people and I will be their God, for they shall return to me with their whole heart.

8 But thus says the LORD: Like the bad figs that are so bad they cannot be eaten, so will I treat King Zedekiah of Judah, his officials, the remnant of Jerusalem who remain in this land, and those who live in the land of Egypt. 9 I will make them a horror, an evil thing, to all the kingdoms of the earth— a disgrace, a byword, a taunt, and a curse in all the places where I shall drive them. 10 And I will send sword, famine, and pestilence upon them, until they are utterly destroyed from the land that I gave to them and their ancestors.

Beginning at Jeremiah 21, Judah has been presented as confused about the choice of life or death that God through Jeremiah placed before them. For instance, King Zedekiah thinks there is life in resisting the Babylonians and to surrender to them will be death. Jeremiah, however, announces that to surrender to Babylon is life and to resist is death (21:8–9). Jehoiakim seems to have life and blessing from God, as he lives in opulence. But it was really his father, Josiah, with whom it was well, because he gave attention to justice and righteousness for the poor and needy; and Jehoiakim is doomed to curse (22:13–19). The prophets who are optimistic and confident about Judah's well-being are heeded, and Jeremiah is rejected. However, God denounces Judah's popular prophets as false and announces through Jeremiah that the insistence of these prophets that "it shall be well with you" only brings Judah closer to doom (23:16–22). What look like life and blessing to most in Judah, God calls death and doom. Those most confused are Judah's kings and prophets, the very persons who should be clearest.

Jeremiah 24 is a prophetic vision that captures the theme of this section of the book about life and blessing, death and curse. The historical setting for this text, indicated in verse 2, is after the first Babylonian deportation that occurred in 597 B.C. but before the final fall of Jerusalem to Babylon in 587 B.C. In 597 B.C., Babylon invaded Judah in response to some actions by Judah's king Jehoiakim that challenged Babylon's dominion over Judah. By the time of Babylon's invasion of Judah in 597 B.C., Jehoiakim had died and his son Jehoiachin was Judah's king. Jehoiachin, along with other Judean leaders, was deported to Babylon; the royal treasury was stripped; and the Temple was looted but not destroyed. Through these events, it must have seemed that those deported to Babylon were being judged by God, plucked up and broken down as God had warned. By contrast, it must have seemed that those who remained in Judah and Jerusalem had been spared God's judgment and continued in God's favor. However, Jeremiah turns this logic of the situation upside down and so inverts the most obvious understanding of life and death, blessing and curse.

In verses 4–7 the good figs are identified as those who were exiled, and it is announced that those exiled, that is, "plucked up," God will "bring . . . back" and "build . . . up" and "plant" (v. 6). There is no claim in these verses that those exiled in 597 B.C. are inherently good or deserve God's favor. Instead, what qualifies those exiled as "good" is God's intention for them: "I will set my eyes upon them for good" (v. 6). The Lord brought Babylon against Judah for judgment, but unexpectedly God declares that those exiled will be regarded as good. There is no indication of any quality of or action by those exiled that might have led God to this changed view of them.

The "good" God intends is in the first instance restoration to the land (v. 6). Beyond return from exile, God also intends a restored relationship, which is expressed through three intertwined phrases in verse 7. In the first phrase, God promises to give those exiled "a heart to know that I am the Lord." One of the accusations God makes through Jeremiah is that Judah has an uncircumcised heart (4:4), a wicked heart (4:14), a heart engraved with sin (17:1–2), which they have been unable to wash or circumcise. In restoring Judah, the Lord intends to do for them what they have been unable to do. God will instill in them another heart, a new will or volition (cf. 31:31–34). The last phrase of verse 7 needs to be understood as the consequence of the gift of a heart promised in the first phrase. God declares that those exiled and given a heart to know God will "return to me with their whole heart," that is, they will at last turn to God and seek relationship, rather than turning away from God as they have been doing.

The middle phrase of verse 7 points to the restored relationship for which God longs and that a changed heart will make possible. The phrase, "they shall be my people and I will be their God," is an expression of covenantal relationship. For example, the phrase "I will take you as my people, and I will be your God" is used in Exodus 6:7, where it is directly linked with the covenant with Israel's ancestors (Exod. 6:2–4). Judah has broken covenant with God and deserves curse (see Jer. 11:1–5). A renewal of covenant relationship will occur, but only because God makes the decision to view those exiled differently, "for good." This divine decision is contrary to the logic of the situation of 597 B.C., in which those exiled seemed to be cursed.

Also against common logic is God's identification as bad figs those who remain in Jerusalem—King Zedekiah and his officials in particular—as well as those who have fled to Egypt. These, it must have seemed, had escaped God's judgment and continued in God's blessing. Verses 8–10 argue the opposite. Zedekiah, we have seen, hoped to escape God's judgment by the Babylonians (21:1–7). Such hope, however, resisted God's intentions and was a further defiance of God. If the common perception is that King Zedekiah and the officials who remain in Jerusalem or who escape Babylonian deportation by fleeing to Egypt (see 42:18ff.) are blessed, God's perception is much different. Verses 8 and 9 in chapter 24 repeat curses used previously in the book of Jeremiah (cf. 24:9 and 19:8; 24:10 and 14:12; 15:2; 18:21; etc.). So, in the events of 597 B.C., those who seem to continue in God's blessing are regarded as cursed by God, and those who seem to be cursed in their exile are regarded by God as good.

The decision of God to identify as "good figs" those exiled in 597 B.C. was surely a scandal. How could those exiled be the "good figs"? Yet God's choice to stake the future with the despised and marginal is consistent with how God is presented in the long biblical drama. In the Old Testament, the Lord chose Abram and Sarai, old and barren (Gen. 11:26–12:3); God chose Jacob the scoundrel (Genesis 27; 32:22–32); God chose the littlest brother, Joseph (Genesis 37); God chose for God's people slaves of the mighty Egyptian Empire (Exodus 1–15); God chose as Israel's king David, the youngest of Jesse's sons (1 Sam. 16:1–13). In the New Testament, Mary anticipated Jesus as one through whom God would humble the exalted and exalt the humble (Luke 1:46–55); Jesus kept company with tax collectors, women, children, the diseased—all marginal persons in his society (Matthew 9; Mark 5); Jesus himself died as a criminal (Luke 23); when Paul thought about the church, he recognized that it included not those judged as wise and powerful but the lowly (1 Cor. 1:26–27). In each case, God has chosen to vest the future with those who would have been popularly regarded as "bad figs."

The Lord's odd perception of who are good and bad figs is well illustrated in the Beatitudes. (The best-known version is in Matt. 5:3–12; also see Luke 6:20–26.) Listen for the awareness of God's inverted perception in these reflections on the Beatitudes by Frederick Buechner:

> If we didn't already know but were asked to guess the kind of people Jesus would pick out for special commendation, we might be tempted to guess one sort or another of spiritual hero—men and women of impeccable credentials morally, spiritually, humanly, and every which way. If so, we would be wrong. . . .
>
> Not the spiritual giants, but "the poor in spirit" as he called them, the ones who spiritually speaking have absolutely nothing to give and absolutely everything to receive like the Prodigal telling his father "I am not worthy to be called thy son" only to discover for the first time all he had in having a father . . .
>
> Not the ones who are righteous but the ones who hope they will be someday and in the meantime are well aware that the distance they still have to go is even greater than the distance they've already come. (*Listening to Your Life*, pp. 256–57)

Jeremiah 25:1–14

This oracle summarizes the prophetic activity of Jeremiah to this point in the book. Verses 1–11 sound very familiar themes.

The first two verses carefully recount the length of Jeremiah's service as a prophet: twenty-three years, from the thirteenth year of Josiah to the fourth of Josiah's son, Jehoiakim. These verses provide information helpful in reconstructing the history of Jeremiah's era. However, the careful counting of twenty-three years of Jeremiah's service is used in verses 3–7 to stress the futility of the prophet's efforts. Verses 3–7 recount God's persistent efforts in attempting to persuade Judah and Israel to repent through Jeremiah and prophets like him: "I have spoken persistently to you . . . " (v. 3); "though the Lord persistently sent you all his servants the prophets . . . " (v. 4); "when they [the prophets] said, 'Turn now . . . ' (v. 5). Yet, each recounting of God's efforts ends with the refrain "you have not listened" (vv. 3, 4, 7). We should not be surprised that God's people have not listened. There has been no evidence in the book that Judah turned and considerable indication that their response to Jeremiah was outright rejection.

Twenty-three years is a long time to speak with no one listening, certainly much longer than almost anyone could endure a relationship in which one was ignored. So, the verdict in verses 8–11 is predictable and repeats many of the judgments and covenant curses from earlier sections of the book: God is directing Judah's history toward "captivity" at the hand of Babylon, which will ruin the land (v. 9; cf. 1:3; Deut. 28:41). Community life will collapse, and marriages that ensure a new generation will cease (25:10; cf. 7:34 and 16:9; Deut. 28:30). The judgment God intends will last a long time, announced both as being "everlasting" (25:9) or as lasting "seventy years" (25:11). The disparity between these two reckonings of the period of judgment may not be as dramatic as we hear it today. "Everlasting" in the Old Testament did not carry the connotation of eternity as we think of it but rather that of the foreseeable future, as long as one can imagine. "Seventy years," which suggests the life span of a human (Ps. 90:10; or, some have suggested, the years a city might last before destruction), may well be an effort by a later editor to soften "everlasting." In either case, "everlasting" or "seventy years," the judgment will last so long that none who experience it will live to see what God intends next. Still, the seventy years does suggest a finite time for God's judgment, for plucking up and tearing down (1:10). The implication is that after seventy years the Lord might intend something else, finally building and planting.

There is a turn in the argument at verse 12. Having announced that Babylon will defeat Judah, God announces that Babylon, too, will be judged after seventy years. Jeremiah has been sent by God as a prophet to the nations (1:10). While Judah is to be first to experience judgment, God's concern extends beyond Judah. Finally, all the nations, even mighty Babylon, will be called to account. Of course, the other side of the argument is that the judgment against Babylon is to occur only after seventy years and does not in any way nullify God's certain judgment of Judah. We need to be careful in our reading not to think that somehow the judgment of Judah is to be short-circuited by God's judgment of Babylon.

Much of this material concerns judgment and the way in which eventually both Judah and Babylon will have to submit to God. Yet, the ultimate concern of this material is not judgment but God's sovereignty. God's purposes are being worked out—through Jeremiah, through Babylon against Judah, and eventually against Babylon. The Lord's reign is portrayed in the book of Jeremiah in global and even cosmic dimensions and is not limited to sovereignty over Judah. Similarly, Matthew's Gospel envisions all the nations gathered for judgment before God, who separates them as sheep and goats (Matt. 25:31–46). Paul sees the whole creation groaning as it awaits redemption (Rom. 8:18–25). God reigns over Israel, over the nations, and over the whole creation. This theme, begun in verses 12–14, is continued through Jeremiah 25.

Brief note needs to be taken of verse 13. The verse provides some clues about the complex process by which the book of Jeremiah came to the form in which we read it. It has often been proposed that verse 13 is related to the incident reported in Jeremiah 36, in which King Jehoiakim burns a scroll containing the words which Jeremiah spoke (36:20–26). Jeremiah subsequently redictates the scroll with additional words added (36:27–32). It is likely that verse 13, with its reference to "this book," is an addition by a later editor who had some written version of Jeremiah's words before him, perhaps the redictated scroll indicated in Jeremiah 36. However, scholars have been unable to agree about which portions of the book as we have it may have been included in either the original or the redictated scroll.

Jeremiah 25:15–29

25:15 **For thus the LORD, the God of Israel, said to me: Take from my hand this cup of the wine of wrath, and make all the nations to whom I send you drink it.** [16] **They shall drink and stagger and go out of their minds because of the sword that I am sending among them.**

[17] **So I took the cup from the LORD's hand, and made all the nations to whom the LORD sent me drink it:** [18] **Jerusalem and the towns of Judah, its kings and officials, to make them a desolation and a waste, an object of hissing and of cursing, as they are today;** [19] **Pharaoh king of Egypt, his servants, his officials, and all his people;** [20] **all the mixed people; all the kings of the land of Uz; all the kings of the land of the Philistines—Ashkelon, Gaza, Ekron, and the remnant of Ashdod;** [21] **Edom, Moab, and the Ammonites;** [22] **all the kings of Tyre, all the kings of Sidon, and the kings of the coastland across the sea;** [23] **Dedan, Tema, Buz, and all who have shaven temples;** [24] **all the kings of Arabia and all the kings of the mixed peoples that live in the desert;** [25] **all the kings of Zimri, all the kings of Elam, and all the kings of Media;** [26] **all the kings of the north, far and near, one after another, and all the kingdoms of the world that are on the face of the earth. And after them the king of Sheshach shall drink.**

[27] **Then you shall say to them, Thus says the LORD of hosts, the God of Israel: Drink, get drunk and vomit, fall and rise no more, because of the sword that I am sending among you.**

[28] **And if they refuse to accept the cup from your hand to drink, then you shall say to them: Thus says the LORD of hosts: You must drink!** [29] **See, I am beginning to bring disaster on the city that is called by my name, and how can you possibly avoid punishment? You shall not go unpunished, for I am summoning a sword against all the inhabitants of the earth, says the LORD of hosts.**

The scene presented in these verses is harsh, crude, and shocking. God is imagined as passing among the nations a "cup of the wine of wrath" from which the nations are forced to drink until they are drunk and vomit. There is a similar scene in this book in which God threatens to fill all the inhabitants of Judah with drunkenness so they will dash against one another self-destructively (13:12–14; see pp. 120–22). In the Old Testament, there are several passages that refer to a cup of wrath the Lord pours out on the wicked when they are called to account (in addition to the texts below, see Ps. 11:6; Lam. 4:21; Ezek. 23:31–34):

> For in the hand of the LORD there is a cup
>   with foaming wine, well mixed;
> he will pour a draught from it
>   and all the wicked of the earth
>   shall drain it down to the dregs.
>
>   (Ps. 75:8)

> Rouse yourself, rouse yourself!
>   Stand up, O Jerusalem,
> you who have drunk at the hand of the LORD
>   the cup of his wrath,
> who have drunk to the dregs
>   the bowl of staggering.
>
>   (Isa. 51:17)

In Psalm 75, the wicked, who are called to account and who must drink a cup of wrath, are from all the earth, from the nations. The Isaiah text, however, which promises Jerusalem restoration, imagines that the Lord makes the people drink from the cup of wrath, similar to Jeremiah 13:12–14.

As God makes the nations drink from the cup, Judah must drink first (Jer. 25:18, 29) and then the nations (vv. 19–26). Thus, the pattern of judgment in these verses parallels that of verses 1–14: Judah is to be judged first, then the nations. The nations mentioned in these verses geographically surround Judah on all sides. Beyond Judah, the list of nations in this chapter begins with Egypt (v. 19), the nation from which Israel was delivered by God from slavery for life in the land of milk and honey (Exod. 3:17). The list ends with Babylon in verse 26, the nation through which Judah is to lose the land. The reference to Babylon is made by spelling the name backward in Hebrew. The implication is that Babylon was so terrible that one needed to be careful even about how one said the name. Certainly, for those who had experienced the Babylonian exile and were reflecting on it in these verses (they are likely not from Jeremiah but from a later editor), Babylon seemed awesome and beyond all accountability.

Yet, the list of nations in verses 17–26 places Judah and all the nations that surround Judah, even Egypt and terrible Babylon, in the same relationship to God. "All the kingdoms of the world that are on the face of the earth" (v. 26) will be made to drink from "the cup of the wine of wrath." All alike "must drink," with no opportunity to refuse (v. 27). God will send among them all a "sword" (vv. 27, 29). Thus, the first two sections of Jeremiah 25 make the same claim: God is sovereign "over nations and kingdoms" (see 1:10). While the Lord directs Judah's history toward "captivity" (1:3), God also directs the course of all the nations—Judah to be sure, but even dreaded Babylon. All stand accountable before the Lord.

It is not possible to read these verses about the "cup of the wine of wrath" and not think about the cup of the Lord's Table. The cup of the Lord's Table seems much different than the cup of wrath in Jeremiah 25. It is a cup of blessing (1 Cor. 10:16) and a cup of covenant (Mark 14:24), which expresses God's gracious offer of relationship restored through Jesus' death and resurrection and anticipates the fullness of God's reign (Mark 14:25; 1 Cor. 11:26). Still, the two meanings of the cup need to be held together as we approach the Lord's Table. Surely, God is sovereign over all nations and kingdoms and holds them all accountable as well as all of us who come to receive the cup at the table. God has every reason to make us drink a cup of wrath and through it know God's reign. Instead, in God's own self the cup of wrath is taken up, the cup that Jesus prayed might pass from him (Mark 14:36). When we come to the Lord's Table, we are offered a cup we do not deserve: a cup of God's blessing, the cup of the new covenant in Christ's blood, which anticipates the fullness of God's reign. Only in God's grace are we offered a cup of blessing rather than a cup of wrath.

Jeremiah 25:30–38

Jeremiah 25 concludes with a third expression of God's sovereignty over the nations through judgment of them. The verses have three parts. First (vv. 30–32), the prophet is commanded to announce God's judgment. The scope of God's judgment is global, again "against all the inhabitants of the earth" (v. 30), "to the ends of the earth" and "with all flesh" (v. 31). Second (v. 33), Jeremiah describes the aftermath of God's judgment. The "slain" will lie everywhere, unburied like "dung on the surface of the ground." The consequences of the judgment of Judah have been described earlier in the book in language quite similar to verse 33 (see 8:2; 9:22; 16:4), in which judgment extends to all the nations over whom God is sovereign. Third (vv. 34–38), the shepherds (that is, kings) of the nations are called to lament because of the devastation caused by the "fierce anger of the Lord" (v. 37). When brought to grief, the kings of the nations, those least likely to imagine themselves accountable, will find they, too, are accountable before God. Again, in earlier sections of the book, there have been laments as a response to God's judgment of Judah (6:26; 8:18–9:3; and 10:19–21, which express God's own grief). In 25:34–38, the lament portrayed is to be voiced by the rulers of the nations in response to God's judgment.

This section of the book of Jeremiah began in Jeremiah 21, where God announced through Jeremiah to Judah, "I am setting before you the way of life and death" (v. 8). At the end of this section of the book, in Jeremiah 25, God sets the ways of life and death not just before Judah but before all "nations and kingdoms" over whom God is sovereign.

"It Is the Lord Who Sent Me"
Jeremiah 26–29

In these chapters, Jeremiah is presented as a prophet sent by the Lord to announce Judah's judgment, captivity in Babylon that will last seventy years. The reason given is that Judah has failed to listen to the prophets whom God has sent. Jeremiah's message of doom is countered in these chapters by optimistic prophets who assure both those in Judah and those already taken captive in 597 B.C. that the Babylonian problem will last only two years. While these prophets are predictably well received, Jeremiah charges that God has not sent them. By Judah's rejection of Jeremiah and embrace of his more optimistic contemporaries, we are taken another step toward understanding the captivity of Judah.

Jeremiah 26:1–19, 24

26:1 **At the beginning of the reign of King Jehoiakim son of Josiah of Judah, this word came from the LORD:** 2 **Thus says the LORD: Stand in the court of the LORD's house, and speak to all the cities of Judah that come to worship in the house of the LORD; speak to them all the words that I command you; do not hold back a word.** 3 **It may be that they will listen, all of them, and will turn from their evil way, that I may change my mind about the disaster that I intend to bring on them because of their evil doings.** 4 **You shall say to them: Thus says the LORD: If you will not listen to me, to walk in my law that I have set before you,** 5 **and to heed the words of my servants the prophets whom I send to you urgently—though you have not heeded—** 6 **then I will make this house like Shiloh, and I will make this city a curse for all the nations of the earth.**

7 **The priests and the prophets and all the people heard Jeremiah speaking these words in the house of the LORD.** 8 **And when Jeremiah had finished speaking all that the LORD had commanded him to speak to all the people, then the priests and the prophets and all the people laid hold of him, saying, "You shall die!** 9 **Why have you prophesied in the name of the LORD, saying, 'This house shall be like Shiloh, and this city shall be desolate, without inhabitant'?" And all the people gathered around Jeremiah in the house of the LORD.**

¹⁰ When the officials of Judah heard these things, they came up from the king's house to the house of the LORD and took their seat in the entry of the New Gate of the house of the LORD. ¹¹ Then the priests and the prophets said to the officials and to all the people, "This man deserves the sentence of death because he has prophesied against this city, as you have heard with your own ears."

¹² Then Jeremiah spoke to all the officials and all the people, saying, "It is the LORD who sent me to prophesy against this house and this city all the words you have heard. ¹³ Now therefore amend your ways and your doings, and obey the voice of the LORD your God, and the LORD will change his mind about the disaster that he has pronounced against you. ¹⁴ But as for me, here I am in your hands. Do with me as seems good and right to you. ¹⁵ Only know for certain that if you put me to death, you will be bringing innocent blood upon yourselves and upon this city and its inhabitants, for in truth the LORD sent me to you to speak all these words in your ears."

¹⁶ Then the officials and all the people said to the priests and the prophets, "This man does not deserve the sentence of death, for he has spoken to us in the name of the LORD our God." ¹⁷ And some of the elders of the land arose and said to all the assembled people, ¹⁸ "Micah of Moresheth, who prophesied during the days of King Hezekiah of Judah, said to all the people of Judah: 'Thus says the LORD of hosts,

Zion shall be plowed as a field;
Jerusalem shall become a heap of ruins,
and the mountain of the house a wooded height.'

¹⁹ Did King Hezekiah of Judah and all Judah actually put him to death? Did he not fear the LORD and entreat the favor of the LORD, and did not the LORD change his mind about the disaster that he had pronounced against them? But we are about to bring great disaster on ourselves!" . . .

²⁴ But the hand of Ahikam son of Shaphan was with Jeremiah so that he was not given over into the hands of the people to be put to death.

This passage carries us through a sequence of events that is initiated by a speech of Jeremiah in the court of the Lord's house at the beginning of Jehoiakim's reign (26:1–6). Jehoiakim became king of Judah in 609 B.C., just after the tragic death of Josiah and at the beginning of a twenty-year period when Judah was to be dominated briefly by Egypt and then by Babylon. Some have suggested that this speech was given on the occasion of Jehoiakim's coronation as king. The speech, which threatens Judah's destruction, draws a hostile response so that Jeremiah is seized and threatened with death (vv. 7–11). Jeremiah defends himself (vv. 12–15), and then "some of the elders of the land" also come to his defense (vv. 16–19). Finally, after a story of another prophet who is actually executed for his prophecy (vv. 20–23), we are told of Jeremiah's release (v. 24).

This passage is often related to Jeremiah 7 and understood as another recounting of the same event. Both texts have Jeremiah speaking in the Temple as people gather for worship (7:2; 26:2); in both, Jeremiah reminds those whom he addresses that God has spoken before but has not been heeded (7:13; 26:5); in both Jeremiah calls Judah and Jerusalem to "amend your ways and doings" (7:3, 5; 26:13); and in both, the destruction of Jerusalem is related to the prior destruction of Shiloh (7:12–14; 26:6, 9). Despite these similarities, however, there is a difference between Jeremiah 7 and 26. Jeremiah 7 focuses more on the words of Jeremiah's speech and, within Jeremiah 7–10, emphasizes that God's people have trusted that which is "false." Jeremiah 26 is less concerned with the words of Jeremiah's speech and instead stresses the reaction to the prophet's speech.

Which, if either, version is the more accurate account is difficult to determine. There is clearly a firm memory in the tradition about the prophet Jeremiah that he spoke in the Temple, threatening its destruction as God had earlier destroyed the worship center of the tribal league at Shiloh. This memory, however, has been passed on with different emphases in Jeremiah 7 and 26. The differences between these two accounts of what must have been the same incident reflect the complex process by which the book of Jeremiah developed into the form in which we read it.

In Jeremiah 26, the prophet's speech in the Temple is recounted by emphasizing that Jeremiah spoke "all the words" that God had commanded (v. 2). While the issue in Jeremiah 7 is if the people will "amend their ways and their doings" (7:3, 5), in Jeremiah 26 the issue is if Judah will "listen" and obey the word of the Lord spoken by God's prophet (vv. 3, 4). As was the case in Jeremiah 7, Jeremiah 26 presents Jeremiah's speech as an "if . . . then" proposition. Jeremiah offers that if Judah will listen, the disaster God threatens may still be avoided (v. 3). However, if God's people refuse to listen, Jeremiah warns, then Jerusalem will be destroyed like Shiloh (vv. 4–6). The destruction of Jerusalem or its survival, death or life, is presented in this chapter as dependent on Judah's willingness to "heed the words of my servants the prophets whom I send to you urgently— though you have not heeded" (v. 5). In Jeremiah 26, the central question is how Judah will respond to Jeremiah, whether they will "heed" or not.

Verses 7–11 indicate the response to Jeremiah by "the priests and the prophets and all the people." While the well-being of Judah depends on heeding the word of the Lord spoken through God's servant Jeremiah, those who hear the prophet's speech respond by saying to Jeremiah, "You

shall die" (v. 8). The desolation of Jerusalem that Jeremiah has threatened
is unthinkable to Judah's leaders, who are confident that God made an
enduring pledge to protect Jerusalem. The Temple liturgy quoted in Jeremiah 7, "the temple of the Lord . . . ," expresses this confidence that God
will never allow Jerusalem's destruction. In Jeremiah 26, the prophet's
speech is heard as treasonous, so he is seized and held (vv. 7–9). Quickly,
the king's "officials" gather to conduct a hearing (vv. 10–11) in the gate of
Temple, a traditional place for a legal matter to be heard in Judah. The
officials function as judges; the prophets and priests are the prosecutors;
and Jeremiah, of course, is the accused.

Because the leaders of Judah cannot imagine God will ever destroy Jerusalem, they think anyone who imagines such a thing cannot possibly be
speaking for the Lord. Given their confidence that God will never destroy
Jerusalem, Jeremiah's accusers are unable to embrace the call of the
prophet to repent and obey the Lord (v. 13), a call that offers a way to avoid
the destruction with which God threatens Judah. In seeking the death of
Jeremiah, they choose death for themselves, God's judgment on Jerusalem
because they fail to "listen" to the word of the Lord spoken by God's servant Jeremiah.

Jeremiah's accusers ask, "Why have you prophesied in the name of the
Lord . . . ?" (v. 9). It is this question that Jeremiah addresses in his response
before the "officials" (vv. 12–15). Both at the beginning and the conclusion of his brief defense, Jeremiah asserts that he spoke as he did because
the "Lord sent me" (vv. 12, 15). The authority by which Jeremiah speaks
is central to the dispute. He claims to announce the destruction of Jerusalem as God's spokesperson. If Jeremiah is sent by God and killed because
of that, then the leaders of Judah will have shed "innocent blood" and will
bring judgment on themselves. Jeremiah's defense is supported by "officials" and "people" who, against the prophets and priests who accused
Jeremiah, argue that Jeremiah does not deserve death (v. 16). The case
against Jeremiah depends on whether he speaks for the Lord or merely
presumes to be God's spokesperson.

Jeremiah's defense is joined by "some of the elders" (v. 17) who, in
good legal fashion, cite a prior case. The prophet Micah, they remember,
once announced to King Hezekiah of Judah that God would destroy Jerusalem (v. 18; cf. Micah 3:12). Hezekiah, however, did not put Micah to
death. Instead, he feared the Lord and entreated the Lord's favor (Jer.
26:19), and the result was that God's mind was changed and the threatened disaster averted. The "elders of the land" who come to Jeremiah's
defense use the case of Hezekiah and Micah to argue that by threatening

to kill Jeremiah, Judah risks a "great disaster" (v. 19). The argument by the elders seems to have been persuasive, for (after an intervening section of text, to be discussed below) Jeremiah is released and not put to death (v. 24).

This chapter may give us some indication of the political conflict in Judah at the time of Jeremiah. The man into whose hands Jeremiah is released, Ahikam son of Shaphan (v. 24), with his family plays an interesting role in the books of Jeremiah and 2 Kings. Also, in Jeremiah 26, the group identified as "the elders of the land" support Jeremiah against his accusers. It is not clear who these elders are or even if Ahikam and his family are among them. In any case, Ahikam and his family are presented in these books as supporters of Jeremiah and, more broadly, supporters of the reforms of King Josiah of Judah. Shaphan, the father of the man to whom Jeremiah is released, was the secretary of King Josiah and among those who, in 2 Kings 22, reported the discovery of a law code to King Josiah of Judah. The law code, believed to be part of the present book of Deuteronomy, led to the reforms by King Josiah, especially the centralization of worship in Jerusalem. Ahikam, to whom Jeremiah is released, also served King Josiah (2 Kings 22:12, 14). Later in the book of Jeremiah, Ahikam's son Gedaliah is remembered as the governor of Judah after the Babylonian captivity (Jeremiah 40). Gedaliah is supported by Jeremiah but assassinated by persons who eventually take Jeremiah, against his will, to Egypt. In the book of Jeremiah, Ahikam and his family are presented as supporters and defenders of the prophet against the hostility of King Josiah's successors and other royal officials who seem not to have supported Josiah's reforms. In Jeremiah 26, the family of Ahikam and "the elders of the land" are presented among those who heed the words of Jeremiah, in contrast to King Jehoiakim, the son of King Josiah, and the prophets and priests who seek Jeremiah's life.

While it may be that information in these verses allows us to see something of the political conflicts in Judah at the time of Jeremiah, Jeremiah 26 as we now have it has a purpose beyond an accurate report of historical events. The editors who shaped Jeremiah 26 after the Babylonian conquest of 587 B.C. knew that Jeremiah was correct about God's judgment of Judah and concluded that Jeremiah must have spoken for the Lord. These editors seem to have had in mind legal material about prophets from Deuteronomy 18:15–22. This legal stipulation concerning prophets is part of the Deuteronomistic law code, which became important in Judah about the time of Jeremiah and later, as the book of Jeremiah was being developed. In part, this stipulation reads:

"I will raise up for them a prophet like you [i.e., Moses] from among their own people; I will put my words in the mouth of the prophet, who shall speak to them everything that I command. Anyone who does not heed the words that the prophet shall speak in my name, I myself will hold account-able. But any prophet who speaks in the name of other gods, or who pre-sumes to speak in my name a word that I have not commanded the prophet to speak—that prophet shall die." You may say to yourself, "How can we recognize a word that the Lord has not spoken?" If a prophet speaks in the name of the Lord but the thing does not take place or prove true, it is a word that the Lord has not spoken. The prophet has spoken it presumptuously; do not be frightened by it. (Deut. 18:18–22)

The judgment Jeremiah had threatened occurred and thus "proved true." The conclusion was obvious: Jeremiah spoke for the Lord. The editors of Jeremiah 26 knew about the destruction of Jerusalem in 587 B.C., as do we who now read the text. Those who edited the book of Jeremiah after the exile of 587 B.C. were able to use the text we have been examining to pro-vide an explanation for the "disaster" that befell Judah. Judah and Jeru-salem were destroyed because the priests, prophets, and many of the people of Judah did not listen to the word of the Lord spoken by God's servant, the prophet Jeremiah, whom God had sent.

Jeremiah 26:20–23

26:20 **There was another man prophesying in the name of the LORD, Uriah son of Shemaiah from Kiriath-jearim. He prophesied against this city and against this land in words exactly like those of Jeremiah.** 21 **And when King Jehoiakim, with all his warriors and all the officials, heard his words, the king sought to put him to death; but when Uriah heard of it, he was afraid and fled and escaped to Egypt.** 22 **Then King Jehoiakim sent Elnathan son of Achbor and men with him to Egypt,** 23 **and they took Uriah from Egypt and brought him to King Jehoiakim, who struck him down with the sword and threw his dead body into the burial place of the common people.**

The story of the prophet Uriah and King Jehoiakim is placed right after the story of Jeremiah's trial for prophesying the destruction of Judah. While Jeremiah is spared execution through the intervention of supporters like Ahikam son of Shaphan and "the elders of the land," King Jehoiakim and the Jerusalem establishment remain hostile toward prophets like Jeremiah. Uriah, this text emphasizes, spoke "in words exactly like those of Jeremiah" (v. 20). The execution of Uriah by King Jehoiakim makes clear that despite a temporary reprieve for Jeremiah, the leadership of Judah reject God's prophets and refuse to listen to their words, so that divine judgment is certain (cf. 26:4–6).

Apart from verses 20–23 in Jeremiah 26, there is no reference in the Old Testament to the prophet Uriah. It may be significant that he was from Kiriath-jearim, which was the site at which the ark of the covenant was kept after the Philistines returned it and before David moved it to Jerusalem (see 1 Sam. 7:2; 2 Samuel 6). Kiriath-jearim may well have been a center for persons who supported views of Israel's relationship with God most like those held by King Josiah. They may have also been critical of the direction of King Jehoiakim (cf. the comments on Anathoth, Jeremiah's hometown, in 1:1, pp. 12–13).

Jeremiah 26 stresses the determination of King Jehoiakim to silence the prophet Uriah. When the king and his officials hear Uriah's words, they seek "to put him to death" (v. 21). Uriah flees to Egypt, but even there he is sought by Jehoiakim, who sends a party to Egypt to bring Uriah back to Jerusalem. The process sounds much like what we call an extradition and suggests some kind of diplomatic relationship between Egypt and Judah. (Jeremiah viewed such diplomatic relationships negatively, as an effort by Judah to secure itself apart from God; see 2:17–18, 37:6–10). Finally, King Jehoiakim has Uriah killed (26:23).

The execution of Uriah underscores several points. First, the actions of King Jehoiakim and King Hezekiah are placed in contrast. When Hezekiah heard from the prophet Micah God's threat to destroy Jerusalem, he feared the Lord and entreated the Lord's favor (v. 19). When King Jehoiakim hears threats of Jerusalem's destruction from Uriah and Jeremiah, he seeks to have these prophets, whom God has sent, put to death. Hezekiah "heeded" God's word, but Jehoiakim does not listen. This favorable portrayal of King Hezekiah in Jeremiah 26 matches that found in 2 Kings 19. In the account of King Hezekiah in 2 Kings, the king heeds God's word from the prophet Isaiah, and Jerusalem is spared destruction by Assyria. These stories demonstrate that King Jehoiakim similarly had an opportunity to heed the words of Jeremiah, but his failure to do so led Judah toward "disaster" and the captivity of Jerusalem, as "the elders of the land" who defended Jeremiah had warned (v. 19).

Second, Uriah's death indicates the grave danger to Jeremiah as he speaks for God to the kings and other leaders in Jerusalem. Jeremiah may escape death this time, but clearly the attitude of the Jerusalem leadership is hostile to God's prophets. They are unwilling to listen, and Jeremiah 26 wants us to understand that when King Jehoiakim opposes Jeremiah, he also opposes God. The destruction of Jerusalem and the captivity of 587

B.C. allowed those who edited the book of Jeremiah a clear perspective on this tragic situation: The king who sought the lives of Jeremiah and Uriah doomed himself and all Judah to a "great disaster" (v. 19), the Babylonian captivity.

Finally, there is also in this chapter an admonition about the future possibilities for Judah beyond the tragedy of the Babylonian captivity. King Hezekiah and King Jehoiakim represent two models by which, after 587 B.C., the people might respond to the word of the Lord spoken by prophets. Jehoiakim does not listen to the word of the Lord and seeks to kill God's messengers. The model of Jehoiakim leads to judgment. Hezekiah, by contrast, on hearing the word of the Lord from God's prophet, fears the Lord and entreats God's favor. Disaster is averted (v. 19). Surely, Jeremiah 26 intends to hold up the model of Hezekiah as the appropriate response to God's word and God's prophets. The church has remembered to the present day that God has called humanity to repentance and new life through prophets and apostles, and most decisively, through the word made flesh in Jesus Christ. Even as God waited to see if the leaders of Judah would heed the word of the Lord, God waits still to see if we will heed that word—the word made flesh in Jesus.

Jeremiah 27:1–22

27:1 **In the beginning of the reign of King Zedekiah son of Josiah of Judah, this word came to Jeremiah from the LORD. ² Thus the LORD said to me: Make yourself a yoke of straps and bars, and put them on your neck. ³ Send word to the king of Edom, the king of Moab, the king of the Ammonites, the king of Tyre, and the king of Sidon by the hand of the envoys who have come to Jerusalem to King Zedekiah of Judah. ⁴ Give them this charge for their masters: Thus says the LORD of hosts, the God of Israel: This is what you shall say to your masters: ⁵ It is I who by my great power and my outstretched arm have made the earth, with the people and animals that are on the earth, and I give it to whomever I please. ⁶ Now I have given all these lands into the hand of King Nebuchadnezzar of Babylon, my servant, and I have given him even the wild animals of the field to serve him. ⁷ All the nations shall serve him and his son and his grandson, until the time of his own land comes; then many nations and great kings shall make him their slave.**

⁸ But if any nation or kingdom will not serve this king, Nebuchadnezzar of Babylon, and put its neck under the yoke of the king of Babylon, then I will punish that nation with the sword, with famine, and with pestilence, says the LORD, until I have completed its destruction by his hand. ⁹ You, therefore, must not listen to your prophets, your diviners, your dreamers, your soothsayers, or your sorcerers, who are saying to you, "You shall not serve the king of Babylon." ¹⁰ For they are prophesying a lie to you, with the result

that you will be removed far from your land; I will drive you out, and you will perish. [11] But any nation that will bring its neck under the yoke of the king of Babylon and serve him, I will leave on its own land, says the LORD, to till it and live there.

[12] I spoke to King Zedekiah of Judah in the same way: Bring your necks under the yoke of the king of Babylon, and serve him and his people, and live. [13] Why should you and your people die by the sword, by famine, and by pestilence, as the LORD has spoken concerning any nation that will not serve the king of Babylon? [14] Do not listen to the words of the prophets who are telling you not to serve the king of Babylon, for they are prophesying a lie to you. [15] I have not sent them, says the LORD, but they are prophesying falsely in my name, with the result that I will drive you out and you will perish, you and the prophets who are prophesying to you.

[16] Then I spoke to the priests and to all this people, saying, Thus says the LORD: Do not listen to the words of your prophets who are prophesying to you, saying, "The vessels of the LORD's house will soon be brought back from Babylon," for they are prophesying a lie to you. [17] Do not listen to them; serve the king of Babylon and live. Why should this city become a desolation? [18] If indeed they are prophets, and if the word of the LORD is with them, then let them intercede with the LORD of hosts, that the vessels left in the house of the LORD, in the house of the king of Judah, and in Jerusalem may not go to Babylon. [19] For thus says the LORD of hosts concerning the pillars, the sea, the stands, and the rest of the vessels that are left in this city, [20] which King Nebuchadnezzar of Babylon did not take away when he took into exile from Jerusalem to Babylon King Jeconiah son of Jehoiakim of Judah, and all the nobles of Judah and Jerusalem— [21] thus says the LORD of hosts, the God of Israel, concerning the vessels left in the house of the LORD, in the house of the king of Judah, and in Jerusalem: [22] They shall be carried to Babylon, and there they shall stay, until the day when I give attention to them, says the LORD. Then I will bring them up and restore them to this place.

In this chapter, Jeremiah "speaks" God's word through an activity that dramatizes his message. (We have encountered this before, for instance, in Jeremiah 13, where the prophet buried a linen loincloth.) Jeremiah places a yoke on his neck (v. 2), which he in turn interprets to indicate that God is giving Judah and its neighbors to serve the king of Babylon as slaves (vv. 5–7). This message that God intends Babylonian domination of the geographic region surrounding Judah coincides with a gathering of envoys from several nations in Jerusalem (vv. 3–4) during the reign of King Zedekiah (597–587 B.C.). It is widely thought that this gathering occurred in 594/93 B.C., at which time Egypt tried to organize a rebellion against Babylon by a number of states that Babylon controlled as vessels.

While we can find the historical developments of 594/93 B.C. in Jeremiah 27, this chapter is not so much interested in reporting accurately the details of a summit conference in Jerusalem as it is in reflecting on why God directed Judah's history to the Babylonian captivity of 587 B.C. Jeremiah 27 continues the concern of prior chapters about responses to God's word by focusing on prophets who contradict Jeremiah's message that demands surrender to Babylon.

Having been ordered by God to place a yoke on his neck, Jeremiah first addresses the envoys of the nations who are gathered in Jerusalem (vv. 3–11), who are to carry Jeremiah's message back to their kings. The yoke Jeremiah places on his neck announces God's intention to the nations that they are to serve the king of Babylon until an appointed time when God will make Babylon itself a slave (vv. 6–7). God's right and ability to decide for Babylonian domination of the nations are justified by the claim that God "made the earth, with the people and animals that are on the earth, and I give it to whomever I please" (v. 5). The phrase "by my great power and my great outstretched arm" is used in Deuteronomy 9:29 to describe how God delivered Israel from Egypt and gave them the land of promise. The phrase as used in Jeremiah 27 suggests God's power, once used to deliver God's people from slavery in Egypt for life in the promised land, will be turned against Judah. Judah refuses to listen to God's prophets, so the Lord is willing to deliver Judah into the hands of the Babylonians.

The concern about the response of the nations to God's word (vv. 8–11) closely parallels the concern of Jeremiah 26 about Judah heeding God's word. These verses indicate the consequences for the nations if they resist Babylon (v. 8) and if they submit (v. 11). Resistance will result in complete destruction of a nation by sword, famine, and pestilence. While it is Babylon that will inflict the imagined destruction, by specifically attributing the destruction of a resisting nation to the Lord (vv. 8, 10, particularly), the emphasis of the text is not narrowly on geopolitical realities but on God's sovereignty and the need for the nations to heed the word of the Lord. Submission, while still resulting in domination by Babylon, will permit a nation to remain on its land "to till it and live there" (v. 11), a less severe consequence than for those who resist.

The consequences of resistance and submission developed in verses 8 and 11 surround a warning to the nations that they "must not listen" to their prophets, diviners, and the like, who promised, "You shall not serve the king of Babylon" (vv. 9–10). This warning is be sounded twice more in Jeremiah 27, in verses 14–15 and 16–18. The conflict between the word of the Lord spoken by Jeremiah that demands submission to Babylon and the word of those prophets who promise quick relief from the Babylonian threat is central to this chapter. In Jeremiah 26, the concern was whether or not Judah would heed God's word. Jeremiah 27 complicates the situation of the preceding chapter by introducing prophets who present a word that contradicts and competes with the word spoken by Jeremiah. The issue in Jeremiah 27 is not simply whether nations will heed God's word but whether they are able to discern the word of the Lord among competing words spoken by persons who all claim to be God's legitimate spokespersons.

The issue of prophets who speak for God and those who speak "lies" (vv. 10, 14) continues in Jeremiah 28 in the confrontation between Jeremiah and Hananiah. The book of Jeremiah was edited and shaped by persons who enjoyed the perspective of time, who had experienced the exile of 587 B.C., and who knew that Jeremiah was correct in announcing Babylonian domination. However, for Jeremiah's contemporaries, who lived prior to the events of 587 B.C., to discern among competing claims regarding who speaks for God must have been quite difficult, and it remains so today. We need to reflect further about this problem as we move through the remainder of Jeremiah 27 and 28.

Having addressed the envoys of the nations, Jeremiah is next presented as he specifically addresses King Zedekiah of Judah (27:12–15). Submission to "the yoke of the king of Babylon" is presented to Zedekiah as a matter of life and death (vv. 12–13; cf. Jer. 21:8–10 and the theme of life and death in Jeremiah 21–24). Jeremiah warns Zedekiah about the prophets who are telling the king of Judah not to serve the king of Babylon. Jeremiah accuses these prophets of lying (vv. 14–15). In Jeremiah 7, the words of the Temple liturgy assuring the inhabitants of Jerusalem that God will never destroy Jerusalem are called "deceptive." In Jeremiah 27, the lie is in the words of prophets who assure Zedekiah and Judah that they will not have to submit to Babylon. Again, the emphasis of these verses is on the response of Zedekiah to the word of the Lord spoken by Jeremiah. Zedekiah's response is made difficult because prophets other than Jeremiah speak words that contradict and compete with Jeremiah's announcement of doom.

Finally, Jeremiah 27 presents God's spokesperson as he addresses "the priests and all this people" of Jerusalem who anticipate the quick return of the Temple fixtures that the Babylonians took in their invasion of Jerusalem of 597 B.C. (vv. 16–22). In some ways, this speech has a different concern from that of the first two speeches in the chapter. In addressing the envoys of the nations and King Zedekiah, Jeremiah is concerned with the decisions of political leaders who might choose to resist the Babylonians. In the final section of the chapter, Jeremiah addresses a group that takes an optimistic view of how Judah's relationship with Babylon will develop.

It is possible to discern in verses 16–22 some indication of the historical situation of Judah in the early 590s B.C. Already in 597 B.C., the Babylonians had entered Jerusalem, looted the Temple, and taken key leaders of Judah captive (see 2 Kings 24:8–17; also pp. 14–15). Those addressed in 27:16–22, priests and people, believed prophets in Judah who announced that "the vessels of the Lord's house will soon be brought back from Babylon" (v. 16). Historically, it may be that the optimism of this group grew from Egyptian efforts to organize Judah and her neighbors to rebel against Babylon (v. 3; also see Jer. 37:1–10).

However, the focus of 27:16–22 is again on the conflict between Jeremiah on the one hand and prophets who imagine Judah's trouble with Babylon will be short-lived on the other. Jeremiah insists that the only hope for Judah is to serve the king of Babylon. To listen to prophets who are "prophesying a lie" with their optimistic vision of the quick return of the Temple vessels will only result in Jerusalem being turned into a desolation (v. 17). Jeremiah is presented as pressing his conflict with the optimistic prophets in two ways (vv. 18–22). First, Jeremiah challenges them to intercede on Judah's behalf that the vessels still left in the Temple not be taken by Babylon. This is to test "if the word of the Lord is with them" (v. 18). Second, Jeremiah announces his version of the Lord's word, which sharply conflicts with the optimistic predictions of those who announce the quick return of the vessels already taken. According to Jeremiah, even the vessels remaining in the Temple after 597 B.C. will be carried to Babylon, where they will remain until God chooses to restore them (vv. 21–22). Clearly, Jeremiah and the optimistic prophets cannot both be the prophets sent by God.

All three sections of Jeremiah 27 present a conflict between Jeremiah, who announces that Judah and the nations must submit to God's reign and surrender to Babylon, and other prophets who conclude that matters are not so dire. Jeremiah declares that Babylon cannot be resisted. As the sovereign of creation, the Lord has decided to give Babylon dominion over Judah and her neighbors. Other prophets referred to in Jeremiah 27 announce that Judah will not have to serve Babylon and that whatever trouble Babylon has caused Judah will be short-lived. Those who edited and shaped the book of Jeremiah did so knowing that the events of 587 B.C. proved Jeremiah correct, a perspective we also enjoy. Yet, in the unfolding story of the prophet in the book, the conflict between Jeremiah and the more optimistic prophets who oppose him is unresolved at the conclusion of Jeremiah 27 and is developed further in Jeremiah 28, through the story of Jeremiah's conflict with a specific prophet, Hananiah.

Jeremiah 28:1–17

28:1 In that same year, at the beginning of the reign of King Zedekiah of Judah, in the fifth month of the fourth year, the prophet Hananiah son of Azzur, from Gibeon, spoke to me in the house of the LORD, in the presence of the priests and all the people, saying, 2 "Thus says the LORD of hosts, the God of Israel: I have broken the yoke of the king of Babylon. 3 Within two years I will bring back to this place all the vessels of the LORD's house, which King Nebuchadnezzar of Babylon took away from this place and carried to Babylon. 4 I will also bring back to this place King Jeconiah son of Jehoiakim of Judah, and all the exiles from Judah who went to Babylon, says the LORD, for I will break the yoke of the king of Babylon."

5 Then the prophet Jeremiah spoke to the prophet Hananiah in the presence of the priests and all the people who were standing in the house of the LORD; 6 and the prophet Jeremiah said, "Amen! May the LORD do so; may the LORD fulfill the words that you have prophesied, and bring back to this place from Babylon the vessels of the house of the LORD, and all the exiles. 7 But listen now to this word that I speak in your hearing and in the hearing of all the people. 8 The prophets who preceded you and me from ancient times prophesied war, famine, and pestilence against many countries and great kingdoms. 9 As for the prophet who prophesies peace, when the word of that prophet comes true, then it will be known that the LORD has truly sent the prophet."

10 Then the prophet Hananiah took the yoke from the neck of the prophet Jeremiah, and broke it. 11 And Hananiah spoke in the presence of all the people, saying, "Thus says the LORD: This is how I will break the yoke of King Nebuchadnezzar of Babylon from the neck of all the nations within two years." At this, the prophet Jeremiah went his way.

12 Sometime after the prophet Hananiah had broken the yoke from the neck of the prophet Jeremiah, the word of the LORD came to Jeremiah: 13 Go, tell Hananiah, Thus says the LORD: You have broken wooden bars only to forge iron bars in place of them! 14 For thus says the LORD of hosts, the God of Israel: I have put an iron yoke on the neck of all these nations so that they may serve King Nebuchadnezzar of Babylon, and they shall indeed serve him; I have even given him the wild animals. 15 And the prophet Jeremiah said to the prophet Hananiah, "Listen, Hananiah, the LORD has not sent you, and you made this people trust in a lie. 16 Therefore thus says the LORD: I am going to send you off the face of the earth. Within this year you will be dead, because you have spoken rebellion against the LORD."

17 In that same year, in the seventh month, the prophet Hananiah died.

Jeremiah 27 introduced the conflict between Jeremiah's message of doom and the claims of other prophets who were more optimistic. Jeremiah 28 presents a specific example of this conflict through the encounter between Jeremiah and Hananiah. As Jeremiah 28 begins, Hananiah, claiming to be God's spokesperson, announces that God has "broken the yoke of the king of Babylon" (vv. 2, 4) and that within two years the vessels that the king of Babylon removed from the Lord's house, along with all of those who were exiled from Judah to Babylon in 597 B.C., will be returned to Judah (vv. 3–4). Hananiah, whose name means "Yahweh is gracious," announces an optimistic version of Judah's future; the Babylonian problem will, in God's grace, soon pass.

Though both Jeremiah and Hananiah claim to speak for God, Hananiah's optimism conflicts with Jeremiah's message of doom. Remember, at the beginning of Jeremiah 27, Jeremiah acts at God's direction to place a yoke on his neck as a sign to indicate that God is giving the nations, including Judah, over to Babylon (27:1–7). Hananiah claims that God has "broken the yoke of the king of Babylon" (vv. 2, 4), and within two years Judah's difficulty with Babylon will be over. Jeremiah 28 explores this conflict between Hananiah and Jeremiah and invites us, too, to ponder how to distinguish among those who claim to speak for God but do so in conflicting ways.

Jeremiah's response to Hananiah is in two parts. First (vv. 5–6), Jeremiah responds to Hananiah by saying, "Amen! May the Lord do so" (v. 6). We have previously encountered the prophet's anguish at having to announce "violence and destruction" to Judah (for instance, 20:7–9). Nothing would please Jeremiah more than for God to relent, to turn back the fearsome "foe from the north" (1:14–15; 4:6; 6:1, 22), to break the yoke of Babylon and cancel plans for Judah's destruction. Jeremiah's first response to Hananiah is to hope, surely with all sincerity, that Hananiah speaks for God. Jeremiah would like to be able himself to announce a reprieve from Babylon, as Hananiah is promising.

Jeremiah, however, is unable to proclaim the optimistic message of Hananiah with integrity, and the second part of Jeremiah's response (vv. 7–9) expresses this reservation. Jeremiah reminds Hananiah that prophets before their own time "prophesied war, famine and pestilence against many countries and great kingdoms" (v. 8). God's prophets, for the most part, have announced not God's deliverance but God's judgment. If Hananiah speaks for God, then he is an exception to the norm. Jeremiah even allows that Hananiah may be the exception, a prophet who announces God's gracious deliverance. However, Jeremiah is deeply suspicious of this possibility and concludes his response by indicating that should a prophet of hope be sent by God, the way it will be known the prophet is such is "when the word of that prophet comes true" (v. 9).

This criterion for identifying a prophet of God as one whose word comes true reflects the passage about prophets from Deuteronomy 18, cited in discussing Jeremiah 26 (pp. 207–8):

> If a prophet speaks in the name of the Lord but the thing does not take place or prove true, it is a word that the Lord has not spoken. (v. 22)

It is likely that this criterion developed out of the experience of the exile of 587 B.C. While Jeremiah's response to Hananiah in verse 9 may be his own words, the response may also reflect the perspective of persons who edited and shaped the book of Jeremiah after 587 B.C. These persons knew that Jeremiah's message of doom had been fulfilled, and from the editors' perspective, the exile proved that Jeremiah was a prophet sent by God. Whether through Jeremiah's own words or those of the editors of the book, Jeremiah 28 recognizes that for the most part God's prophets have announced not grace but judgment. The weight of history is against Hananiah, and only if his optimistic word were to come true could Hananiah prove his claim to speak for God.

The first nine verses of Jeremiah 28 present Jeremiah and Hananiah in direct conflict. The final verses of the chapter indicate how that conflict intensified before coming to a sudden and startling resolution (v. 17). It is Hananiah who escalates the conflict. To underscore his announcement that God has "broken the yoke of the king of Babylon" (vv. 2, 4), Hananiah performs a symbolic act that directly contradicts Jeremiah's earlier act of placing a yoke on his neck (see 27:1–8). Hananiah "took the yoke from the neck of the prophet Jeremiah, and broke it" (28:10). Hananiah thus gives visible expression to his optimistic message that in just two more years, Babylon will be through.

After this escalation of the conflict Jeremiah withdraws, but then, at an unspecified later time (v. 12), he counters Hananiah with considerable resolve (vv. 12–16). God will replace the wooden bars with forged iron bars, warns Jeremiah, as a way to emphasize that the nations will serve Babylon as God intends and as Jeremiah announced. Babylon will not go away as Hananiah has promised but will exercise total dominion, at least for a while (remember 27:7), because that is what God intends. So total will be Babylon's domination that even the wild beasts of the nations will serve the king of Babylon (28:14).

Jeremiah not only disputes the content of Hananiah's message but also attacks Hananiah's claim that he speaks for God. Jeremiah charges that Hananiah is not sent by the Lord and is causing Judah to "trust in a lie" (v. 15). The accusation that the Lord has not sent Hananiah complements Jeremiah's announcement that God will judge Judah because the people have failed to listen to the prophets whom God had sent urgently (26:5).

The punishment Jeremiah announces for Hananiah, whom God has "not sent," is that God will send Hananiah off the face of the earth; that is, Hananiah will die (28:16). Hananiah has announced that the Babylonian threat will disappear in two years. Jeremiah announces that Hananiah will die within one year. Death is the punishment specified in Deuteronomy 18:20 for prophets who presume to speak for God but do not. This story of the conflict between Jeremiah and Hananiah comes to a sudden end at verse 17 with the report that Hananiah died "in that same year," just as Jeremiah announced. The announcement of Hananiah's death resolves in Jeremiah's favor the conflict presented in this chapter. Jeremiah, not Hananiah, is God's spokesperson. Jeremiah's message of judgment, not Hananiah's optimism, points the course along which God is directing Judah's history.

With the conclusion of this story about the confrontation between Jeremiah and Hananiah, we are left with two questions. First, how are we to account for the conflict between Jeremiah and Hananiah, both of whom claimed to speak for God? Second, how might this story help us in our time when we are confronted with persons who claim to speak for God but do so in conflicting ways?

There were other optimistic prophets in Judah before Hananiah. For instance, Isaiah, a prophet in Judah from approximately 740–700 B.C., at times promised God's protection of Judah. When a coalition of nations threatened Judah around 735 B.C., Isaiah counseled Judah's king Ahaz about those who planned to overthrow him, "It shall not stand, and it shall not come to pass" (Isa. 7:7). Later, when Assyria besieged Jerusalem around 700 B.C., Isaiah counseled King Hezekiah, "He shall not come into the city" (Isa. 37:33). So, Hananiah was not the first prophet in Judah who had spoken an optimistic or comforting word.

It is likely that Hananiah, along with Isaiah before him, based his confidence about Jerusalem's security on a widely held belief that God would protect forever both Jerusalem and the kings of Jerusalem who followed King David. We hear such confidence about Jerusalem expressed, for instance, in Psalm 46 ("the city" is Jerusalem):

> There is a river whose streams make glad the city of God,
>   the holy habitation of the Most High.
> God is in the midst of the city; it shall not be moved;
>   God will help it when the morning dawns.
>
> (vv. 4–5)

Comparable notions about Jerusalem can be found in Psalms 48:1, 8; 87:3 and in Jeremiah 7, discussed earlier. Similarly, an expression of God's commitment to Judah's kings after David is found in 2 Samuel 7, which uses the word *forever* repeatedly (e.g., 2 Sam. 7:16, 29). So, Hananiah was not without some basis for his confidence in God's protection of Jerusalem from the Babylonians.

Jeremiah, as discussed earlier, was most influenced by a point of view that emphasized not so much God's protection of Judah as what the Lord had done for Israel (especially remembering the exodus from Egypt) and the ways in which the people were accountable before God. Jeremiah would have surely been aware of the viewpoint of Hananiah. However, when Jeremiah considered Judah as he knew it—its idolatry, its lack of concern for the poor, its efforts to secure itself through foreign alliances, its self-assured religious practices that discounted the possibility of accountability before God—he was convinced, against Hananiah, that in their moment of history, God was about to call Judah to account. Of course, Hananiah's words of comfort and assurance were easier to accept than Jeremiah's. It is no surprise that the people of Judah rejected Jeremiah and prophets like him and embraced Hananiah, who assured them that all was well. However, Jeremiah 28 is clear that more often than not, God's prophets "prophesied war, famine, and pestilence," and that one needs to be suspicious of "the prophet who prophesies peace" (vv. 8–9).

Understanding the basis of the conflict between Jeremiah and Hananiah may help us with the issue of how we might respond when persons who claim that they speak for God offer very different perspectives. We need to be careful about generalizing from the specific instance presented to us in Jeremiah 28. Like those who witnessed the conflict between Jeremiah and Hananiah, we need to decide in each situation, with all its complexity and uncertainty, who speaks for God. Still, Jeremiah 28 suggests to us that it is well to be suspicious of those who, like Hananiah, speak words of comfort and reassurance that we want to hear and that are easy for us. Rather, "from ancient times" (v. 8) the persons more likely to have been sent by God are those whose message is discomforting and disturbing— "war, famine, and pestilence"—like the hard words of Jeremiah, who announced that God intended a long dominion for Babylon over Judah and the nations. We, like the people of ancient Judah, are drawn to the assurance of the Hananiahs among us. Jeremiah 28 claims that God is more likely to speak to us through the hard words of the Jeremiahs, who announce that God is disrupting and ending the world in which we are so comfortable.

Jeremiah 29:1–23

29:1 **These are the words of the letter that the prophet Jeremiah sent from Jerusalem to the remaining elders among the exiles, and to the priests, the prophets, and all the people, whom Nebuchadnezzar had taken into exile from Jerusalem to Babylon.** 2 **This was after King Jeconiah, and the queen mother, the court officials, the leaders of Judah and Jerusalem, the artisans, and the smiths had departed from Jerusalem.** 3 **The letter was sent by the hand of Elasah son of Shaphan and Gemariah son of Hilkiah, whom King Zedekiah of Judah sent to Babylon to King Nebuchadnezzar of Babylon. It said:** 4 **Thus says the LORD of hosts, the God of Israel, to all the exiles whom I have sent into exile from Jerusalem to Babylon:** 5 **Build houses and live in them; plant gardens and eat what they produce.** 6 **Take wives and have sons and daughters; take wives for your sons, and give your daughters in marriage, that they may bear sons and daughters; multiply there, and do not decrease.** 7 **But seek the welfare of the city where I have sent you into exile, and pray to the LORD on its behalf, for in its welfare you will find your welfare.** 8 **For thus says the LORD of hosts, the God of Israel: Do not let the prophets and the diviners who are among you deceive you, and do not listen to the dreams that they dream,** 9 **for it is a lie that they are prophesying to you in my name; I did not send them, says the LORD.**

10 **For thus says the LORD: Only when Babylon's seventy years are completed will I visit you, and I will fulfill to you my promise and bring you back to this place.** 11 **For surely I know the plans I have for you, says the LORD, plans for your welfare and not for harm, to give you a future with hope.** 12 **Then when you call upon me and come and pray to me, I will hear you.** 13 **When you search for me, you will find me; if you seek me with all your heart,** 14 **I will let you find me, says the LORD, and I will restore your fortunes and gather you from all the nations and all the places where I have driven you, says the LORD, and I will bring you back to the place from which I sent you into exile.**

15 **Because you have said, "The LORD has raised up prophets for us in Babylon,"—** 16 **Thus says the LORD concerning the king who sits on the throne of David, and concerning all the people who live in this city, your kinsfolk who did not go out with you into exile:** 17 **Thus says the LORD of hosts, I am going to let loose on them sword, famine, and pestilence, and I will make them like rotten figs that are so bad they cannot be eaten.** 18 **I will**

pursue them with the sword, with famine, and with pestilence, and will make them a horror to all the kingdoms of the earth, to be an object of cursing, and horror, and hissing, and a derision among all the nations where I have driven them, [19] because they did not heed my words, says the LORD, when I persistently sent to you my servants the prophets, but they would not listen, says the LORD. [20] But now, all you exiles whom I sent away from Jerusalem to Babylon, hear the word of the LORD: [21] Thus says the LORD of hosts, the God of Israel, concerning Ahab son of Kolaiah and Zedekiah son of Maaseiah, who are prophesying a lie to you in my name: I am going to deliver them into the hand of King Nebuchadrezzar of Babylon, and he shall kill them before your eyes. [22] And on account of them this curse shall be used by all the exiles from Judah in Babylon: "The LORD make you like Zedekiah and Ahab, whom the king of Babylon roasted in the fire," [23] because they have perpetrated outrage in Israel and have committed adultery with their neighbors' wives, and have spoken in my name lying words that I did not command them; I am the one who knows and bears witness, says the LORD.

Jeremiah 29 concerns an exchange of letters between Jeremiah and those persons who were taken captive to Babylon in 597 B.C. (vv. 1–2). The chapter as we have it is complicated and may include portions of a number of different letters that were woven together by an editor. For instance, one letter from Jeremiah to those exiled in 597 B.C. may be found in verses 1–15, with its conclusion in verses 21–23. (Notice that you can read from v. 15 over to v. 21, which picks up the flow from v. 15; this may mean that vv. 16–20 were not part of Jeremiah's letter and were inserted by an editor.) Verses 24–28 seem to be a letter sent by Jeremiah to a man named Shemaiah who was exiled, but Jeremiah's letter in these verses consists mostly of a quotation of a letter Shemaiah sent from Babylon to the priest Zephaniah in Jerusalem (vv. 26–28). Finally, verses 31–32 include a second letter Jeremiah sent to the exiles after he had heard the priest Zephaniah read Shemaiah's letter from exile.

Though Jeremiah 29 is complicated, it continues the theme begun in Jeremiah 26 about who it is that God sent to announce God's intentions for Judah. Three times in Jeremiah 29, in verses 9, 19, and 31, there is direct concern with whom God did or did not "send" as a spokesperson.

Regarding Jeremiah's first letter, it was sent by Jeremiah to Babylon in the hands of two men identified as Elasah son of Shaphan and Gemariah son of Hilkiah (v. 3). At the end of Jeremiah 26, after the legal proceeding when Jeremiah had preached in the Temple, it was reported that Jeremiah was released to Ahikam son of Shaphan. It seems that Elasah, one of the men who carried Jeremiah's letter to Babylon, was a brother of Ahikam and part of a family that had been supportive of King Josiah's reforms and of Jeremiah. It has been suggested that Gemariah may have been a son of the high priest Hilkiah (not Jeremiah's father), who was also connected with Josiah's reform, having found the scroll in the Temple (2 Kings 22:8). It is difficult to know if the historical details of Jeremiah 29 are accurate; but if they are, they give us another glimpse of the political situation of Jeremiah's time. The accounts suggest that Jeremiah was supported by a group of persons in Judah who had connections with the reform efforts of King Josiah and who, by Jeremiah's time, were a strong minority voice in Judah's politics.

The content of Jeremiah's first letter to those exiled in Babylon deals with several matters: the relationship of those exiled to Babylon (vv. 5–9), the future of Judah beyond Babylon (vv. 10–14), and a condemnation of two persons who claimed to be prophets among the Babylonian exiles (vv. 20–23). While verses 16–19 may have been added by an editor who was trying to piece together the various letters included in Jeremiah 29, these verses, as we will see, are important to this chapter.

Jeremiah's first letter addresses the issue of how those who were already taken captive to Babylon in 597 B.C. are to live as exiles (vv. 5–9). In verse 5, a fresh twist is given to the "build and plant" phrase from Jeremiah's call (1:10), where the words signaled God's intention to restore the nations after God had "plucked them up and pulled them down." In addressing those already exiled to Babylon in 597 B.C., Jeremiah urges the exiles to "build" and "plant" houses and gardens in Babylon, to establish families and settle into Babylon for the long haul (29:6). By building and planting in Babylon and establishing their families there, those whom God has already "plucked up" from the land will be submitting to God's sovereign intentions for Babylonian domination.

There is a connection with the preceding chapter and Hananiah's optimistic prediction that the exile will last but two years. Jeremiah's counsel that those already exiled "build and plant" in Babylon undercuts any hope that the exile will be short. Further, Jeremiah's condemnation of "the prophets and diviners who are among you" (29:8) suggests that among those exiled in Babylon are prophets who share Hananiah's optimistic viewpoint about the exile. Some scholars have even suggested that the prophets in Babylon were urging some kind of rebellion. As he did with Hananiah, Jeremiah in his letter dismisses optimistic prophets with God's declaration "I did not send them" (v. 9). Jeremiah understands that God demands Judah submit to Babylon, and so, Jeremiah insists that for those exiled to Babylon in 597 B.C., it is the time to build houses and plant gardens in Babylon. Jeremiah's condemnation of those who claim to be prophets among the exiles is developed further in verses 21–23, which include the likely conclusion of Jeremiah's first letter. We come to these verses shortly.

What Jeremiah counsels those who have been exiled goes beyond simply settling in for the long haul. Rather, Jeremiah demands that those exiled seek the "welfare" of Babylon "and pray to the Lord on its behalf" (v. 7). It is ironic that Jeremiah was told not to pray for Judah (see 7:16; 11:14; 14:11), but those exiled in Babylon are to pray for Babylon's "welfare" (the Hebrew word is *shālôm* and suggests peace, prosperity, wholeness). Concern for Babylon's welfare demands more than resigned acceptance of a long exile. Babylon is to be not merely a place of sojourn to be endured but a place of involvement and concern, where those exiled from Judah are to live seeking the "welfare" even of hated Babylon. Indeed, Jeremiah links the welfare of Judaean exiles with the welfare of Babylon (v. 7). The Lord, who is sovereign over nations and kingdoms (1:10), demands that the exiles participate in God's concern for all nations and kingdoms, including Babylon.

Perhaps a comparison for us is how we relate to persons or groups from whom we feel estrangement, other racial or social groups, for instance. One way of relating is to accept out of necessity that we now live in a pluralistic world where we must inevitably relate to people we do not particularly like. Another way of relating is to see those who are different from us as a gift from God who enrich us, and so to embrace and welcome diversity and relationships with others as for our "welfare" and the welfare of God's creation. Jeremiah calls on those already exiled in Babylon not merely to accept their plight but to embrace it as a gift from God for their welfare.

Jeremiah's sense of the wholeness of God's creation is captured in another setting by the writer of the New Testament letter to the Ephesians. In a context in which the hostility was not between Judaeans and Babylonians but between Jews and Gentiles, the author of Ephesians wrote:

> But now in Christ Jesus you who once were far off [i.e., Gentiles] have been brought near by the blood of Christ. For he is our peace; in his flesh he has made both groups into one and has broken down the dividing wall, that is, the hostility between us. . . . So he came and proclaimed peace to you who were far off and peace to those who were near. . . . So then you are no longer strangers and aliens, but you are citizens and saints and also members of the household of God. (2:13–14, 17, 19)

Ephesians speaks of the "peace" that we in the church know though Jesus Christ. Jeremiah anticipated the fullness of the gospel of Jesus Christ when he urged exiled Judaeans of his time to seek the welfare (that is, peace) of Babylon and to consider even hated Babylon "home." God's imagination is not bound by the dividing walls of hostility constructed by human conflicts. In God's reign, Judaeans and Babylonians as well as Gentiles and Jews are to live in peace. Jeremiah's letter to the exiles presses us to ask, in God's global vision, whose welfare God calls us to seek and with whom God is inviting us to live in peace.

Surely, the prophets condemned in verse 8 must have delivered a very different message from Jeremiah's admonition to seek Babylon's welfare. The prophets Jeremiah condemned may have announced, like Hananiah, that the exile in Babylon would not last long. Jeremiah perceives that these prophets urge that which works against God's sovereign intentions, against Judah's submission to Babylon. About these prophets, Jeremiah announces on God's behalf, "I did not send them" (29:9).

Finally, Jeremiah's first letter addresses the problem of despair, the sense among those exiled that they have no future (vv. 10–14). The affirmation of these verses is that God, who urged Judah to seek the welfare of Babylon, also has intentions for the welfare of Judah, for Judah's "future with hope" beyond Babylonian dominion (v. 11). God, who sent Judah into exile, will finally be attentive to Judah (v. 12), restore Judah's fortunes, and gather them from the nations (v. 14). These verses anticipate Jeremiah 30–33, whose theme is God's restoration of Judah's fortunes after 587 B.C.

While Jeremiah's first letter to those exiled in 597 B.C. likely concluded with verses 21–23, the editor who pieced together Jeremiah 29 added verses 16–19. In the way we now have Jeremiah 29, verses 16–23 form a distinct section in which Jeremiah addresses first those who were left behind in Jerusalem (vv. 16–19) and then those exiled in Babylon (vv. 20–23).

The material that addresses those who remained in Jerusalem (vv. 16–19) is very much like Jeremiah 24; there is even a reference to "rotten figs" (29:17; see 24:2, 8). While those who escaped exile when Babylon invaded Judah in 597 B.C. may think they are somehow favored by God, verses 16–19 threaten those who remain in Jerusalem with terrible judgment and covenant curse. Another military invasion is anticipated with the threat of "sword, . . . famine, . . . and pestilence." (This curse has been used extensively in the book since it was first introduced in 14:12.) However, this curse will result in a second, that Judah will become "an object of cursing, and horror, and hissing" among the nations. This language is drawn from the covenant curse in Deuteronomy 28:37. For those who have remained in Jerusalem and may think themselves favored by God, a double judgment is announced. The reason for such harsh judgment is given in verse 19, which links this material to previous chapters. Judah will experience covenant curse because they have failed to heed God's word, have failed to listen to God's prophets. (The language of verse 29:19 is almost identical to that in 26:5.)

Verses 20–23 (which include the conclusion of Jeremiah's first letter) address those already exiled to Babylon and are concerned with two prophets among the exiles (remember v. 8). Practically nothing is known about Ahab and Zedekiah or what, specifically, they did to deserve the severe condemnation of Jeremiah found in these verses. The clearest charge is that they have "spoken in my name lying words that I did not command" (v. 23), an accusation similar to that which Jeremiah leveled against Hananiah (28:15) and against the optimistic prophets of Judah (27:14). After reading about the optimistic prophets of Judah and about Hananiah, we can surmise that these prophets in Jeremiah 29 must have announced an early end to the exile, even though we cannot know this with certainty. Verses 20–23 complement verses 16–19. Just as God will judge Jerusalem because those who remained behind after 597 B.C. will not listen to the prophets whom God sends, so the two prophets among those exiled will be punished because they presume to speak for God, who has not sent them.

The same issues with which we have been concerned for several chapters of Jeremiah again surface and challenge us: as we seek to discern who is and is not God's prophet in our time; with caution about those who claim to speak for God but whose word is comfortable and to our liking; with encouragement to heed well the hard words of those we would like to dismiss but who may well be the servants through whom God speaks to us.

Jeremiah 29:24–32

29:24 **To Shemaiah of Nehelam you shall say:** [25] **Thus says the LORD of hosts, the God of Israel: In your own name you sent a letter to all the people who are in Jerusalem, and to the priest Zephaniah son of Maaseiah, and to all the priests, saying,** [26] **The LORD himself has made you priest instead of the priest Jehoiada, so that there may be officers in the house of the LORD to control any madman who plays the prophet, to put him in the stocks and the collar.** [27] **So now why have you not rebuked Jeremiah of Anathoth who plays the prophet for you?** [28] **For he has actually sent to us in Babylon, saying, "It will be a long time; build houses and live in them, and plant gardens and eat what they produce."**

²⁹ **The priest Zephaniah read this letter in the hearing of the prophet Jeremiah.** ³⁰ **Then the word of the LORD came to Jeremiah:** ³¹ **Send to all the exiles, saying, Thus says the LORD concerning Shemaiah of Nehelam: Because Shemaiah has prophesied to you, though I did not send him, and has led you to trust in a lie,** ³² **therefore thus says the LORD: I am going to punish Shemaiah of Nehelam and his descendants; he shall not have anyone living among this people to see the good that I am going to do to my people, says the LORD, for he has spoken rebellion against the LORD.**

Verses 24–32 indicate that there was an exchange of letters that involved Jeremiah; Shemaiah of Nehelam, who had been exiled to Babylon in 597 B.C.; and Zephaniah son of Maaseiah, a priest in Jerusalem. Apparently, the letters exchanged among these parties became public. While the entire exchange of letters is difficult to reconstruct, we can find in these verses what Shemaiah, writing from Babylon to the priest Zephaniah in Jerusalem, said about Jeremiah and how Jeremiah responded when he heard Shemaiah's letter.

Shemaiah wrote from Babylon to the priest Zephaniah in Jerusalem. It sounds as if Zephaniah had recently assumed his priestly position (v. 26) and Shemaiah was not very pleased about how Zephaniah was handling his duties. Shemaiah wrote to admonish Zephaniah, particularly displeased that the priest was not able "to control" Jeremiah (v. 26), whom Shemaiah called a "madman" who "plays the prophet for you." Shemaiah did not think Jeremiah was a prophet. He was angered by the letter Jeremiah had sent to those exiled in 597 B.C. that said the exile would be long and the exiles needed to build houses and plant gardens (v. 28; see vv. 5–7). Shemaiah would have had considerable sympathy with those among the Jerusalem leadership who thought Jeremiah should be put to death because he prophesied the destruction of Jerusalem (26:7–9). For Shemaiah, Jeremiah was a Babylonian sympathizer and a traitor to the cause of Judah who could not possibly speak for God.

Shemaiah's attitude should not surprise us at all. It is quite common that those in church and in society who question the comfortable assumption that all is well are rejected as "mad" or as sympathizers with an enemy who cannot possibly speak for God. In our own century, Dietrich Bonhoeffer, who spoke out against the evil of the Third Reich, was jailed and executed as a traitor. Nelson Mandela and other brave persons of color in South Africa who opposed apartheid were imprisoned, tortured, and in some cases killed as dangers to society. Martin Luther King Jr. was branded a communist, hounded by law-enforcement agencies, often imprisoned, and finally killed. To imagine that God might be about dis-ordering and reordering the world is a dangerous business, and through Shemaiah we hear one who is frightened by what Jeremiah announces as God's spokesperson.

The priest Zephaniah shared Shemaiah's letter with Jeremiah (v. 29). Once again, it may be that we can hear in this something of the political intrigue in Jerusalem at this time. Zephaniah's sympathies must have been much more with Jeremiah than with Shemaiah. In any case, when Jeremiah heard Shemaiah's letter, he wrote again to those in Babylon. He condemned Shemaiah as he had Hananiah (Jeremiah 28), the optimistic prophets of Judah (Jeremiah 27), and Ahab and Zedekiah (29:21–23). Jeremiah declared that God had "not sent" Shemaiah (cf. 27:15; 28:15; 29:9), that Shemaiah led those exiled to "trust in a lie" (cf. 27:10, 16; 28:15; 29:9, 23), and that Shemaiah spoke "rebellion against the Lord" (29:32; Jeremiah made the same charge against Hananiah in 28:16).

The judgment Jeremiah announced against Shemaiah reflected Shemaiah's critique of Jeremiah. Shemaiah had objected to Jeremiah's assertion that the exile would be long. The judgment Jeremiah announced for Shemaiah was that neither Shemaiah nor his descendants would live to see the "good" God would eventually do for Judah. Though the exile would be long, Jeremiah had promised, God would restore the fortunes of the people and gather them again in the land (v. 14). However, for Shemaiah, who rebelled against God's plucking up and resisted building and planting in Babylon, there would not be building and planting in the land, and he would not participate Judah's restoration.

To this point, the emphasis of the book of Jeremiah has been on plucking up and tearing down. Not surprisingly, Jeremiah's announcement of God's judgment met with considerable resistance. It was difficult for citizens of Judah like Shemaiah to imagine that only by embracing God's judgment could there be any hope for restoration, for building and planting. In Jeremiah 30–33, the emphasis of the book shifts to God's intention to restore the fortunes of Judah and Israel after the exile. As we read of God's intention to restore Judah in the next chapters of Jeremiah, we need to remember Shemaiah and Jeremiah's word to him that restoration is a promise for those who experience God's judgment, and not a negation of judgment.

Works Cited

Bonhoeffer, Dietrich. *The Cost of Discipleship*. Translated by R. H. Fuller. New York: Macmillan Co., 1963.

———. *Life Together*. Translated by John W. Doberstein. San Francisco: Harper & Brothers, 1954.

Brueggemann, Walter A."The Book of Jeremiah: Portrait of a Prophet." *Interpretation* 37 (1983): 130–45.

———. *Jeremiah 1—25: To Pluck Up and Pull Down*. International Theological Commentary. Grand Rapids: Wm. B. Eerdmans Publishing Co., 1988.

———. *The Prophetic Imagination*. Philadelphia: Fortress Press, 1978.

Buechner, Frederick. *Listening to Your Life: Daily Meditations with Frederick Buechner*. Complied by George Connor. San Francisco: Harper-Collins, 1992.

The Church of South India. *The Book of Common Worship*. London: Oxford University Press, 1963.

Cone, James. *A Black Theology of Liberation*. Twentieth Anniversary Edition. Maryknoll, N.Y.: Orbis Books, 1986.

Fretheim, Terence. *The Suffering of God*. Overtures to Biblical Theology. Philadelphia: Fortress Press, 1984.

The Heidelberg Catechism. Four hundredth Anniversary Edition. Philadelphia: United Church Press, 1962.

Heschel, Abraham. *The Prophets*. Volume 1. New York: Harper & Row, 1962.

Holladay, William. *Jeremiah I*. Hermeneia. Edited by Paul D. Hanson. Philadelphia: Fortress Press, 1986.

Kavanaugh, John Francis. *Following Christ in a Consumer Society: The Spirituality of Cultural Resistance*. Maryknoll, N.Y.: Orbis Books, 1981.

Luther, Martin. *Small Catechism: A Handbook for Christian Doctrine*. St. Louis: Concordia Publishing House, 1943. (The quotation comes from the section of the book "A Short Explanation of Dr. Martin Luther's *Small Catechism*," pp. 37–221.)

———. *The Large Catechism*. Translated by J. N. Lenker. Minneapolis: Augsburg Publishing House, 1935.

Newbigin, Lesslie. *Foolishness to Greeks: The Gospel and Western Culture*. Grand Rapids: Wm. B. Eerdmans Publishing Co., 1986.

Placher, William. "Narratives of a Vulnerable God." *Princeton Seminary Bulletin* 19 (1993): 134–51.

Thompson, John A. *The Book of Jeremiah*. The New International Commentary on the Old Testament. Grand Rapids: Wm. B. Eerdmans Publishing Co., 1980.

Wallis, James. *Agenda for a Biblical People*. New York: Harper & Row, 1976.

Wolff, Hans Walter. "The Kerygma of the Yahwist." Translated by Wilbur A. Bemware. In *The Vitality of Old Testament Traditions*, by Walter A. Brueggemann and Hans Walter Wolff. Philadelphia: Fortress Press, 1975.

The hymn "Blessed Jesus, at Your Word" is by Tobias Clausnitzer, 1663, and is found in *Hymns, Psalms, and Spiritual Songs*, 454. Louisville, Ky.: Westminster/John Knox Press, 1990.

The hymn "Make Me a Captive, Lord" is by George Matheson, 1890, and is found in *Hymns, Psalms, and Spiritual Songs*, 378.

The hymn "There Is a Balm in Gilead," an African American spiritual, is found in *Hymns, Psalms, and Spritual Songs*, 394.

For Further Reading

Blenkinsopp, Joseph. *A History of Prophecy in Israel*. Revised and Enlarged. Louisville, Ky.: Westminster/John Knox, 1996.

Bright, John. *A History of Israel*. 3d ed. Philadelphia: Westminster Press, 1981.

———. *Jeremiah*. Anchor Bible 21. Garden City, N.Y.: Doubleday & Co., 1965.

Calvin, John. *Commentaries on the Book of the Prophet Jeremiah and the Lamentations*. 6 vols. Translated and edited by the Reverend John Owen. Edinburgh: T. Constable for the Calvin Translation Society, 1852.

Clements, Ronald E. *Jeremiah*. Interpretation: A Bible Commentary for Teaching and Preaching. Edited by James Luther Mays. Atlanta: John Knox, 1988.